WRITING ANALYSES OF LITERATURE

James P. Degnan

William Heffernan

University of Santa Clara

Holt, Rinehart and Winston, Inc.

New York   Chicago   San Francisco   Atlanta
Dallas   Montreal   Toronto   London   Sydney

Copyright © 1969 by James P. Degnan and William Heffernan
All rights reserved
Library of Congress Catalog Card Number: 69-16081
SBN: 03-075475-5
Printed in the United States of America
1 2 3 4 5 6 7 8 9

PREFACE

The question most often asked writing instructors by their students—especially in courses involving writing analyses of literature—is, "What exactly do you want?" The goal of this book is to help the instructor answer this question as simply and quickly as possible.

Since *Writing Analyses of Literature* is *primarily* a guide for *writing about* literature rather than for reading literature, many may wish to use it as a supplement to, rather than a substitute for, the conventional anthology and as a book designed primarily to teach students to read literature. However, since *Writing Analyses of Literature* is also a small anthology of literature as well as a general guide to reading literature, it can be used by itself.

A glance at the table of contents reveals the simplicity of the book's approach. Instead of pages of abstract editorial explanation, of "rules," *telling* the student what the instructor wants, the student is quickly *shown* what the instructor wants: that is, the student is presented with a work of literature and a sample analysis of that work. From the beginning, the student has in mind a clear picture—the sample analysis—of what the instructor wants rather than the hazy notion that results from general "rules." Possessing this picture, the student is encouraged to write a comparable analysis on a work of literature similar to the one discussed in the sample analysis.

The fact that most of the sample papers in this text are relatively short—roughly from 500 to 1500 words—indicates our desire to be particularly helpful to the instructor in the ordinary literature-composition course, that is, the instructor who typically assigns papers of such lengths. We have found that in the few other books designed specifically to help the instructor teach the art of literary analysis, the sample papers—if they exist at all—are either too short or too long to be used effectively.

By concentrating on formalistic writing assignments—for example, assignments in writing about close readings, assignments in analyzing imagery, structure, and prosody—we do not mean to imply that we think formalistic criticism* the only kind or necessarily the most important kind

*See glossary for definitions of asterisked terms.

of literary criticism. Further—as should be obvious from our selection of works to be analyzed—we do not pretend that *all* literature lends itself naturally to formalistic criticism. We have concentrated on formalistic assignments because: (1) such assignments are and should be a major concern in most literature-composition courses and (2) a simple guide to writing such assignments has long been needed.

While time in the typical literature-composition course will probably prevent the student from doing all the assignments suggested in *Writing Analyses of Literature,* the editors are convinced that if the student can master even a few of the assignments he will receive a good introduction to writing practical literary criticism. We believe, in fact, that it is often far more valuable for the student, especially the student learning to write analyses of literature, to do one assignment well—that is, to rewrite and resubmit a paper, after the paper has been edited by his instructor (several times if necessary) until that paper succeeds—rather than go on to new assignments.

The editors, of course, assume that the instructor will use the book any way he sees fit: he can follow the book literally as he would a syllabus for a writing program; he can use all or only a few of the assignments; or he can substitute favorite assignments of his own for some of the book's assignments. Our intention is to provide the instructor with a book of essentials for writing literary analyses—a book that, free of cumbersome apparatus and editorial intrusions, offers the instructor the maximum amount of flexibility to teach his course according to the particular needs of his students.

Further, while the editors obviously agree with the interpretations in the sample analyses, we do not expect the instructor or the student necessarily to agree with these interpretations. Our purpose has been to present samples of *organization,* not necessarily of interpretation. We suggest, in fact, that an interesting supplementary assignment might be for the instructor, if he disagrees with an interpretation, to have his students, using textual evidence (which he may provide or have the students discover for themselves), write papers arguing with that interpretation. We assume that the instructor will emphasize in his class discussions the weaknesses as well as the strengths of the sample papers; for our hope is that the sample papers will serve as objects for emulation as well as for imitation.

J. P. D.
W. H.

Santa Clara, California
January 1969

SUGGESTIONS
FOR USING
THIS TEXT

Before beginning to write his analysis of a work of literature, even before reading the sample analyses provided in the book, the student should thoroughly understand the selections upon which the sample analyses are written. For example, prior to writing his first assignment—the summary-paraphrase of John Donne's "Batter My Heart, Three-Personed God"—the student should thoroughly understand George Meredith's "Lucifer in Starlight"; that is, he must comprehend not only the poem's paraphraseable content, but its imagery, prosody, structure, tone, basic irony, and so forth, as well. Such understanding usually comes after (a) the student (perhaps using the suggestions mentioned in the introductions to poetry and to the short story and drama) has carefully read the work and (b) after he has carefully discussed his reading with his instructor.

Thoroughly understanding the works of literature upon which the sample analyses are written prepares the student to read and understand—hopefully, with little or no help from his instructor—the similar works of literature that he is instructed to analyze. Thus, after carefully reading and thoroughly discussing with his instructor "Lucifer in Starlight" the student reads and discusses the sample analysis of that poem and the editors' comments on the sample analysis; then the student carefully reads Donne's "Batter My Heart, Three-Personed God" and writes an analysis on this poem, an analysis similar in organization to the analysis of "Lucifer in Starlight."

While for the sake of originality most instructors understandably prefer that their students do for themselves the job of prewriting—of reading and understanding the work of literature they are to write about—the editors believe that occasionally students might write on material that has been partially or even thoroughly discussed in class. For example, the instructor might conduct a thorough discussion of Donne's "Batter My Heart, Three-Personed God" as well as of "Lucifer in Starlight" before having the student write on the Donne poem. While such a writing assignment may be little more than an exercise in organizing notes, organizing notes coherently, concisely, and clearly, is a skill not to be entirely despised.

Besides the works of literature upon which the sample analyses are written, the instructor might also include other similar works in his prewriting discussions. For example, in Assignment 3: Analysis of Imagery, the instructor might discuss some of the poems in the Further Assignments section, such as "The Windhover: To Christ Our Lord," "The Silken Tent," or "That Time of Year," all of which appear in Appendix II; or the instructor may wish to use poems from outside the text. In any event, a thorough discussion of a poem or poems similar to the one the student is to write about is obviously most desirable.

Briefly, the general plan for using *Writing Analyses of Literature* is as follows: (a) The student reads carefully and discusses thoroughly the works of literature (and perhaps other similar works assigned by the instructor) upon which the sample analyses are written. (b) Using the sample analyses as his guides (along with his instructor's suggestions, the editors' comments, and the general suggestions for understanding literature that appear in the book's introductions to poetry and to the short story and drama), the student writes comparable analyses on works of literature similar to the selections analyzed in the sample analyses.

CONTENTS

Part I

POETRY

INTRODUCTION
TO POETRY

As editors of this text we do not pretend that there is any method, any book of rules, for writing analyses of literature. We do believe that all successful analyses have two common characteristics: (1) they answer the questions the individual literary work of art raises, and (2) they demonstrate how the parts of a literary work of art function to develop the whole of that work. Successfully written literary analysis, therefore, like successful oral literary analysis, is largely a matter of intelligently and imaginatively raising and answering questions and of constantly demonstrating how the parts of a poem, play or story *function,* how they work to advance the purpose of a literary work of art. Further, we believe that all successful analyses, especially all analyses of poems, result from sedulous *prewriting,* that is, from a thorough mastery of the individual text before writing.

What does such mastery involve? Again, there is no method, no formula or book of rules, that will guarantee successful prewriting; however, there are a few helpful general rules of procedure. For example, to master the kinds of poems that appear in this text you should do at least the following:

1. Read the poems word by word, line by line, *many* times.
2. Carefully use such standard reference works as the *Oxford English Dictionary* and a good encyclopedia so that you know *thoroughly* all the possibilities of meaning, connotative and denotative,*[1] of every word and allusion.
3. Constantly ask yourself the question, how does this part—for example, this word, image, symbol, sentence structure, mark of punctuation, and so forth— function to develop the whole?

[1] See Glossary for definitions of asterisked terms.

3

4. *Imagine* the poem, that is, see the literal picture, hear the literal sounds the poem creates.

Poetry is poetry because it makes abstractions concrete; and it should be appreciated for its concreteness, for, to quote the poet-critic John Ciardi, "*how* it means," as well as for *what* it means. For instance, in Matthew Arnold's well-known poem "Dover Beach" there is a famous image* of a "darkling plain." Asked what this "plain" is, the careless reader typically answers "the materialistic world" or "a world devoid of meaning" or some similar abstraction. Literally, however, the "plain" *is* Dover Beach, that is, the slate beach lying before the poet's eyes. If we are to read the poem as poetry and not merely as some sort of vague philosophy we first must *see* the image of the beach, as Arnold obviously wants us to, and only secondly speculate as to what the beach may symbolize.

The editors' intention in suggesting that the student write first on poetry and then move on to the more discursive kinds of literature, for example, the short story and the play, is to discourage, from the beginning, the kind of abstract response to literature mentioned above. In any event, we believe it obvious that the art of close reading—the art of questioning possibilities of meaning in every word and line, of appreciating the function which the part plays in developing the whole of a literary work of art—is much more easily acquired through the study of poems than through the study of the more discursive kinds of literature. And, of course, it is this art of close reading that the student must master before he can write successful analyses of poems or of any other kind of literature.

Although every poem, like every other individual work of literature, raises its own unique questions and must, therefore, be approached as a unique object, the following general suggestions and questions may be helpful to the student in prewriting for poetry assignments:

1. What is the purpose* of the poem?
2. What is the situation in the poem? What is the occasion? What is the time and place?
3. Is the situation dramatic?* If so, who is the speaker, and to whom is he speaking?
4. What is the tone* of the poem, that is, the attitude of the poet?
5. Discuss the function of the poem's diction, of its images and symbols, its allusions, its pattern of imagery.
6. What is the form* of the poem? What is the relationship between form and meaning in the poem?
7. Paraphrase the poem, that is, if the poem lends itself to paraphrase.
8. Discuss the significance of sound patterns in the poem, that is, the poem's meter.

9. Discuss the function of paradox* and irony* in the poem.
10. Discuss the appropriateness of the poem's figures of speech: its metaphors, similes, and personifications.

ASSIGNMENT 1: THE SUMMARY-PARAPHRASE

Without going into a detailed analysis of the poem's parts, for example, imagery, rhythm, meter, and so on, the summary-paraphrase should answer these general questions: What is happening in the poem? What is the poem trying to say? The summary-paraphrase should also construe any images that might confuse the reader's basic understanding of what *literally* is happening and being said in the poem.

LUCIFER IN STARLIGHT

George Meredith

On a starred night Prince Lucifer uprose
Tired of his dark dominion swung the fiend
Above the rolling ball in cloud part screened,
Where sinner hugged the specter of repose.
Poor prey to his hot fit of pride were those.   5
And now upon his western wing he leaned,
Now his huge bulk o'er Afric's sands careened,
Now the black planet shadowed Arctic snows.
Soaring through wider zones that pricked his scars
With memory of the old revolt from Awe,   10
He reached a middle height, and at the stars,
Which are the brain of heaven, he looked, and sank.
Around the ancient track marched, rank on rank,
The army of unalterable law.

SAMPLE SUMMARY-PARAPHRASE

Weary of being condemned to his "dark dominion" of hell, Lucifer, motivated by a "hot fit of pride," one starry night flies from hell intending to crash heaven, to reoccupy the kingdom of God from which he was long before expelled for another "hot fit of pride"—a fit that led him to attempt usurping God's throne. Described as a "huge bulk" and a "black planet"— images suggesting the enormity of his influence over earth—Lucifer flies first over earth, the "rolling ball" where his "poor prey," the sinners who have been his victims so long lie sleeping; passes to "wider zones" that rekindle in him the painful memories of his original expulsion from heaven; reaches a "middle height," from which perspective he looks at the stars, recognizes that they symbolize an orderly universe—a universe in which all things have their proper place, including himself; and finally, sinks back to his proper place, his "dark dominion," utterly frustrated in his attempt to reoccupy heaven, to destroy the orderly operation of the universe.

What Meredith is doing in "Lucifer in Starlight" is creating a new version of an old myth, a myth made famous by Milton in *Paradise Lost*. According to that myth, Lucifer is defeated by supernatural forces, by God and his angels; however, in Meredith's poem, Lucifer is defeated by natural forces, by the "stars," the "army of unalterable law." What the poem says then, in part, is simply that in a universe that is per se orderly (the universe, for example, of the eighteenth-century Deists) supernatural forces, God and his angels, are not necessary to keep evil and anarchy, symbolized by Lucifer, in their proper place.

COMMENTS ON THE SAMPLE
SUMMARY-PARAPHRASE

The summary-paraphrase, without going into a detailed analysis of the poem's parts, for instance, imagery, rhythm, meter, and so forth, should answer the general questions: What is happening in the poem? What is the poem trying to say? Also, the summary-paraphrase should explain any images that might confuse the reader's basic understanding of what literally is happening and being said in the poem.

The writer of the sample summary-paraphrase has raised and answered the two key questions mentioned above. He has also, without going into detailed analysis, clarified certain images that need clarification if we are to understand the poem's basic action.* For example, without showing how the individual images* work in the total imagistic pattern of the poem, the writer explains what Meredith means by such images as "poor prey," "rolling ball," and "black planet." Were the writer doing a detailed analysis of imagery, he would have raised and answered such questions as: What is the significance of Lucifer's being defeated on a starry night? What is the significance of Lucifer being the name of a star? Does the fact that planets are condemned to fixed orbits and that Lucifer metaphorically is a "black planet" have any thematic significance? However, to repeat, the function of the summary-paraphrase is to tell us what *literally* is happening and being said in the poem.

The key questions raised and answered by the writer of the summary-paraphrase in paragraph two are: Why does Lucifer sink at the sight of the stars? How can the stars properly be called an army? What is the relationship between Milton's treatment of Lucifer's fall and Meredith's treatment of his rise and fall? Further, the writer explains in paragraph two specifically that Meredith's treatment of Lucifer's defeat is analogous to the Deist's explanation of evil in the universe, thus making it much easier for the reader to see how the parts—the imagery, diction, and so on—work to develop the poem's meaning. Given this summary-paraphrase the reader wishing to do a more detailed analysis of the poem will find his task considerably easier.

Rhetorically, for the most part, the summary-paraphrase of Meredith's poem is chronologically organized; Lucifer's flight, as in the poem, is traced from beginning to end. Notice that the writer summarizes the poem's action in present tense, a rhetorical device giving both immediacy and unity to the composition. Notice also that the flight is described in one periodic sentence, another device giving unity or tightness to the composition.

BATTER MY HEART, THREE-PERSONED GOD

John Donne

Batter my heart, three-personed God, for you
As yet but knock, breathe, shine, and seek to mend;
That I may rise and stand, o'erthrow me, and bend
Your force to break, blow, burn, and make me new.
I, like an usurped town, to another due,   5
Labor to admit you, but oh, to no end;
Reason, your viceroy in me, me should defend,
But is captived and proves weak or untrue.
Yet dearly I love you and would be loved fain,
But am betrothed unto your enemy;   10
Divorce me, untie or break that knot again,

Take me to you, imprison me, for I,
Except you enthrall me, never shall be free,
Nor ever chaste except you ravish me.

Assignment: Write a summary-paraphrase of Donne's "Batter My Heart, Three-Personed God." Your summary-paraphrase should attempt to answer (though not necessarily in the same order) the following questions:

1. What literally is the poet asking of God?
2. What are the stages in the development of his prayer?
3. What is the poetic significance of the prayer being addressed to a "three-personed God"?
4. Upon what basic paradox does the poem turn?
5. What are the stages in the development of the poem's basic pattern of imagery?

Further Assignment: Write a summary-paraphrase of any other poem in this text, including those in Appendix II.

ASSIGNMENT 2: ANALYSIS OF DOMINANT IMAGE

The student who wishes to understand the poem's purpose must go beyond literal summary or paraphrase to the poem's imagery. While the patterns of images, of sense impressions, which lead the student to this purpose may be quite complicated, and may involve many different images, the poet will often simplify the reader's task of understanding and appreciating the poem by developing these images around a central or dominant image. For example, while the images in the following poem, "White Christmas," are numerous and varied—"cotton wool," "obese folds," "stalactites," "old stone circles," "tinned milk," "sackcloth and ashes"—all of these images are united by their relationship to the image of snow, the dominant image in the poem.

WHITE CHRISTMAS

W. R. Rodgers

Punctually at Christmas the soft plush
Of sentiment snows down, embosoms all
The sharp and pointed shapes of venom, shawls
The hills and hides the shocking holes of this
Uneven world of want and wealth, cushions   5

From *Awake! and Other Poems* by W. R. Rodgers. Reprinted by permission of Martin Secker & Warburg Limited.

With cosy wish like cotton-wool the cool
Arm's-length interstices of caste and class,
And into obese folds subtracts from sight
All truculent acts, bleeding the world white.

Punctually that glib pair, Peace and Goodwill,   10
Emerges royally to take the air,
Collect the bows, assimilate the smiles,
Of waiting men. It is a genial time;
Angels, like stalactites, descend from heaven;
Bishops distribute their own weight in words,   15
Congratulate the poor on Christlike lack;
And the member for the constituency
Feeds the five thousand, and has plenty back.

Punctually, to-night, in old stone circles
Of set reunion, families stiffly sit   20
And listen: this is the night and this the happy time
When the tinned milk of human kindness is
Upheld and holed by radio-appeal:
Hushed are hurrying heels on hard roads,
And every parlour's a pink pond of light   25
To the cold and travelling man going by
In the dark, without a bark or a bite.

But punctually to-morrow you will see
All this silent and dissembling world
Of stilted sentiment suddenly melt   30
Into mush and watery welter of words
Beneath the warm and moving traffic of
Feet and actual fact. Over the stark plain
The silted mill-chimneys once again spread
Their sackcloth and ashes, a flowing mane   35
Of repentance for the false day that's fled.

SAMPLE ANALYSIS OF A DOMINANT IMAGE

W. R. Rodgers' poem "White Christmas" is a searing indictment of a hypocritical society that glibly produces the ersatz morality of the Christmas season because it is socially useful; and then, just as easily, condones a return to the post-Christmas world where men go on displaying their inhumanity rather than their good will. The poem ironically concludes that the grim, cruel, unpretentious post-Christmas world, described in the poem's final stanza, is more honest than the world of sham altruism merchandised at Christmas.

The poem's dominant image, snow, makes Rodgers' ironical indictment forceful. A traditional Christmas image, in the poem snow does not call forth the true Christmas sentiments, that is, genuine peace and good will; instead snow evokes sham sentiments or sentimentality, which deceitfully covers or hides the real cruelty of life ("embosoms all / The sharp and pointed shapes of venom"), obscuring everything that is painful. Snow (Christmas sentimentality) does not remove "truculent acts," Rodgers tells us, it merely "subtracts [them] from sight." It enables the obese rich to go on "bleeding the world white:" thus, the whiteness of snow, instead of having its traditional connotations of purity and innocence, suggests a deathly and unnatural pallor. Ironically, this pallor contrasts with "The warm and moving traffic of / Feet and actual fact" of the last stanza, associated with a harsh post-Christmas world.

Snow not only hides injustice, it temporarily fills gaps: the social gaps between classes, the material gaps between those who have and those who have not. Snow shawls

> The hills and hides the shocking holes of this
> Uneven world of want and wealth, cushions
> With cosy wish like cotton-wool the cool
> Arm's-length interstices of caste and class, . . .

It acts as a buffer to prevent the shocking clashes and daily frictions between classes. This Christmas sentimentality has social utility, since it is responsible for the appearance of a temporary equality that, in fact, really does not exist; it allows us to forget how far apart are the worlds of wealth and want. Rodgers' indictment reminds us that even the usual callous behavior of the rich to the poor is preferable to this deception. Two qualities of snow are developed in this passage: its coolness, and its fluffiness. Snow's coolness emphasizes its duplicity since coolness ill suits snow's assumed role of blanketing, or making warm the coolness, or standoffishness, of men. Snow's fluffiness ("plush," "cushions," "cozy") suggests a comfort given to consciences by the Christmas spirit. The verbs ("embosoms," "shawls," "cushions") add a maternal note to the comforting, implying, perhaps, that this "soft plush" allows the wealthy subscribers to Christmas sentimentality to temporarily assume the character of innocent children unheedful of the self-created differences between men.

Precisely at the start of the working day, the snow of sentiment (as if on schedule) punctually melts,

Into mush and watery welter of words
Beneath the warm and moving traffic of
Feet and actual fact.

In the world of the last stanza sordid, but honest, blackness replaces whiteness.

The silted mill-chimneys once again spread
Their sackcloth and ashes, a flowing mane
Of repentance for the false day that's fled.

As if doing penance for its former hypocrisy, the earth resumes its real sordid character with the plume of black smoke flowing from the mill-chimney.

While snow is not explicitly mentioned in the middle stanzas, its qualities—coolness, fluffiness, and color—appear subsumed in other images. For example, the coldness hinted at in stanza one is developed in stanza three where angels are compared to "stalactites." Stalactites are cold and hard like icicles (the form melted snow sometimes takes), suggesting that these angels bring no meaningful message nor warm tidings. The line "Hushed are hurrying heels on hard roads" implies snow's fluffiness, which prevents people comfortably housed in parlors from hearing anything but the mechanized radio appeals. Snow muffles the sound of the footsteps of the "cold and travelling man" (perhaps a modern-day Christ who has been unable to find room at the inn). Finally, even the saccharine and commercial "tinned milk" of stanza three is linked by color to snow.

In "White Christmas" W. R. Rodgers ironically reverses the comforting sentiments of the popular Bing Crosby Christmas tune, and reveals through the dominant image of snow, the hypocrisy of the Christmas sentiment. A black but honest Christmas, he implies would be far better.

COMMENTS ON SAMPLE ANALYSIS
OF A DOMINANT IMAGE*

If a student wishes to understand the poem's purpose, he must go beyond literal summary or paraphrase to the poem's imagery. While the patterns of images, which lead the student to the poem's purpose may be quite complicated, and may involve many different images, the poet will often simplify the reader's task of understanding and appreciating the poem by developing these images around a central or dominant image. In W. R. Rodgers' poem "White Christmas," for example, while the images are numerous and varied: "cotton-wool," "obese folds," "stalactites," "old stone circles," "tinned milk," "sackcloth and ashes," all of the images are united by their relationship to the image of snow, the dominant image in the poem.

Notice in the opening paragraph of the sample analysis how the writer has identified the dominant image and demonstrated its relationship to the poem's purpose. He has answered such questions as: What does snow stand for in the poem? Why is it called "plush?" Why does it "embosom," "shawl," "hide," "subtract from sight," and "cushion?" When it melts, why is snow described as "mush and watery welter of words?" In order to explain the relationship between snow and other secondary images in the poem, the writer has had to ask himself some additional questions: Why is the smoke from mill-chimneys described as "a flowing mane / Of repentance?" How are Angels like stalactites? Why is the milk of human kindness "tinned?" Why is the "travelling man" ignored? Of course, the writer has not exhausted all the possible relationships between the secondary images and the dominant image. For example, he could have explored the relationship between the weighty Bishops of the second stanza, and snow's "obese folds" in stanza one.

Notice how in the second and third paragraphs the writer calls the reader's attention to the primary functions of snow: hiding, filling, and cushioning, and how he postpones a discussion of the less important images, those in which snow is present only by implication, until the fifth paragraph. Also, notice how each paragraph returns to the essential purpose of the poem—an indictment of the rich who find it to their advantage to subscribe to Christmas sentimentality.

STILL, CITIZEN SPARROW

Richard Wilbur

Still, citizen sparrow, this vulture which you call
Unnatural, let him but lumber again to air
Over the rotten office, let him bear
The carrion ballast up, and at the tall

Tip of the sky lie cruising. Then you'll see   5
That no more beautiful bird is in heaven's height,

No wider more placid wings, no watchfuller flight;
He shoulders nature there, the frightfully free,

The naked-headed one. Pardon him, you
Who dart in the orchard aisles, for it is he   10
Devours death, mocks mutability,
Has heart to make an end, keeps nature new.

Thinking of Noah, childheart, try to forget
How for so many bedlam hours his saw
Soured the song of birds with its wheezy gnaw,   15
And the slam of his hammer all the day beset

The people's ears. Forget that he could bear
To see the towns like coral under the keel,
And the fields so dismal deep. Try rather to feel
How high and weary it was, on the waters where   20

He rocked his only world, and everyone's.
Forgive the hero, you who would have died
Gladly with all you knew; he rode that tide
To Ararat; all men are Noah's sons.

Assignment: Write an analysis of the dominant image, the vulture, in Richard Wilbur's "Still, Citizen Sparrow." Your analysis should attempt to answer the following questions:

1. What does the vulture represent?
2. Are the descriptions of the vulture in stanza three to be taken figuratively? For example, is the phrase "naked-headed one" merely a literal description of the vulture?
3. Why does the poet ask the sparrow to pardon the vulture (line 9), and to forgive Noah, the hero (line 22)?
4. Why is the vulture's office called "unnatural" by the sparrow, while the poet says the vulture "shoulders nature"?
5. While there is no explicit mention of the vulture in the last three stanzas, does that mean that the image is absent? What, for example, connects the description in lines 4 and 5 with the description in lines 20 and 21?
6. Is there any connection between the vulture's bearing "carrion ballast" (line 4), and the poem's concluding statement "all men are Noah's sons" (line 24)?

Further Assignment: Write a dominant image analysis of one of the following poems:

1. Robert Frost's "Birches." Focus on the image of the birches.

2. Gerard Manley Hopkins' "The Windover: To Christ Our Lord." Focus on the combined motion-light image.
3. Robert Frost's "The Silken Tent." Focus on the tent image.
4. Shakespeare's "That Time of Year." Focus on the light image.
5. A. E. Housman's "Terence, This is Stupid Stuff." Focus on the image of beer.

These poems are all included in Appendix II.

ASSIGNMENT 3: ANALYSIS OF IMAGERY

What is the purpose of the poem? How does the poem's imagery, that is, its pattern of sense impressions, of pictures, of diction, contribute to the fulfillment of that purpose? These are the major general questions the writer of the analysis of imagery must raise and answer.

DESIGN

Robert Frost

I found a dimpled spider, fat and white,
On a white heal-all, holding up a moth
Like a white piece of rigid satin cloth—
Assorted characters of death and blight
Mixed ready to begin the morning right,
Like the ingredients of a witches' broth—
A snow-drop spider, a flower like froth,
And dead wings carried like a paper kite.
What had that flower to do with being white,
The wayside blue and innocent heal-all?
What brought the kindred spider to that height,
Then steered the white moth thither in the night?
What but design of darkness to appall?—
If design govern in a thing so small.

SAMPLE ANALYSIS OF IMAGERY

The purpose of Frost's poem, "Design," is to raise and to answer the question: If design governs in a thing so small as the systematic destruction of a moth by a spider, then isn't it appalling to think that design (nature, God, whatever supernatural being rules the universe) also governs the activities of higher beings too? Actually, Frost's question is rhetorical, for by the time the reader finishes "Design" he has been shown with painstaking care that design *does* govern; and the implication in the final part of the poem is that man, realizing that "design of darkness" does rule, *should* be appalled.

From the beginning until the end of "Design" the poet designs the poem so that we cannot help but be appalled by what "Design" shows us. First of all we see the literal design or picture of a white moth being devoured by a white spider on a white flower

> I found a dimpled spider, fat and white,
> On a white heal-all, holding up a moth
> Like a white piece of rigid satin cloth—
> Assorted characters of death and blight
> Mixed ready to begin the morning right, . . .

That all is white—including the spider which we generally think of as black or brown and the heal-all which is supposed to be blue—makes an ugly picture even uglier. Whiteness is associated with innocence, but in this poem the whiteness is sinister because it is the cause of the moth's destruction. Something supernatural or preternatural used whiteness to deceive the moth, to trap him, the imagery seems to suggest. But behind the mere physical deception is a design more sinister, the design of nature, which created the moth to feed on the flower (the moth is the character of "blight" later suggested in the poem), just as the same design of nature created the spider to feed on the moth. In other words, what Frost seems to be saying is that there are no innocent characters in nature; that all nature (and perhaps human life as well) is a matter of kill or be killed, a matter of scheming or *designing*.

The sinister suggestion conveyed by the image of whiteness and the reference to the spider as "dimpled and fat" (suggesting the innocence of a baby), is continued through the first part of the poem by the image of the "white satin cloth," the "assorted characters of death and blight," and the image of the "morning right." All of these images suggest, again, design; but this time they suggest a design of ceremony. The way the spider holds the moth like "a white satin cloth" before devouring him suggests a kind of

Black Mass, a kind of Unholy Communion. Possibly Frost intends for us to see this as an unholy ceremony because his use of "morning right" is perhaps a pun;* "rite" as well as *right* being intended. That the moth, flowers, and spider are "characters" implies that they are in a drama which fits in with the notion of their being in a preternatural ritual or ceremony. Dramas are directed and produced, *designed,* not by the actors but generally by someone outside the stage; so again the notion of a sinister influence is suggested.

Adding still further to the suggestion that what we have in "Design" is an unholy ceremony designed by some wicked, preternatural agent, is the image that the "characters"—the moth, spider, and flower—are "like the ingredients of a witches' broth." A witches' broth is a carefully *designed* recipe created by evil to effect evil. "A snow-drop spider" fits appropriately into the "broth" because of his poisonous nature; the flower like a "froth" suggests the foam in the "broth" and connotes frothing at the mouth, and the "paper kite" image besides being a picture of the dead moth (he is like a triangular paper kite) suggests his helplessness, his victimization.

The last stanza of "Design" raises the question which I mentioned earlier

> What had that flower to do with being white
> The wayside blue and innocent heal-all?
> What brought the kindred spider to that height,
> Then steered the white moth thither in the night?
> What but design of darkness to appall?—
> If design govern in a thing so small.

What design does govern in a thing so small, can be seen in this stanza as well as in stanza one. Frost uses ironic terms like "steered" and "kindred" to show us, again, design. The moth was directed to the flower, "steered," and he was in league with the "design of nature to appall" in that he was *kin* to the flower and spider, but related not as "kindred" usually are thought to be related, by family love, but by the need to feed on one another. Does Frost suggest, they are one and the same?

COMMENTS ON SAMPLE ANALYSIS OF IMAGERY

What is the purpose of "Design?" How does the poem's imagery, that is, its pattern of sense impressions, of pictures, of diction, contribute to the fulfillment of that purpose? These are the general questions that the writer of the sample paper analyzing imagery has raised and answered.

After clearly and succinctly stating the poem's purpose, the writer proceeds in chronological order simultaneously to summarize the poem's action and to explicate in detail the poem's imagery. Notice that the writer, in paragraphs two and three, explicates so as to give the reader a picture of the poem's general setting, of the stage upon which the ironic drama of design is played. Analyzing in detail the over-all significance of the poem's dominant image—the image of *whiteness*—these paragraphs function to give the reader a sense of the over-all imagistic shape of the poem and thus prepare the reader for the close scrutiny of particular images that follows.

Above all, the sample paper is notable for its coherence, that is, its sticking to the point, the point which, of course, is made in paragraph one. Notice in the transition from paragraph one to paragraph two how the explicator has meaningfully repeated key words from paragraph one like "design," and "appalled." Notice the same meaningful repetition* in the other paragraph transitions.

Meaningful repetition (in contrast to needless repetition) is, of course, one of many rhetorical devices for achieving coherence in literary compositions. Using it, however, or using any other rhetorical device successfully, involves the writer's knowing clearly *before* he writes *exactly* what point he's trying to make in his composition.

Another feature of the sample paper is that it evidences clearly its writer's scrupulous use of the dictionary. Almost every word in the poem is closely scrutinized for its possibilities of contributing to the poem's total effect. Puns are noted (with the rather outstanding exception of the pun on "appall" in the next to last line) and commented upon as are other meaningfully ambiguous* words.

Assignment: Write an analysis of the imagery in John Donne's "Batter My Heart, Three-Personed God" (pages 8–9). Your analysis should answer the same questions as those answered in your paraphrase of the poem as well as the following questions:

1. What is the purpose of the poem?
2. Can the purpose be stated in the form of a basic Christian paradox?* If so, what is that paradox?
3. Of what importance, if any, is the poet's basically Christian attitude to the fulfillment of purpose in the poem?
4. What are examples of meaningful ambiguities in the poem's diction? of puns? How do these ambiguities and puns function to fulfill the poem's purpose?
5. Are the poem's dominant images, that is, those depicting pillage and ravishment, logically developed? Does the poem's purpose justify the use of such strong images?

Further Assignment: Write an analysis of imagery on any of the following poems:

1. Robert Lowell's "Colloquy in Black Rock."
2. John Donne's "A Valediction Forbidding Mourning."
3. Gerard Manley Hopkins' "Spring and Fall: To a Young Child."
4. Matthew Arnold's "Dover Beach."
5. Robert Frost's "A Soldier."
6. George Meredith's "Lucifer in Starlight."

The first five poems above are included in Appendix II; "Lucifer in Starlight" is on page 6.

ASSIGNMENT 4:
ANALYSIS
OF STRUCTURE*

The writer of the analysis of structure should answer these major questions about the poem: What is the structural problem? How is it solved? What is the relationship between the structure, that is, the organization or rhetoric of the poem, and the meaning of the poem?

LAPIS LAZULI

William Butler Yeats

I have heard that hysterical women say
They are sick of the palette and fiddle-bow
Of poets that are always gay,
For everybody knows or else should know
That if nothing drastic is done   5
Aeroplane and Zeppelin will come out,
Pitch like King Billy bomb-balls in
Until the town lie beaten flat.

All perform their tragic play,
There struts Hamlet, there is Lear,   10
That's Ophelia, that Cordelia;
Yet they, should the last scene be there,
The great stage curtain about to drop,

If worthy their prominent part in the play,
Do not break up their lines to weep.   15
They know that Hamlet and Lear are gay;
Gaiety transfiguring all that dread.
All men have aimed at, found and lost;
Black out; Heaven blazing into the head:
Tragedy wrought to its uttermost.   20
Though Hamlet rambles and Lear rages,
And all the drop scenes drop at once
Upon a hundred thousand stages,
It cannot grow by an inch or an ounce.

On their own feet they came, or on shipboard,   25
Camel-back, horse-back, ass-back, mule-back,
Old civilisations put to the sword.
Then they and their wisdom went to rack:
No handiwork of Callimachus,
Who handled marble as if it were bronze,   30
Made draperies that seemed to rise
When sea-wind swept the corner, stands;
His long lamp-chimney shaped like the stem
Of a slender palm, stood but a day;
All things fall and are built again,   35
And those that build them again are gay.

Two Chinamen, behind them a third,
Are carved in lapis lazuli,
Over them flies a long-legged bird,
A symbol of longevity;   40
The third, doubtless a serving-man,
Carries a musical instrument.

Every discoloration of the stone,
Every accidental crack or dent,
Seems a water-course or an avalanche,   45
Or lofty slope where it still snows
Though doubtless plum or cherry-branch
Sweetens the little half-way house
Those Chinamen climb towards, and I
Delight to imagine them seated there;   50
There, on the mountain and the sky,
On all the tragic scene they stare.
One asks for mournful melodies;
Accomplished fingers begin to play.

Their eyes mid many wrinkles, their eyes,   55
Their ancient, glittering eyes, are gay.

SAMPLE ANALYSIS OF STRUCTURE

Yeats' purpose in "Lapis Lazuli" is to demonstrate that history is an endless sequence of cycles (or spirals, elsewhere called *gyres* by Yeats)—cycles of destruction and creation. Yeats associates cycles of creation with gaiety and cycles of destruction with violence and decay: violence—as in the aerial bombardment in stanza one and in the destruction of civilization by the sword in stanza three; decay—as in the lapis lazuli medallion of stanza four ("Every discoloration of the stone, / Every accidental crack or dent, . . .") and in the Chinamen carved on its face ("Their eyes mid many wrinkles, their eyes, / Their ancient, glittering eyes, are gay.") Gaiety, the poem implies, is like the insight gained by the heroes of Greek tragedy, a state of mind reached by those who, while recognizing that the essential tragedy of life is that all human accomplishments are ephemeral, that is, subject to destruction, nevertheless, continue to bear this painful knowledge nobly, insisting that life has meaning.

To make this purpose clear, that is, to emphasize the single purpose implicit in the diverse subjects of the poem's stanzas—the irrelevance of art in wartime (stanza one), Shakespeare's tragedies (stanza two), the successive collapse of civilizations (stanza three), and the lapis lazuli medallion (stanzas four and five)—Yeats uses the appropriate rhetorical or structural device: contrast. Within each stanza, images of destruction ("beaten," "blazing," "rack," "dent") contrast with images of creation ("palette and fiddle-bow," "Hamlet and Lear," "civilisations," "build") to suggest the poem's underlying purpose: to demonstrate that history is a sequence of alternating cycles of destruction and creation. These contrasting patterns of imagery give the poem a spiral-like structure which says implicitly what Yeats is saying explicitly: "All things fall and are built again, / And those that build them again are gay."

Contrast, however, is not the only structural device in "Lapis Lazuli." Yeats also employs inverse chronological order to organize his material. The poem moves backward in time with references in stanza one to World War I, in stanza two to Elizabethan England, and in stanza three to the Greece of fifth century B.C. Finally, the last two stanzas suggest the ancient civilization of China. In addition, like Walt Whitman's "Passage to India," Yeats' poem moves backward to the beginnings of civilization not only in time, but also in space, shifting gradually from the Western setting of stanza one toward the East with each successive stanza. This chronological and spatial structure aids Yeats in emphasizing his essential point that, even though civilizations may rise and fall, the spirit of gaiety transcends them all.

The structure of "Lapis Lazuli," resting on contrast, chronological and spatial order, subtly demonstrates Yeats' purpose: that the history of man, despite its surface confusion, does have coherence and meaning, not for the hysterical, but for those who, like the Chinamen, can be gay while hearing "mournful melodies."

COMMENTS ON THE SAMPLE ANALYSIS OF STRUCTURE

Writing about a poem's structure is a difficult task since structure involves what poet John Ciardi has called the "act of language," that is, the technique which, while inseparable from the poem's meaning, always remains the most difficult part of that meaning to articulate. In this sample paper the writer is concerned with that portion of technique called structure, that is, how the poem is organized.

Before writing the paper, the writer had asked and answered three important questions about the poem: What is the structural problem? How is it solved? What is the relationship between the structure and the poem's meaning? The first paragraph deals with poem's meaning; by repeating this meaning in every paragraph, the writer shows how it is related to each of the three structural devices. The second paragraph exposes the structural problem, and paragraphs two and three give the solution to the problem.

Notice in the second paragraph how the writer has implied a definition of structure—the rhetorical devices which hold together the parts of the poem—and how, in his subsequent analysis, he stays within this definition. For example, the writer refrains from explicating the imagery mentioned in the second paragraph since imagery itself does not come within the terms of the definition. Finally, the last paragraph sums up the structural devices used in the poem, and again relates them to the poem's meaning.

TWO TRAMPS IN MUD TIME

Robert Frost

Out of the mud two strangers came
And caught me splitting wood in the yard.
And one of them put me off my aim

By hailing cheerily "Hit them hard!"
I knew pretty well why he dropped behind   5
And let the other go on a way.
I knew pretty well what he had in mind:
He wanted to take my job for pay.

Good blocks of beech it was I split,
As large around as the chopping block;   10
And every piece I squarely hit
Fell splinterless as a cloven rock.
The blows that a life of self-control
Spares to strike for the common good
That day, giving a loose to my soul,   15
I spent on the unimportant wood.

The sun was warm but the wind was chill.
You know how it is with an April day
When the sun is out and the wind is still,
You're one month on in the middle of May.   20
But if you so much as dare to speak,
A cloud comes over the sunlit arch,
A wind comes off a frozen peak,
And you're two months back in the middle of March.

A bluebird comes tenderly up to alight   25
And fronts the wind to unruffle a plume
His song so pitched as not to excite
A single flower as yet to bloom.
It is snowing a flake: and he half knew
Winter was only playing possum.   30
Except in color he isn't blue,
But he wouldn't advise a thing to blossom.

The water for which we may have to look
In summertime with a witching-wand,
In every wheelrut's now a brook,   35
In every print of a hoof a pond.
Be glad of water, but don't forget
The lurking frost in the earth beneath
That will steal forth after the sun is set
And show on the water its crystal teeth.   40

The time when most I loved my task
These two must make me love it more
By coming with what they came to ask.
You'd think I never had felt before

The weight of an ax-head poised aloft,   45
The grip on earth of outspread feet,
The life of muscles rocking soft
And smooth and moist in vernal heat.

Out of the woods two hulking tramps
(From sleeping God knows where last night,   50
But not long since in the lumber camps).
They thought all chopping was theirs of right.
Men of the woods and lumberjacks,
They judged me by their appropriate tool.
Except as a fellow handled an ax,   55
They had no way of knowing a fool.

Nothing on either side was said.
They knew they had but to stay their stay
And all their logic would fill my head:
As that I had no right to play   60
With what was another man's work for gain.
My right might be love but theirs was need.
And where the two exist in twain
Theirs was the better right—agreed.

But yield who will to their separation,   65
My object in living is to unite
My avocation and my vocation
As my two eyes make one in sight.
Only where love and need are one,
And the work is play for mortal stakes,   70
Is the deed ever really done
For Heaven and the future's sakes.

Assignment: Write an analysis of the structure of Robert Frost's "Two Tramps in Mud Time." In writing your analysis answer the following questions:

1. What is the function of the seasonal description in the third, fourth and fifth stanzas?
2. Are these stanzas digressive, or do they contribute something important to the poem's purpose?
3. What rhetorical device connects these stanzas, and how does it relate to the poem's concluding stanzas?
4. What is the rhetorical relationship between "need" and "love" in stanza eight?
5. Does this relationship continue into stanza nine?
6. How does the exposition of the poem's purpose in stanza nine comment on the earlier description of chopping wood in stanza two?

Further Assignment: Write an analysis of the structure of one of the following poems:

1. Robert Frost's "Birches"
2. Walt Whitman's "Passage to India"
3. Percy Bysshe Shelley's "Ode to the West Wind"
4. W. H. Auden's "The Fall of Rome"
5. William Wordsworth's "Lines Composed a Few Miles Above Tintern Abbey"
6. W. H. Auden's "In Memory of W. B. Yeats"

These poems are all included in Appendix II.

ASSIGNMENT 5: ANALYSIS OF PROSODY*

Essentially, the writer of the analysis of prosody is trying to answer the question: How does a poem's sound contribute to the poem's sense? How, for example, do meter, rhythm, and sound patterns like alliteration, assonance, onomatopoeia, and so forth, contribute to the development of the poem's purpose?

I LIKE TO SEE IT LAP THE MILES

Emily Dickinson

I like to see it lap the miles,
And lick the valleys up,
And stop to feed itself at tanks;
And then, prodigious, step

Around a pile of mountains,   5
And, supercilious, peer
In shanties by the sides of roads;
And then a quarry pare

To fit its sides, and crawl between,
Complaining all the while   10
In horrid, hooting stanza;
Then chase itself down hill

29

And neigh like Boanerges;
Then, punctual as a star,
Stop—docile and omnipotent—   15
At its own stable door.

SAMPLE ANALYSIS OF PROSODY

"I Like to See it Lap the Miles" is a *tour de force* in which Emily Dickinson has effectively marshalled the major resources of prosody—meter,* stanza* form, rhyme,* alliteration* and assonance*—to describe the movement of a railroad train, or, as it is metaphorically identified in the poem, the iron horse.

One of the most impressive parts of her performance, impressive because of its simple functionalism, is her use of metrical variations on the standard ballad stanza* form—a quatrain with alternating lines of iambic tetrameter and iambic trimeter rhyming *a b c b*—which the poetess has altered for her own purposes, namely, to illustrate the alterations in the movement of the train. For example, in the first three stanzas the train is shown moving rapidly, the rapidity conveyed through essentially regular meter built on monosyllabic or disyllabic words (there are only five words of more than two syllables in the entire poem); and, in the first few lines, through alliterating liquids, which suggest the steady rhythm of the moving train:

$$\overline{\text{I líke}} \mid \overline{\text{to sée}} \mid \overline{\text{it láp}} \mid \overline{\text{the míles,}}$$
$$\text{And líck} \mid \text{the vál} \mid \text{leys úp,}$$

But in the fourth stanza when the train slows down, the verse, like the train, chugs to a halt with substituted spondaic* and pyrrhic* feet in the last two lines:

$$\text{Stóp —dóc} \mid \text{ile and} \mid \text{om níp} \mid \text{o tént—}$$
$$\text{At its} \mid \text{own stá} \mid \text{ble dóor.}$$

Significantly, the train slows on polysyllabic words—"docile and omnipotent" — suggesting latent power rather than rapid movement. Paralleling her use of alliteration in stanza one, in this last stanza the poetess modulates her sound effects describing the chugging train, first by having vowel sounds alliterate: the [a] sound in stop and docile, the [o] sound in omnipotent and own; and, second by an increase in sonority between the last pair of vowel sounds [o] and [e], and the poem's final vowel sound [ə] in door, the increase in sonority describing the last burst of noise from the train as it comes to complete rest.

Not only has Miss Dickinson made alterations in the basic ballad meter, but she has also altered the basic ballad form. Instead of the usual complete rhyme and end-stopped lines* in the second and fourth lines of the ballad quatrain, the poetess uses run-on lines* and slant rhyme* to maintain the rapid movement suggested by the regular iambic meter* and alliteration. Try, for example, substituting full rhyme* for the slant rhyme, "stare" for "peer" in line six. There is a noticeable halt after the complimentary rhyme "pare." Another significant innovation on the ballad stanza is the functional use of the breaks between stanzas to describe the train's actions. For example, the precariousness of "stép / A round a pile of móun tains" is conveyed not only by the suppression of the normal stress at the end of the fifth line, but by the break at the end of the stanza after "step." Literally, the reader must step from stanza to stanza. Similarly, the break between the second and third stanzas suggests paring a quarry, that is riding through a mountain pass.

Emily Dickinson's poem almost exhausts the prosodaic resources of the ballad, and it ably demonstrates the subtle possibilities between the subject of the verse and the versification itself.

COMMENTS ON SAMPLE PROSODAIC ANALYSIS

Before writing the prosodaic analysis, the writer had to do a considerable amount of work. He had to scan the poem, that is, first, mark off the accented and unaccented syllables in each line; and second, identify the basic foot, and count the number of feet in each line. (See the glossary for an explanation of metrical feet.)

The writer also had to distinguish between mechanical scansion—a faulty method of scansion when the basic metrical pattern or ground meter, as poet Karl Shapiro calls it, is indiscriminately imposed on all the lines—and the actual meter, when the reader acknowledges the relatively greater importance of some of the words in the line. For example, notice the distinction between this mechanical scansion of the last two lines of Emily Dickinson's poem:

Stop—dóc | īle aňd | om nip | o teńt—
At its | own sta | ble dóor.

and the actual scansion where stress is placed on the important words actually emphasized in reading:

Stóp dóc | īle aňd | om níp | o teńt—
At its | own sta | ble dóor.

It is not sufficient simply to mark off these variations; he must ask why the poet has introduced them, and whether they are appropriate to the subject and mood of the lines.

Once the ground meter had been identified, the writer then had to note the stanza form, that is, the number of lines comprising the stanza and the rhyming pattern. If the poem uses a traditional stanza form, the writer must take note of it; in this case the ballad stanza form had been used, and the writer noted significant departures from the standard form—for example, the use of slant instead of full rhyme. Again, the writer noted the effect of this variation.

Finally, the poem called attention to its own sound effects in the line "horrid, hooting stanza;" consequently, the writer looked for such sound effects as alliteration and assonance (which he discussed), onomatopoeia,* euphony and cacaphony (which he did not mention).

At this point, the writer was ready to begin writing his essay. In organizing his material, he found it helpful to combine the discussion of meter and alliteration (paragraph two), so that the reader would be made aware of how these two elements combine to describe the train.

BUICK

Karl Shapiro

As a sloop with a sweep of immaculate wings on her delicate spine
And a keel as steel as a root that holds in the sea as she leans,
Leaning and laughing, my warm hearted beauty, you ride, you ride,
You tack on the curves with parabola speed and a kiss of goodbye,
Like a thoroughbred sloop, my new high-spirited spirit, my kiss.   5

As my foot suggests that you leap in the air with your hips of a girl,
My finger that praises your wheel and announces your voices of song,
Flouncing your skirts, you blueness of joy, you flirt of politeness,
You leap, you intelligence, essence of wheelness with silvery nose,
And your platinum clocks of excitement stir like the hairs of a fern.   10

But now with your eyes that enter the future of roads you forget;
Where you turned on the stinging lathes of Detroit and Lansing at night
And shrieked at the torch in your secret parts and the amorous tests,
But now with your eyes that enter the future of roads you forget;
You are all instinct with your phosphorous glow and your streaking hair.   15

And now when we stop it is not as the bird from the shell that I leave
Or the leathery pilot who steps from his bird with a sneer of delight,
And not as the ignorant beast do you squat and watch me depart,
But with exquisite breathing you smile, with satisfaction of love,
And I touch you again as you tick in the silence and settle in sleep.   20

Assignment: Write a prosodaic analysis of Karl Shapiro's "Buick." Answer the following questions in writing your analysis:

1. What is the basic meter Shapiro employs?
2. Is it appropriate or inappropriate to his subject? Why?
3. Where does he introduce variations in the meter? To what effect?
4. Where do alliteration and assonance occur, and what are their effects? Where do pauses (caesura) occur in the lines?
5. Why does the poet repeat certain words, such as sloop, ride, kiss, leap, hair, spirit, bird?
6. Why is the poem divided into stanzas?

Further Assignment: Write a prosodaic analysis of one of the following poems:

1. William Carlos Williams' "The Dance"
2. Robert Frost's "Stopping By Woods on a Snowy Evening"
3. Randall Jarrell's "The Death of the Ball Turret Gunner"
4. Theodore Roethke's "My Papa's Waltz"
5. John Ciardi's "Gulls Land and Cease to Be"

These poems are included in Appendix II.

Part II

SHORT STORY
and
DRAMA

INTRODUCTION TO THE SHORT STORY AND DRAMA

Although James Joyce's "An Encounter" has been called a "poem in prose" and Ibsen's *Hedda Gabler,* because of its organic tightness, can legitimately be called poetic, obviously, no story or play is a poem; both genres differ greatly from poems as both differ greatly from one another. However, writing formalistic analyses of these three genres—poems, stories and plays—involves essentially the same basic procedure: that is, demonstrating how the parts of the individual work of literature serve to develop the whole of the work, demonstrating, in short, how part functions to fulfill purpose. Therefore, many of the techniques you may have acquired in analyzing poems will be useful to you in analyzing stories and plays.

The major difference between analyzing short stories and plays—both essentially dramatic genres involving characters in conflict*—and analyzing poems is that stories and plays raise considerably different questions than do poems. Therefore, the questions you must raise in preparation for writing analyses of stories and plays—your prewriting questions—will be considerably different from those raised in prewriting for poetry analyses.

The art of prewriting for stories and plays, like the art of prewriting for poems, is largely a matter of responding to *particular* works of art, of answering the *particular* questions that a *particular* story or play may raise. However, in prewriting for stories and plays, the following general questions and suggestions may be helpful:

1. Whose story or play is it? Who is the protagonist,* the character in whom we

see a *change* (usually psychological) as a result of the conflict or the action of the story or play?

2. Who is the antagonist?* What is the conflict? Do the protagonist and the antagonist represent universal values? If so, what are those values? Does the external conflict of the story reflect an internal, and perhaps more significant, conflict?

3. What is the symbolic function of the story's or play's events? Of the story's or play's major and minor characters? Of the story's or play's title?

4. What is the tone* of the story or play, that is, the author's attitude toward his audience? How does the tone function to achieve the author's purpose?

5. Discuss the stages of development in the story or play: the exposition,* complication,* resolution,* denouement,* for example. Discuss the *change* or the *awareness* that comes to the protagonist as a result of the story's or play's action.

6. Discuss the significance of point of view* in the story. Why, for example, is it important that a story be told from an omniscient, first person, third person, or effaced narrator point of view?

7. What is the social-historical, moral-philosphical significance of the story or play?

8. What is the significance of the setting (in time and place) and of the details of the setting or set to the story or play?

ASSIGNMENT 6: ANALYSIS OF CHARACTER AND CONFLICT

Writing the analysis of character and conflict involves answering questions like the following: What is the major conflict in the story, novel, or play? Is the conflict mainly internal or external? Who is the protagonist? Who is the antagonist (or antagonists)? Are the protagonist and antagonist representative of universal values? What change, if any, takes place within the protagonist as a result of the conflict? What is the symbolic function of the minor characters in the story? What is the symbolic function of the story's action? How does the title help to define the story's conflict?

AN ENCOUNTER

James Joyce

It was Joe Dillon who introduced the Wild West to us. He had a little library made up of old numbers of *The Union Jack, Pluck* and *The Halfpenny Marvel.* Every evening after school we met in his back garden and arranged Indian battles. He and his fat young brother Leo, the idler, held the loft of the stable while we tried to carry it by storm; or we fought a pitched battle on the grass. But, however well we fought, we never won siege or battle and all our bouts ended with Joe Dillon's war dance of victory. His parents went to eight-o'clock mass every morning in Gardiner Street and the peaceful odour of Mrs. Dillon was prevalent in the hall of the house. But he played too fiercely for us who were younger and more timid. He looked like some kind of an Indian when he capered round the garden, an old tea-cosy on his head, beating a tin with his fist and yelling:

"Ya! yaka, yaka, yaka!"

Everyone was incredulous when it was reported that he had a vocation for the priesthood. Nevertheless it was true.

A spirit of unruliness diffused itself among us and, under its influence, differences of culture and constitution were waived. We banded ourselves together, some boldly, some in jest and some almost in fear: and of the number of these latter, the reluctant Indians who were afraid to seem studious or lacking in robustness, I was one. The adventures related in the literature of the Wild West were remote from my nature but, at least, they opened doors of escape. I liked better some American detective stories which were traversed from time to time by unkempt fierce and beautiful girls. Though there was nothing wrong in these stories and though their intention was sometimes literary they were circulated secretly at school. One day when Father Butler was hearing the four pages of Roman History clumsy Leo Dillon was discovered with a copy of *The Halfpenny Marvel.*

"This page or this page? This page? Now, Dillon up! *'Hardly had the day'* . . . Go on! *'Hardly had the day dawned'.* . . Have you studied it? What have you there in your pocket?"

Everyone's heart palpitated as Leo Dillon handed up the paper and everyone assumed an innocent face. Father Butler turned over the pages, frowning.

"What is this rubbish?" he said. *"The Apache Chief!* Is this what you read instead of studying your Roman History? Let me not find any more of this wretched stuff in this college. The man who wrote it, I suppose, was some wretched fellow who writes these things for a drink. I'm surprised at boys like you, educated, reading such stuff. I could understand it if you were . . . National School boys. Now, Dillon, I advise you strongly, get at your work or . . ."

This rebuke during the sober hours of school paled much of the glory of the Wild West for me and the confused puffy face of Leo Dillon awakened one of my consciences. But when the restraining influence of the school was at a distance I began to hunger again for wild sensations, for the escape which those chronicles of disorder alone seemed to offer me. The mimic warfare of the evening became at last as wearisome to me as the routine of school in the morning because I wanted real adventures to happen to myself. But real adventures, I reflected, do not happen to people who remain at home: they must be sought abroad.

The summer holidays were near at hand when I made up my mind to break out of the weariness of school-life for one day at least. With Leo Dillon and a boy named Mahony I planned a day's miching. Each of us saved up sixpence. We were to meet at ten in the morning on the Canal Bridge. Mahony's big sister was to write an excuse for him and Leo Dillon was to tell his brother to say he was sick. We arranged to go along the Wharf Road until we came to the ships, then to cross in the ferryboat and walk out to see the Pigeon House. Leo Dillon was afraid we might meet Father Butler or someone out of the college; but Mahony asked, very sensibly, what would Father Butler be doing out at the Pigeon House. We were reassured: and I brought the first stage of the plot to an end by collecting sixpence from the other two, at the same time showing them my own sixpence. When we were making the last arrangements on the eve we were all vaguely excited. We shook hands, laughing, and Mahony said:

"Till to-morrow, mates!"

That night I slept badly. In the morning I was first-comer to the bridge as I lived nearest. I hid my books in the long grass near the ashpit at the end of the garden where nobody ever came and hurried along the canal bank. It was a mild sunny morning in the first week of June. I sat up on the coping of the bridge admiring my frail canvas shoes which I had diligently pipe-clayed overnight and watching the docile horses pulling a tramload of business people up the hill. All the branches of the tall trees which lined the mall were gay with little light green leaves and the sunlight slanted through them on to the water. The granite stone of the bridge was beginning to be warm and I began to pat it with my hands in time to an air in my head. I was very happy.

When I had been sitting there for five or ten minutes I saw Mahony's gray suit approaching. He came up the hill, smiling, and clambered up beside me on the bridge. While we were waiting he brought out the catapult which bulged from his inner pocket and explained some improvements which he had made in it. I asked him why he had brought it and he told me he had brought it to have some gas with the birds. Mahony used slang freely, and spoke of Father Butler as Old Bunser. We waited on for a quarter of an hour more but still there was no sign of Leo Dillon. Mahony, at last, jumped down and said:

"Come along. I knew Fatty'd funk it."

"And his sixpence . . . ?" I said.

"That's forfeit," said Mahony. "And so much the better for us—a bob and a tanner instead of a bob."

We walked along the North Strand Road till we came to the Vitriol Works and then turned to the right along the Wharf Road. Mahony began to play the Indian as soon as we were out of public sight. He chased a crowd of ragged girls, brandishing his unloaded catapult and, when two ragged boys began, out of chivalry, to fling stones at us, he proposed that we should charge them. I objected that the boys were too small, and so we walked on, the ragged troop screaming after us: *"Swaddlers! Swaddlers!"* thinking that we were Protestants because Mahony, who was dark-complexioned, wore the silver badge of a cricket club in his cap. When we came to the Smoothing Iron we arranged a siege; but it was a failure because you must have at least three. We revenged ourselves on Leo Dillon by saying what a funk he was and guessing how many he would get at three o'clock from Mr. Ryan.

We came then near the river. We spent a long time walking about the noisy streets flanked by high stone walls, watching the working of cranes and engines and often being shouted at for our immobility by the drivers of groaning carts. It was noon when we reached the quays and, as all the labourers seemed to be eating their lunches, we bought two big currant buns and sat down to eat them on some metal piping beside the river. We pleased ourselves with the spectacle of Dublin's commerce—the barges signalled from far away by their curls of wooly smoke, the brown fishing fleet beyond Ringsend, the big white sailing-vessel which was being discharged on the opposite quay. Mahony said it would be right skit to run away to sea on one of those big ships and even I, looking at the high masts, saw, or imagined, the geography which had been scantily dosed to me at school gradually taking substance under my eyes. School and home seemed to recede from us and their influences upon us seemed to wane.

We crossed the Liffey in the ferryboat, paying our toll to be transported in the company of two labourers and a little Jew with a bag. We were serious to the point of solemnity, but once during the short voyage our eyes met and we laughed. When we landed we watched the discharging of the graceful three-master which we had observed from the other quay. Some bystanders said that she was a Norwegian vessel. I went to the stern and tried to decipher the legend upon it but, failing to do so, I came back and examined the foreign sailors to see had any of them green eyes for I had some confused notion. . . . The sailors' eyes were blue and grey and even black. The only sailor whose eyes could have been called green was a tall man who amused the crowd on the quay by calling out cheerfully every time the planks fell:

"All right! All right!"

When we were tired of this sight we wandered slowly into Ringsend. The day had grown sultry, and in the windows of the grocers' shops musty biscuits lay bleaching. We bought some biscuits and chocolate which we ate sedulously as we wandered through the squalid streets where the families of the fishermen live. We could find no dairy and so we went into a huckster's shop and bought a bottle of raspberry lemonade each. Refreshed by this, Mahony chased a cat down a lane, but the cat escaped into a wide field. We both felt rather tired and when we reached the field we made at once for a sloping bank over the ridge of which we could see the Dodder.

It was too late and we were too tired to carry out our project of visiting the Pigeon House. We had to be home before four o'clock lest our adventure should be discovered. Mahony looked regretfully at his catapult and I had to suggest going home by train before he regained any cheerfulness. The sun went in behind some clouds and left us to our jaded thoughts and the crumbs of our provisions.

There was nobody but ourselves in the field. When we had lain on the bank for some time without speaking I saw a man approaching from the far end of the field. I watched him lazily as I chewed one of those green stems on which girls tell fortunes. He came along by the bank slowly. He walked with one hand upon his hip and in the other hand he held a stick with which he tapped the turf lightly. He was shabbily dressed in a suit of greenish-black and wore what we used to call a jerry hat with a high crown. He seemed to be fairly old for his moustache was ashen-gray. When he passed at our feet he glanced up at us quickly and then continued his way. We followed him with our eyes and saw that when he had gone on for perhaps fifty paces he turned about and began to retrace his steps. He walked towards us very slowly, always tapping the ground with his stick, so slowly that I thought he was looking for something in the grass.

He stopped when he came level with us and bade us good-day. We answered him and he sat down beside us on the slope slowly and with great care. He began to talk of the weather, saying that it would be a very hot summer and adding that the seasons had changed greatly since he was a boy—a long time ago. He said that the happiest time of one's life was undoubtedly one's schoolboy days and that he would give anything to be young again. While he expressed these sentiments which bored us a little we kept silent. Then he began to talk of school and of books. He asked us whether we had read the poetry of Thomas Moore or the works of Sir Walter Scott and Lord Lytton. I pretended that I had read every book he mentioned so that in the end he said:

"Ah, I can see you are a bookworm like myself. Now," he added, pointing to Mahony who was regarding us with open eyes, "he is different; he goes in for games."

He said he had all Sir Walter Scott's works and all Lord Lytton's works at home and never tired of reading them. "Of course," he said, "there were some of Lord Lytton's works which boys couldn't read." Mahony asked why couldn't boys read them—a question which agitated and pained me because I was afraid the man would think I was as stupid as Mahony. The man, however, only smiled. I saw that he had great gaps in his mouth between his yellow teeth. Then he asked us which of us had the most sweethearts. Mahony mentioned lightly that he had three totties. The man asked me how many I had. I answered that I had none. He did not believe me and said he was sure I must have one. I was silent.

"Tell us," said Mahony pertly to the man, "how many have you yourself?"

The man smiled as before and said that when he was our age he had lots of sweethearts.

"Every boy," he said, "has a little sweetheart."

His attitude on this point struck me as strangely liberal in a man of his age. In my heart I thought that what he said about boys and sweethearts was reasonable. But I disliked the words in his mouth and I wondered why he shivered once or twice as if he feared something or felt a sudden chill. As he proceeded I noticed that his accent was good. He began to speak to us about girls, saying what nice soft hair they had and how soft their hands were and how all girls were not so good as they seemed to be if one only knew. There was nothing he liked, he said, so much as looking at a nice young girl, at her nice white hands and her beautiful soft hair. He gave me the impression that he was repeating something which he had learned by heart or that, magnetised by some words of his own speech, his mind was slowly circling round and round in the same orbit. At times he spoke as if he were simply alluding to some fact that everybody knew, and at other times he lowered his voice and spoke mysteriously as if he were telling us something secret which he did not wish others to overhear. He repeated his phrases over and over again, varying them and surrounding them with his monotonous voice. I continued to gaze towards the foot of the slope, listening to him.

After a long while his monologue paused. He stood up slowly, saying that he had to leave us for a minute or so, a few minutes, and, without changing the direction of my gaze, I saw him walking slowly away from us towards the near end of the field. We remained silent when he had gone. After a silence of a few minutes I heard Mahony exclaim:

"I say! Look what he's doing!"

As I neither answered nor raised my eyes Mahony exclaimed again:

"I say . . . He's a queer old josser!"

"In case he asks us for our names," I said, "let you be Murphy and I'll be Smith."

We said nothing further to each other. I was still considering whether I would go away or not when the man came back and sat down beside us again. Hardly had he sat down when Mahony, catching sight of the cat which had escaped him, sprang up and pursued her across the field. The man and I watched the chase. The cat escaped once more and Mahony began to throw stones at the wall she had escaladed. Desisting from this, he began to wander about the far end of the field, aimlessly.

After an interval the man spoke to me. He said that my friend was a very rough boy and asked did he get whipped often at school. I was going to reply indignantly that we were not National School boys to be whipped, as he called it; but I remained silent. He began to speak on the subject of chastising boys. His mind, as if magnetised again by his speech, seemed to circle slowly round and round its new centre. He said that when boys were that kind they ought to be whipped and well whipped. When a boy was rough and unruly there was nothing would do him any good but a good sound whipping. A slap on the hand or a box on the ear was no good: what he wanted was to get a nice warm whipping. I was surprised at this sentiment and involuntarily glanced up at his face. As I did so I met the gaze of a pair of bottle-green eyes peering at me from under a twitching forehead. I turned my eyes away again.

The man continued his monologue. He seemed to have forgotten his recent liberalism. He said that if ever he found a boy talking to girls or having a girl for a sweetheart he would whip him and whip him; and that would teach him not to be talking to girls. And if a boy had a girl for a sweetheart and told lies about it then he would give him such a whipping as no boy ever got in this world. He said that there was nothing in this world he would like so well as that. He described to me how he would whip such a boy as if he were unfolding some elaborate mystery. He would love that, he said, better than anything in this world; and his voice, as he led me monotonously through the mystery, grew almost affectionate and seemed to plead with me that I should understand him.

I waited till his monologue paused again. Then I stood up abruptly. Lest I should betray my agitation I delayed a few moments pretending to fix my shoe properly and then, saying that I was obliged to go, I bade him goodday. I went up the slope calmly but my heart was beating quickly with fear that he would seize me by the ankles. When I reached the top of the slope I turned round and, without looking at him, called loudly across the field:

"Murphy!"

My voice had an accent of forced bravery in it and I was ashamed of my paltry strategem. I had to call the name again before Mahony saw me and hallooed in answer. How my heart beat as he came running across the field to me! He ran as if to bring me aid. And I was penitent; for in my heart I had always despised him a little.

SAMPLE ANALYSIS OF CHARACTER
AND CONFLICT

Why the narrator-protagonist of "An Encounter" has always—as he confesses in the last line of the story—despised Mahony a little, is a key question to be answered in order to define the major conflict of the story. That a sensitive, intelligent and imaginative person such as the narrator would naturally "despise . . . a little" the callous, crude, and rather cruel Mahony—a boy who bullies smaller children, is cruel to animals, and is rude to older people—is certainly part of the answer. However, Joyce's story suggests a more complex and universal answer: that is, that the narrator's despising Mahony "a little" is a statement of the age old antipathy (an antipathy that derives from a mixture of repulsion and attraction, of contempt and envy) that the man of thought feels for the man of action; the man of imagination for the man of common sense; the man of conscience for the man of instinct; the civilized man for the primitive man. Thus, in "An Encounter" the major conflict is between the values represented by the narrator (conscience, imagination, and so forth) and those represented by Mahony (action, instinct, and so forth).

Although there are a few hints of an overt, a public conflict between the two boys—for example, the narrator's protesting against Mahony's bullying of the smaller children—basically the story's conflict takes place in the consciousness of the narrator-protagonist. Within the person of the narrator, the reader sees, throughout the story, a struggle that the narrator himself is not clearly aware of: the struggle mentioned above, the struggle between the narrator's values and Mahony's. A helpful metaphor for dramatizing this struggle occurs early in the story when the narrator refers to himself as a "reluctant Indian" (this in describing his attitude toward the Wild West games at the Dillon's); Mahony, on the other hand, slightly later (at the beginning of the hooky playing adventure) is described as enthusiastically adopting the role of "the Indian," that is, *instinctively* becoming the natural, amoral, asocial man—the primitive, the savage. Instinctively, for example, Mahony pockets Leo Dillon's sixpence, intimidates the smaller children, looks for birds to shoot with his slingshot, chases the cat, calls Father Butler (symbol of church and school and tradition) "Old Bunser," and is rude to the old pervert. None of this bothers Mahony's conscience; none of this causes him a moment's reflection; he simply behaves this way naturally and effortlessly. The narrator, on the other hand—the "reluctant Indian"—cannot instinctively and naturally enjoy the hooky playing adventure: he is too intelligent, too imaginative, too sensitive to other people's rights and feelings; he is too conscientious, too civilized, too bound, in short, to what Freud calls the demands of the super ego. The narrator, for example, wonders why Mahony brings along the slingshot (a symbol of the aggressiveness Mahony possesses and the narrator lacks); the narrator is conscientiously puzzled about the right thing to do with Leo Dillon's money; the narrator finds Mahony's free use of slang worth commenting on; the narrator conscientiously reminds Mahony that it's not fair to bully the smaller children; and, finally, the narrator worries about hurting the feelings of the old pervert.

What Joyce is rather brilliantly articulating with this metaphor—the Indian metaphor—is not only the narrator's central problem and the story's major conflict, but—if we can believe Freud—the central problem of civilized man: that is, in order to be civilized, man must check, must repress, his natural impulses, his appetites, his instincts and aggressive tendencies; and in so doing, in trying, for example, to live by *conscience,* by codes and laws and ideals, by conventions and traditions, by the demands of the super ego, civilized man (like the narrator) runs the risk of frustration, neurosis, and ultimately, of perverting his nature.

The conflict between what Mahony represents and what the narrator represents resolves itself in the final scene of the story—the story's major recognition scene. Here the narrator—explicitly for the first time in the story—confesses his real feelings for Mahony and admits, albeit grudgingly, his dependence on Mahony—that is, his dependence on the strengths Mahony represents. In this scene Mahony brings aid to the narrator, and the narrator, in his conscientious way, feels "penitent" or guilty for having "always despised him [Mahony] a little." The "aid" Mahony brings, of course, is the aid the man of action brings to the man of thought, the aid to act, the aid to escape the spell of the pervert. The narrator's inability to break away easily from the pervert is, on one level, attributable to his sensitivity—to his good manners (developed according to the super ego) that prohibit his hurting the old man's feelings by rudely taking leave; however, on a more significant level, the narrator's inability to break away can be attributed to his fascination with the pervert. Whereas the old man with his literary pretentions and compulsive monologues simply bores Mahony— who commonsensically dismisses him as a "queer old josser" and then runs off in his characteristically *natural* way to chase a cat—the old man appeals to the narrator's imagination (a faculty not highly developed in Mahony), to his intellectual curiosity. Besides being interested in and sympathizing with the pervert, the narrator to some extent *identifies* with the pervert. Both he and the pervert, for example, are described as "bookworms" whereas Mahony is described by the pervert as "different; he goes in for games." (Again we see the mind-body duality.) From the narrator's point of view, the pervert is well spoken and well read (though the pervert's taste in literature is apparently for romanticism of a decadent kind); and the narrator immediately hopes that the old man will think well of him—that is, not think him "as *stupid* as Mahony."

Perversion is a sickness of civilization—a sickness caused by overcivilization, by the development of the mind and imagination and conscience at the expense of the *natural,* instinctive life; and the pervert in "An Encounter" functions as a symbol of overcivilization, of decadence. That the narrator-protagonist *encounters* the pervert, momentarily finds himself in league with the pervert (that is, men of breeding and intelligence pitted against a barbarian), and ultimately needs Mahony's "aid" to escape the spell of the pervert, is Joyce's way of showing through symbolic action the central conflict in the narrator's consciousness and the central and universal problem of civilized man. If we ask ourselves what *happens* in the story—at least on this level of the story's action—we can answer that as a result of the "encounter" the boy learns that his virtues (sensitivity, intelligence, imagination, conscientiousness, and so on) have in them the seeds of the vices the old man represents; that, in short, he could become what the old man is. That the "green eyes" belong to the pervert and not to the sailors—conventional romantic hero figures, figures boys identify with—is a major irony that supports the above reading. The boy's reluctant acceptance of his *need* for Mahony thus becomes symbolically the boy's reluctant acceptance of the truth that, if he is to achieve genuine maturity, he must *balance* the conflicting demands of his nature.

COMMENTS ON THE SAMPLE CHARACTER AND CONFLICT ANALYSIS

If you will study the sample analysis carefully you will see that the writer has raised and answered questions necessary not only for an analysis of a particular story but for analyses of all stories. For example, he raises such questions as: What is the major conflict in the story? Is the conflict mainly external or internal, that is, does it take place mainly outside or inside the mind of the main character, of the protagonist? Whose story is it? Who is the protagonist, the character *changed* as a result of the story's conflict? Who is the antagonist or the protagonist's main adversary? Are the protagonist and the antagonist representative of universal types? What conflicting universal values do they represent? What change takes place in the protagonist? What new awareness comes to him as a result of the story's action, of his conflict with the antagonist? What is the symbolic function of the other characters in the story? How do they help develop the story's purpose? What is the symbolic function of the external action in the story, for instance, of Mahony's running across the field to bring aid and of his chasing the cat?

Although the writer of the sample paper fails to raise other major questions (What is the function of the title in defining the conflict? What is the function of the narrator's suggesting that Mahony and he give false names, false identities, to the pervert? What is the symbolic function of the hooky trip itself?) by and large he has done a thorough job of raising and answering the questions his analysis demands.

Rhetorically, the sample paper is basically an essay of comparison and contrast. The writer begins with a major question which leads him smoothly to the main job of answering that question, of contrasting the narrator and Mahony. Notice how the writer has selected a key Joyce metaphor—"the reluctant Indian,"—a particular symbol from the text, and then developed this metaphor with pertinent extra textual detail, for example, the super ego, id categories. Using these major categories, the writer is able to organize smoothly his main points of contrast and to demonstrate the universal conflict behind the particular conflict of the two boys. Notice also that the writer always carefully documents his generalizations with ample evidence, a number of details from the text. He does not merely state; he *demonstrates;* he *proves* through the scrupulous use of concrete details and examples.

Assignment: Focusing on Tesman and Lövborg write an analysis of character and conflict in *Hedda Gabler.* Your analysis should attempt to answer such questions as the following:

1. What conflicting universal values are represented by Tesman and Lövborg?
2. How does the conflict between what Tesman represents and what Lövborg represents provide a reflection of the conflict within the mind of Hedda?
3. Does the conflict between Tesman's values and Lövborg's values illustrate what Friedrich Nietzsche in *The Birth of Tragedy* calls the eternal struggle between the Apollonian and the Dionysian* spirits?
4. How do the manuscripts of Tesman and Lövborg symbolically define the conflict in values that exists between the two men?

HEDDA GABLER

Henrik Ibsen

CHARACTERS

George Tesman
Hedda Tesman, his wife
Miss Juliana Tesman, his aunt
Mrs. Elvsted
Judge Brack
Eilert Lövborg
Berta, servant at the Tesmans'

The scene of the action is Tesman's villa, in the west end of Christiania.

Act I

Scene: *A spacious, handsome, and tastefully furnished drawing room, decorated in dark colors. In the back, a wide doorway with curtains drawn back, leading into a smaller room decorated in the same style as the drawing room. In the right-hand wall of the front room, a folding door leading out to the hall. In the opposite wall, on the left, a glass door, also with curtains drawn back. Through the panes can be seen part of a verandah outside, and trees covered with autumn foliage. An oval table, with a cover on it, and surrounded by chairs, stands well forward. In front, by the wall on the right, a wide stove of dark porcelain, a high-backed armchair, a cushioned footrest, and two foot-stools. A settee, with a small round table in front of it, fills the upper right-hand corner. In front, on the left, a little way from the wall, a sofa. Farther back than the glass door, a piano. On either side of the doorway at the back a whatnot with terra-cotta and majolica ornaments. Against the back wall of the inner room a sofa, with a table, and one or two chairs. Over the sofa hangs the portrait of a handsome elderly man in a General's uniform. Over the table a hanging lamp, with an opal glass shade. A number of bouquets are arranged about the drawing room, in vases and glasses. Others lie upon the tables. The floors in both rooms are covered with thick carpets. Morning light. The sun shines in through the glass door.*

MISS JULIANA TESMAN, *with her bonnet on and carrying a parasol, comes in from the hall, followed by* BERTA, *who carries a bouquet wrapped in paper.* MISS TESMAN *is a comely and pleasant-looking lady of about sixty-*

five. She is nicely but simply dressed in a gray walking costume. BERTA *is a middle-aged woman of plain and rather countrified appearance.*

Miss Tesman. [*Stops close to the door, listens, and says softly.*] Upon my word, I don't believe they are stirring yet!

Berta. [*Also softly.*] I told you so, Miss. Remember how late the steamboat got in last night. And then, when they got home!—good Lord, what a lot the young mistress had to unpack before she could get to bed.

Miss Tesman. Well, well—let them have their sleep out. But let us see that they get a good breath of the fresh morning air when they do appear. [*She goes to the glass door and throws it open.*]

Berta. [*Beside the table, at a loss what to do with the bouquet in her hand.*] I declare there isn't a bit of room left. I think I'll put it down here, Miss. [*She places it on the piano.*]

Miss Tesman. So you've got a new mistress now, my dear Berta. Heaven knows it was a wrench to me to part with you.

Berta. [*On the point of weeping.*] And do you think it wasn't hard for me too, Miss? After all the blessed years I've been with you and Miss Rina.

Miss Tesman. We must make the best of it, Berta. There was nothing else to be done. George can't do without you, you see—he absolutely can't. He has had you to look after him ever since he was a little boy.

Berta. Ah, but, Miss Julia, I can't help thinking of Miss Rina lying helpless at home there, poor thing. And with only that new girl, too! She'll never learn to take proper care of an invalid.

Miss Tesman. Oh, I shall manage to train her. And of course, you know, I shall take most of it upon myself. You needn't be uneasy about my poor sister, my dear Berta.

Berta. Well, but there's another thing, Miss. I'm so mortally afraid I shan't be able to suit the young mistress.

Miss Tesman. Oh, well—just at first there may be one or two things—

Berta. Most like she'll be terrible grand in her ways.

Miss Tesman. Well, you can't wonder at that—General Gabler's daughter! Think of the sort of life she was accustomed to in her father's time. Don't you remember how we used to see her riding down the road along with the General? In that long black habit—and with feathers in her hat?

Berta. Yes, indeed—I remember well enough—! But good Lord, I should never have dreamt in those days that she and Master George would make a match of it.

Miss Tesman. Nor I. But, by-the-bye, Berta—while I think of it: in future you mustn't say Master George. You must say Dr. Tesman.

Berta. Yes, the young mistress spoke of that too—last night— the moment they set foot in the house. Is it true, then, Miss?

Miss Tesman. Yes, indeed it is. Only think, Berta—some foreign university has made him a doctor—while he has been abroad, you understand. I hadn't heard a word about it, until he told me himself upon the pier.

Berta. Well, well, he's clever enough for anything, he is. But I didn't think he'd have gone in for doctoring people too.

Miss Tesman. No, no, it's not that sort of doctor he is. [*Nods significantly.*] But let me tell you, we may have to call him something still grander before long.

Berta. You don't say so! What can that be, Miss?

Miss Tesman. [*Smiling.*] H'm—wouldn't you like to know! [*With emotion.*] Ah, dear, dear—if my poor brother could only look up from his grave now, and see what his little boy has grown into! [*Looks around.*] But bless me, Berta—why have you done this? Taken the chintz covers off all the furniture?

Berta. The mistress told me to. She can't abide covers on the chairs, she says.

Miss Tesman. Are they going to make this their everyday sitting room then?

Berta. Yes, that's what I understood—from the mistress. Master George— the doctor—he said nothing.

[GEORGE TESMAN *comes from the right into the inner room, humming to himself, and carrying an unstrapped empty portmanteau. He is a middle-sized, young-looking man of thirty-three, rather stout, with a round, open, cheerful face, fair hair and beard. He wears spectacles, and is somewhat carelessly dressed in comfortable indoor clothes.*]

Miss Tesman. Good morning, good morning, George.

Tesman. [*In the doorway between the rooms.*] Aunt Julia! Dear Aunt Julia! [*Goes up to her and shakes hands warmly.*] Come all this way—so early! Eh?

Miss Tesman. Why of course I had to come and see how you were getting on.

Tesman. In spite of your having had no proper night's rest?

Miss Tesman. Oh, that makes no difference to me.

Tesman. Well, I suppose you got home all right from the pier? Eh?

Miss Tesman. Yes, quite safely, thank goodness. Judge Brack was good enough to see me right to my door.

Tesman. We were so sorry we couldn't give you a seat in the carriage. But you saw what a pile of boxes Hedda had to bring with her.

Miss Tesman. Yes, she had certainly plenty of boxes.

Berta. [*To* TESMAN.] Shall I go in and see if there's anything I can do for the mistress?

Tesman. No, thank you, Berta—you needn't. She said she would ring if she wanted anything.

Berta. [*Going towards the right.*] Very well.

Tesman. But look here—take this portmanteau with you.

Berta. [*Taking it.*] I'll put it in the attic. [*She goes out by the hall door.*]

Tesman. Fancy, Aunty—I had the whole of that portmanteau chock full of copies of documents. You wouldn't believe how much I have picked up from all the archives I have been examining—curious old details that no one has had any idea of—

Miss Tesman. Yes, you don't seem to have wasted your time on your wedding trip, George.

Tesman. No, that I haven't. But do take off your bonnet, Auntie. Look here! Let me untie the strings—eh?

Miss Tesman. [*While he does so.*] Well, well—this is just as if you were still at home with us.

Tesman. [*With the bonnet in his hand, looks at it from all sides.*] Why, what a gorgeous bonnet you've been investing in!

Miss Tesman. I bought it on Hedda's account.

Tesman. On Hedda's account? Eh?

Miss Tesman. Yes, so that Hedda needn't be ashamed of me if we happened to go out together.

Tesman. [*Patting her cheek.*] You always think of everything, Aunt Julia. [*Lays the bonnet on a chair beside the table.*] And now, look here—suppose we sit comfortably on the sofa and have a little chat, till Hedda comes.

[*They seat themselves. She places her parasol in the corner of the sofa.*]

Miss Tesman. [*Takes both his hands and looks at him.*] What a delight it is to have you again, as large as life, before my very eyes, George! My George—my poor brother's own boy!

Tesman. And it's a delight for me, too, to see you again, Aunt Julia! You, who have been father and mother in one to me.

Miss Tesman. Oh, yes, I know you will always keep a place in your heart for your old aunts.

Tesman. And what about Aunt Rina? No improvement—eh!

Miss Tesman. Oh, no—we can scarcely look for any improvement in her case, poor thing. There she lies, helpless, as she has lain for all these years. But heaven grant I may not lose her yet awhile! For if I did, I don't know what I should make of my life, George—especially now that I haven't you to look after any more.

Tesman. [*Patting her back.*] There, there, there—!

Miss Tesman. [*Suddenly changing her tone.*] And to think that here you are a married man, George!—And that you should be the one to carry off Hedda Gabler, the beautiful Hedda Gabler! Only think of it—she, that was so beset with admirers!

Tesman. [*Hums a little and smiles complacently.*] Yes, I fancy I have several good friends about town who would like to stand in my shoes— eh?

Miss Tesman. And then this fine long wedding tour you have had! More than five—nearly six months—

Tesman. Well, for me it has been a sort of tour of research as well. I have had to do so much grubbing among old records—and to read no end of books too, Auntie.

Miss Tesman. Oh, yes, I suppose so. [*More confidentially, and lowering her voice a little.*] But listen now, George—have you nothing—nothing special to tell me?

Tesman. As to our journey?

Miss Tesman. Yes.

Tesman. No, I don't know of anything except what I have told you in my letters. I had a doctor's degree conferred on me—but that I told you yesterday.

Miss Tesman. Yes, yes, you did. But what I mean is—haven't you any— any—expectations—?

Tesman. Expectations?

Miss Tesman. Why, you know, George—I'm your old auntie!

Tesman. Why, of course I have expectations.

Miss Tesman. Ah!

Tesman. I have every expectation of being a professor one of these days.

Miss Tesman. Oh, yes, a professor—

Tesman. Indeed, I may say I am certain of it. But my dear Auntie—you know all about that already!

Miss Tesman. [*Laughing to herself.*] Yes, of course I do. You are quite right there. [*Changing the subject.*] But we were talking about your journey. It must have cost a great deal of money, George?

Tesman. Well, you see—my handsome traveling scholarship went a good way.

Miss Tesman. But I can't understand how you can have made it go far enough for two.

Tesman. No, that's not so easy to understand—eh?

Miss Tesman. And especially traveling with a lady—they tell me that makes it ever so much more expensive.

Tesman. Yes, of course—it makes it a little more expensive. But Hedda had to have this trip, Auntie! She really had to. Nothing else would have done.

Miss Tesman. No, no I suppose not. A wedding tour seems to be quite indispensable nowadays. But tell me now—have you gone thoroughly over the house yet?

Tesman. Yes, you may be sure I have. I have been afoot ever since daylight.

Miss Tesman. And what do you think of it all?

Tesman. I'm delighted! Quite delighted! Only I can't think what we are to do with the two empty rooms between this inner parlor and Hedda's bedroom.

Miss Tesman. [*Laughing.*] Oh, my dear George, I dare say you may find some use for them—in the course of time.

Tesman. Why of course you are quite right, Aunt Julia! You mean as my library increases—eh?

Miss Tesman. Yes, quite so, my dear boy. It was your library I was thinking of.

Tesman. I am specially pleased on Hedda's account. Often and often, before we were engaged, she said that she would never care to live anywhere but in Secretary Falk's villa.

Miss Tesman. Yes, it was lucky that this very house should come into the market, just after you had started.

Tesman. Yes, Aunt Julia, the luck was on our side, wasn't it—eh?

Miss Tesman. But the expense, my dear George! You will find it very expensive, all this.

Tesman. [*Looks at her, a little cast down.*] Yes, I suppose I shall, Aunt!

Miss Tesman. Oh, frightfully!

Tesman. How much do you think? In round numbers?—Eh?

Miss Tesman. Oh, I can't even guess until all the accounts come in.

Tesman. Well, fortunately, Judge Brack has secured the most favorable terms for me—so he said in a letter to Hedda.

Miss Tesman. Yes, don't be uneasy, my dear boy. Besides, I have given security for the furniture and all the carpets.

Tesman. Security? You? My dear Aunt Julia—what sort of security could you give?

Miss Tesman. I have given a mortgage on our annuity.

Tesman. [*Jumps up.*] What! On your—and Aunt Rina's annuity!

Miss Tesman. Yes, I knew of no other plan, you see.

Tesman. [*Placing himself before her.*] Have you gone out of your senses, Auntie! Your annuity—it's all that you and Aunt Rina have to live upon.

Miss Tesman. Well, well, don't get so excited about it. It's only a matter of form you know—Judge Brack assured me of that. It was he that was kind enough to arrange the whole affair for me. A mere matter of form, he said.

Tesman. Yes, that may be all very well. But nevertheless—

Miss Tesman. You will have your own salary to depend upon now. And, good heavens, even if we did have to pay up a little—! To eke things out a bit at the start—! Why, it would be nothing but a pleasure to us.

Tesman. Oh, Auntie—will you never be tired of making sacrifices for me!

Miss Tesman. [*Rises and lays her hands on his shoulders.*] Have I had any other happiness in this world except to smooth your way for you, my dear boy? You, who have had neither father nor mother to depend on. And now we have reached the goal, George! Things have looked black enough for us, sometimes; but, thank heaven, now you have nothing to fear.

Tesman. Yes, it is really marvelous how everything has turned out for the best.

Miss Tesman. And the people who opposed you—who wanted to bar the way for you—now you have them at your feet. They have fallen, George. Your most dangerous rival—his fall was the worst. And now he has to lie on the bed he has made for himself—poor misguided creature.

Tesman. Have you heard anything of Eilert? Since I went away, I mean.

Miss Tesman. Only that he is said to have published a new book.

Tesman. What! Eilert Lövborg! Recently—eh?

Miss Tesman. Yes, so they say. Heaven knows whether it can be worth anything! Ah, when your new book appears—that will be another story, George! What is it to be about?

Tesman. It will deal with the domestic industries of Brabant during the Middle Ages.

Miss Tesman. Fancy—to be able to write on such a subject as that.

Tesman. However, it may be some time before the book is ready. I have all these collections to arrange first, you see.

Miss Tesman. Yes, collecting and arranging—no one can beat you at that. There you are my poor brother's own son.

Tesman. I am looking forward eagerly' to setting to work at it; especially now that I have my own delightful home to work in.

Miss Tesman. And, most of all, now that you have got the wife of your heart, my dear George.

Tesman. [*Embracing her.*] Oh, yes, yes, Aunt Julia. Hedda—she is the best part of all! [*Looks towards the doorway.*] I believe I hear her coming— eh?

[HEDDA *enters from the left through the inner room. She is a woman of nine-and-twenty. Her face and figure show refinement and distinction. Her complexion is pale and opaque. Her steel-gray eyes express a cold, unruffled repose. Her hair is of an agreeable medium brown, but not particularly abundant. She is dressed in a tasteful, somewhat loose-fitting morning gown.*]

Miss Tesman. [*Going to meet* HEDDA.] Good morning, my dear Hedda! Good morning, and a hearty welcome.

Hedda. [*Holds out her hand.*] Good morning, dear Miss Tesman! So early a call! That is kind of you.

Miss Tesman. [*With some embarrassment.*] Well—has the bride slept well in her new home?

Hedda. Oh yes, thanks. Passably.

Tesman. [*Laughing.*] Passably! Come, that's good, Hedda! You were sleeping like a stone when I got up.

Hedda. Fortunately. Of course one has always to accustom one's self to new surroundings, Miss Tesman—little by little. [*Looking towards the left.*] Oh—there the servant has gone and opened the verandah door, and let in a whole flood of sunshine.

Miss Tesman. [*Going towards the door.*] Well, then, we will shut it.

Hedda. No, no, not that! Tesman, please draw the curtains. That will give a softer light.

Tesman. [*At the door.*] All right—all right. There now, Hedda, now you have both shade and fresh air.

Hedda. Yes, fresh air we certainly must have, with all these stacks of flowers—. But—won't you sit down, Miss Tesman?

Miss Tesman. No, thank you. Now that I have seen that everything is all right here—thank heaven! I must be getting home again. My sister is lying longing for me, poor thing.

Tesman. Give her my very best love, Auntie; and say I shall look in and see her later in the day.

Miss Tesman. Yes, yes, I'll be sure to tell her. But by-the-bye, George— [*Feeling in her dress pocket*]—I have almost forgotten—I have something for you here.

Tesman. What is it, Auntie? Eh?

Miss Tesman. [*Produces a flat parcel wrapped in newspaper and hands it to him.*] Look here, my dear boy.

Tesman. [*Opening the parcel.*] Well, I declare! Have you really saved them for me, Aunt Julia! Hedda! isn't this touching—eh?

Hedda. [*Beside the whatnot on the right.*] Well, what is it?

Tesman. My old morning shoes! My slippers.

Hedda. Indeed. I remember you often spoke of them while we were abroad.

Tesman. Yes, I missed them terribly. [*Goes up to her.*] Now you shall see them, Hedda!

Hedda. [*Going towards the stove.*] Thanks, I really don't care about it.

Tesman. [*Following her.*] Only think—ill as she was, Aunt Rina embroidered these for me. Oh, you can't think how many associations cling to them.

Hedda. [*At the table.*] Scarcely for me.

Miss Tesman. Of course not for Hedda, George.

Tesman. Well, but now that she belongs to the family, I thought—

Hedda. [*Interrupting.*] We shall never get on with this servant, Tesman.

Miss Tesman. Not get on with Berta?

Tesman. Why, dear, what puts that in your head? Eh?

Hedda. [*Pointing.*] Look there! She has left her old bonnet lying about on a chair.

Tesman. [*In consternation, drops the slippers on the floor.*] Why, Hedda—

Hedda. Just fancy, if any one should come in and see it.

Tesman. But Hedda—that's Aunt Julia's bonnet.

Hedda. Is it!

Miss Tesman. [*Taking up the bonnet.*] Yes, indeed it's mine. And what's more, it's not old, Madame Hedda.

Hedda. I really did not look closely at it, Miss Tesman.

Miss Tesman. [*Trying on the bonnet.*] Let me tell you it's the first time I have worn it—the very first time.

Tesman. And a very nice bonnet it is too—quite a beauty!

Miss Tesman. Oh, it's no such great thing, George. [*Looks around her.*] My parasol—? Ah, here. [*Takes it.*] For this is mine too—[*Mutters.*]—not Berta's.

Tesman. A new bonnet and a new parasol! Only think, Hedda!

Hedda. Very handsome indeed.

Tesman. Yes, isn't it? But Auntie, take a good look at Hedda before you go! See how handsome she is!

Miss Tesman. Oh, my dear boy, there's nothing new in that. Hedda was always lovely. [*She nods and goes towards the right.*]

Tesman. [*Following.*] Yes, but have you noticed what splendid condition she is in? How she has filled out on the journey?

Hedda. [*Crossing the room.*] Oh, do be quiet—!

Miss Tesman. [*Who has stopped and turned.*] Filled out?

Tesman. Of course you don't notice it so much now that she has that dress on. But I, who can see—

Hedda. [*At the glass door, impatiently.*] Oh, you can't see anything.

Tesman. It must be the mountain air in the Tyrol—

Hedda. [*Curtly, interrupting.*] I am exactly as I was when I started.

Tesman. So you insist; but I'm quite certain you are not. Don't you agree with me, Auntie?

Miss Tesman. [*Who has been gazing at her with folded hands.*] Hedda is lovely—lovely—lovely. [*Goes up to her, takes her head between both hands, draws it downwards, and kisses her hair.*] God bless and preserve Hedda Tesman—for George's sake.

Hedda. [*Gently freeing herself.*] Oh! Let me go.

Miss Tesman. [*In quiet emotion.*] I shall not let a day pass without coming to see you.

Tesman. No you won't, will you, Auntie? Eh?

Miss Tesman. Good-by—good-by!

[*She goes out by the hall door.* TESMAN *accompanies her. The door remains half open.* TESMAN *can be heard repeating his message to Aunt Rina and his thanks for the slippers.*

[*In the meantime,* HEDDA *walks about the room raising her arms and clenching her hands as if in desperation. Then she flings back the curtains from the glass door, and stands there looking out.*

[*Presently* TESMAN *returns and closes the door behind him.*]

Tesman. [*Picks up the slippers from the floor.*] What are you looking at, Hedda?

Hedda. [*Once more calm and mistress of herself.*] I am only looking at the leaves. They are so yellow—so withered.

Tesman. [*Wraps up the slippers and lays them on the table.*] Well you see, we are well into September now.

Hedda. [*Again restless.*] Yes, to think of it! Already in—in September.

Tesman. Don't you think Aunt Julia's manner was strange, dear? Almost solemn? Can you imagine what was the matter with her? Eh?

Hedda. I scarcely know her, you see. Is she often like that?

Tesman. No, not as she was today.

Hedda. [*Leaving the glass door.*] Do you think she was annoyed about the bonnet?

Tesman. Oh, scarcely at all. Perhaps a little, just at the moment—

Hedda. But what an idea, to pitch her bonnet about in the drawing room! No one does that sort of thing.

Tesman. Well you may be sure Aunt Julia won't do it again.

Hedda. In any case, I shall manage to make my peace with her.

Tesman. Yes, my dear, good Hedda, if you only would.

Hedda. When you call this afternoon, you might invite her to spend the evening here.

Tesman. Yes, that I will. And there's one thing more you could do that would delight her heart.

Hedda. What is it?

Tesman. If you could only prevail on yourself to say *du*[1] to her. For my sake, Hedda? Eh?

Hedda. No, no, Tesman—you really mustn't ask that of me. I have told you so already. I shall try to call her "Aunt"; and you must be satisfied with that.

Tesman. Well, well. Only I think now that you belong to the family, you—

Hedda. H'm—I can't in the least see why—

[*She goes up towards the middle doorway.*]

Tesman. [*After a pause.*] Is there anything the matter with you, Hedda? Eh?

Hedda. I'm only looking at my old piano. It doesn't go at all well with all the other things.

Tesman. The first time I draw my salary, we'll see about exchanging it.

Hedda. No, no—no exchanging. I don't want to part with it. Suppose we put it there in the inner room, and then get another here in its place. When it's convenient, I mean.

Tesman. [*A little taken aback.*] Yes—of course we could do that.

Hedda. [*Takes up the bouquet from the piano.*] These flowers were not here last night when we arrived.

Tesman. Aunt Julia must have brought them for you.

Hedda. [*Examining the bouquet.*] A visiting card. [*Takes it out and reads.*] "Shall return later in the day." Can you guess whose card it is?

Tesman. No. Whose? Eh?

Hedda. The name is "Mrs. Elvsted."

Tesman. Is it really? Sheriff Elvsted's wife? Miss Rysing that was.

Hedda. Exactly. The girl with the irritating hair, that she was always showing off. An old flame of yours, I've been told.

Tesman. [*Laughing.*] Oh, that didn't last long; and it was before I knew you, Hedda. But fancy her being in' town!

Hedda. It's odd that she should call upon us. I have scarcely seen her since we left school.

Tesman. I haven't seen her either for—heaven knows how long. I wonder how she can endure to live in such an out-of-the-way hole—eh?

Hedda. [*After a moment's thought says suddenly.*] Tell me, Tesman—isn't it somewhere near there that he—that—Eilert Lövborg is living?

---

[1] *Du:* thou, the familiar form of the pronoun *you.*

Tesman. Yes, he is somewhere in that part of the country.

[BERTA *enters by the hall door.*]

Berta. That lady, ma'am, that brought some flowers a little while ago, is here again. [*Pointing.*] The flowers you have in your hand, ma'am.
Hedda. Ah, is she? Well, please show her in.

[BERTA *opens the door for* MRS. ELVSTED, *and goes out herself.* MRS. ELVSTED *is a woman of fragile figure, with pretty, soft features. Her eyes are light blue, large, round, and somewhat prominent, with a startled, inquiring expression. Her hair is remarkably light, almost flaxen, and unusually abundant and wavy. She is a couple of years younger than* HEDDA. *She wears a dark visiting dress, tasteful, but not quite in the latest fashion.*]

Hedda. [*Receives her warmly.*] How do you do, my dear Mrs. Elvsted? It's delightful to see you again.
Mrs. Elvsted. [*Nervously, struggling for self-control.*] Yes, it's a very long time since we met.
Tesman. [*Gives her his hand.*] And we too—eh?
Hedda. Thanks for your lovely flowers—
Mrs. Elvsted. Oh, not at all—I would have come straight here yesterday afternoon; but I heard that you were away—
Tesman. Have you just come to town? Eh?
Mrs. Elvsted. I arrived yesterday, about midday. Oh, I was quite in despair when I heard that you were not at home.
Hedda. In despair! How so?
Tesman. Why, my dear Mrs. Rysing—I mean Mrs. Elvsted—
Hedda. I hope that you are not in any trouble?
Mrs. Elvsted. Yes, I am. And I don't know another living creature here that I can turn to.
Hedda. [*Laying the bouquet on the table.*] Come—let us sit here on the sofa—
Mrs. Elvsted. Oh, I am too restless to sit down.
Hedda. Oh no, you're not. Come here. [*She draws* MRS. ELVSTED *down upon the sofa and sits at her side.*]
Tesman. Well? What is it, Mrs. Elvsted?
Hedda. Has anything particular happened to you at home?
Mrs. Elvsted. Yes—and no. Oh—I am so anxious you should not misunderstand me—
Hedda. Then your best plan is to tell us the whole story, Mrs. Elvsted.
Tesman. I suppose that's what you have come for—eh?

Mrs. Elvsted. Yes, yes—of course it is. Well then, I must tell you—if you don't already know—that Eilert Lövborg is in town, too.

Hedda. Lövborg—!

Tesman. What! Has Eilert Lövborg come back? Fancy that, Hedda!

Hedda. Well, well—I hear it.

Mrs. Elvsted. He has been here a week already. Just fancy—a whole week! In this terrible town, alone! With so many temptations on all sides.

Hedda. But my dear Mrs. Elvsted—how does he concern you so much?

Mrs. Elvsted. [*Looks at her with a startled air, and says rapidly.*] He was the children's tutor.

Hedda. Your children's?

Mrs. Elvsted. My husband's. I have none.

Hedda. Your step-children's, then?

Mrs. Elvsted. Yes.

Tesman. [*Somewhat hesitatingly.*] Then was he—I don't know how to express it—was he—regular enough in his habits to be fit for the post? Eh?

Mrs. Elvsted. For the last two years his conduct has been irreproachable.

Tesman. Has it indeed? Fancy that, Hedda!

Hedda. I hear it.

Mrs. Elvsted. Perfectly irreproachable, I assure you! In every respect. But all the same—now that I know he is here—in this great town—and with a large sum of money in his hands—I can't help being in mortal fear for him.

Tesman. Why did he not remain where he was? With you and your husband? Eh?

Mrs. Elvsted. After his book was published he was too restless and unsettled to remain with us.

Tesman. Yes, by-the-bye, Aunt Julia told me he had published a new book.

Mrs. Elvsted. Yes, a big book, dealing with the march of civilization—in broad outline, as it were. It came out about a fortnight ago. And since it has sold so well, and been so much read—and made such a sensation—

Tesman. Has it indeed? It must be something he has had lying by since his better days.

Mrs. Elvsted. Long ago, you mean?

Tesman. Yes.

Mrs. Elvsted. No, he has written it all since he has been with us—within the last year.

Tesman. Isn't that good news. Hedda? Think of that.

Mrs. Elvsted. Ah, yes, if only it would last!

Hedda. Have you seen him here in town?

Mrs. Elvsted. No, not yet. I have had the greatest difficulty in finding out his address. But this morning I discovered it at last.

Hedda. [*Looks searchingly at her.*] Do you know, it seems to me a little odd of your husband—h'm—

Mrs. Elvsted. [*Starting nervously.*] Of my husband! What?

Hedda. That he should send you to town on such an errand—that he does not come himself and look after his friend.

Mrs. Elvsted. Oh no, no—my husband has no time. And besides, I—I had some shopping to do.

Hedda. [*With a slight smile.*] Ah, that is a different matter.

Mrs. Elvsted. [*Rising quickly and uneasily.*] And now I beg and implore you, Mr. Tesman—receive Eilert Lövborg kindly if he comes to you! And that he is sure to do. You see you were such great friends in the old days. And then you are interested in the same studies—the same branch of science—so far as I can understand.

Tesman. We used to be, at any rate.

Mrs. Elvsted. That is why I beg so earnestly that you—you too—will keep a sharp eye upon him. Oh, you will promise me that, Mr. Tesman—won't you?

Tesman. With the greatest of pleasure, Mrs. Rysing—

Hedda. Elvsted.

Tesman. I assure you I shall do all I possibly can for Eilert. You may rely upon me.

Mrs. Elvsted. Oh, how very, very kind of you! [*Presses his hands.*] Thanks, thanks, thanks! [*Frightened.*] You see, my husband is very fond of him!

Hedda. [*Rising.*] You ought to write to him, Tesman. Perhaps he may not care to come to you of his own accord.

Tesman. Well, perhaps it would be the right thing to do, Hedda? Eh?

Hedda. And the sooner the better. Why not at once?

Mrs. Elvsted. [*Imploringly.*] Oh, if you only would!

Tesman. I'll write this moment. Have you his address. Mrs.—Mrs. Elvsted.

Mrs. Elvsted. Yes. [*Takes a slip of paper from her pocket, and hands it to him.*] Here it is.

Tesman. Good, good. Then I'll go in—[*Looks about him.*] By-the-bye—my slippers? Oh, here. [*Takes the packet, and is about to go.*]

Hedda. Be sure you write him a cordial, friendly letter. And a good long one too.

Tesman. Yes, I will.

Mrs. Elvsted. But please, please don't say a word to show that I have suggested it.

Tesman. No, how could you think I would? Eh? [*He goes out to the right, through the inner room.*]

Hedda. [*Goes up to* MRS. ELVSTED, *smiles, and says in a low voice.*] There. We have killed two-birds with one stone.

Mrs. Elvsted. What do you mean?

Hedda. Could you not see that I wanted him to go?

Mrs. Elvsted. Yes, to write the letter—

Hedda. And that I might speak to you alone.

Mrs. Elvsted. [*Confused.*] About the same thing?

Hedda. Precisely.

Mrs. Elvsted. [*Apprehensively.*] But there is nothing more, Mrs. Tesman! Absolutely nothing!

Hedda. Oh, yes, but there is. There is a great deal more—I can see that. Sit here—and we'll have a cosy, confidential chat. [*She forces* MRS. ELVSTED *to sit in the easy chair beside the stove, and seats herself on one of the footstools.*]

Mrs. Elvsted. [*Anxiously, looking at her watch.*] But, my dear Mrs. Tesman—I was really on the point of going.

Hedda. Oh, you can't be in such a hurry. Well? Now tell me something about your life at home.

Mrs. Elvsted. Oh, that is just what I care least to speak about.

Hedda. But to me, dear—? Why, weren't we schoolfellows?

Mrs. Elvsted. Yes, but you were in the class above me. Oh, how dreadfully afraid of you I was then!

Hedda. Afraid of me?

Mrs. Elvsted. *Yes,* dreadfully. For when we met on the stairs you used always to pull my hair.

Hedda. Did I, really?

Mrs. Elvsted. Yes, and once you said you would burn it off my head.

Hedda. Oh, that was all nonsense, of course.

Mrs. Elvsted. Yes, but I was so silly in those days. And since then, too—we have drifted so far—far apart from each other. Our circles have been so entirely different.

Hedda. Well then, we must try to drift together again. Now listen! At school we said *du* to each other; and we called each other by our Christian names—

Mrs. Elvsted. No, I am sure you must be mistaken.

Hedda. No, not at all! I can remember quite distinctly. So now we are going to renew our old friendship. [*Draws the footstool closer to* MRS. ELVSTED.] There now! [*Kisses her cheek.*] You must say *du* to me and call me Hedda.

Mrs. Elvsted. [*Presses and pats her hands.*] Oh, how good and kind you are! I am not used to such kindness.

Hedda. There, there, there! And I shall say *du* to you, as in the old days, and call you my dear Thora.

Mrs. Elvsted. My name is Thea.

Hedda. Why, of course! I meant Thea. [*Looks at her compassionately.*] So you are not accustomed to goodness and kindness, Thea? Not in your own home?

Mrs. Elvsted. Oh, if I only had a home! But I haven't any; I have never had a home.

Hedda. [*looks at her for a moment.*] I almost suspected as much.

Mrs. Elvsted. [*Gazing helplessly before her.*] Yes—yes—yes.

Hedda. I don't quite remember—was it not as housekeeper that you first went to Mr. Elvsted's?

Mrs. Elvsted. I really went as governess. But his wife—his late wife—was an invalid—and rarely left her room. So I had to look after the housekeeping as well.

Hedda. And then—at last—you became mistress of the house.

Mrs. Elvsted. [*Sadly.*] Yes, I did.

Hedda. Let me see—about how long ago was that?

Mrs. Elvsted. My marriage?

Hedda. Yes.

Mrs. Elvsted. Five years ago.

Hedda. To be sure; it must be that.

Mrs. Elvsted. Oh, those five years—! Or at all events the last two or three of them! Oh, if you² could only imagine—

Hedda. [*Giving her a little slap on the hand.*] De? Fie, Thea!

Mrs. Elvsted. Yes, yes, I will try—Well if —you could only imagine and understand—

Hedda. [*Lightly.*] Eilert Lövborg has been in your neighborhood about three years, hasn't he?

Mrs. Elvsted. [*Looks at her doubtfully.*] Eilert Lövborg? Yes—he has.

Hedda. Had you known him before, in town here?

Mrs. Elvsted. Scarcely at all. I mean—I knew him by name of course.

Hedda. But you saw a good deal of him in the country?

Mrs. Elvsted. Yes, he came to us every day. You see, he gave the children lessons; for in the long run I couldn't manage it all myself.

Hedda. No, that's clear. And your husband—? I suppose he is often away from home?

Mrs. Elvsted. Yes. Being Sheriff, you know, he has to travel about a good deal in his district.

Hedda. [*Leaning against the arm of the chair.*] Thea—my poor, sweet Thea—now you must tell me everything—exactly as it stands.

Mrs. Elvsted. Well then, you must question me.

Hedda. What sort of a man is your husband, Thea? I mean—you know—in everyday life. Is he kind to you?

---

² Mrs. Elvsted here uses the formal pronoun *De,* whereupon Hedda rebukes her. In her next speech Mrs. Elvsted says *du.*

Mrs. Elvsted. [*Evasively.*] I am sure he means well in everything.

Hedda. I should think he must be altogether too old for you. There is at least twenty years' difference between you, is there not?

Mrs. Elvsted. [*Irritably.*] Yes, that is true, too. Everything about him is repellent to me! We have not a thought in common. We have no single point of sympathy—he and I.

Hedda. But is he not fond of you all the same? In his own way?

Mrs. Elvsted. Oh, I really don't know. I think he regards me simply as a useful property. And then it doesn't cost much to keep me. I am not expensive.

Hedda. That is stupid of you.

Mrs. Elvsted. [*Shakes her head.*] It cannot be otherwise—not with him. I don't think he really cares for any one but himself—and perhaps a little for the children.

Hedda. And for Eilert Lövborg, Thea.

Mrs. Elvsted. [*Looking at her.*] For Eilert Lövborg? What puts that into your head?

Hedda. Well, my dear—I should say, when he sends you after him all the way to town—[*Smiling almost imperceptibly.*] And besides, you said so yourself, to Tesman.

Mrs. Elvsted. [*With a little nervous twitch.*] Did I? Yes, I suppose I did. [*Vehemently, but not loudly.*] No—I may just as well make a clean breast of it at once! For it must all come out in any case.

Hedda. Why, my dear Thea—?

Mrs. Elvsted. Well, to make a long story short: My husband did not know that I was coming.

Hedda. What! Your husband didn't know it!

Mrs. Elvsted. No, of course not. For that matter, he was away from home himself—he was traveling. Oh, I could bear it no longer, Hedda! I couldn't indeed—so utterly alone as I should have been in the future.

Hedda. Well? And then?

Mrs. Elvsted. So I put together some of my things—what I needed most—as quietly as possible. And then I left the house.

Hedda. Without a word?

Mrs. Elvsted. Yes—and took the train straight to town.

Hedda. Why, my dear, good Thea—to think of you daring to do it!

Mrs. Elvsted. [*Rises and moves about the room.*] What else could I possibly do?

Hedda. But what do you think your husband will say when you go home again?

Mrs. Elvsted. [*At the table, looks at her.*] Back to him.

Hedda. Of course.

Mrs. Elvsted. I shall never go back to him again.

Hedda. [*Rising and going towards her.*] Then you have left your home—for good and all?

Mrs. Elvsted. Yes. There was nothing else to be done.

Hedda. But then—to take flight so openly.

Mrs. Elvsted. Oh, it's impossible to keep things of that sort secret.

Hedda. But what do you think people will say of you, Thea?

Mrs. Elvsted. They may say what they like for aught *I* care. [*Seats herself wearily and sadly on the sofa.*] I have done nothing but what I had to do.

Hedda. [*After a short silence.*] And what are your plans now? What do you think of doing?

Mrs. Elvsted. I don't know yet. I only know this, that I must live here, where Eilert Lövborg is—if I am to live at all.

Hedda. [*Takes a chair from the table, seats herself beside her, and strokes her hands.*] My dear Thea—how did this—this friendship—between you and Eilert Lövborg come about?

Mrs. Elvsted. Oh, it grew up gradually. I gained a sort of influence over him.

Hedda. Indeed?

Mrs. Elvsted. He gave up his old habits. Not because I asked him to, for I never dared do that. But of course he saw how repulsive they were to me; and so he dropped them.

Hedda. [*Concealing an involuntary smile of scorn.*] Then you have reclaimed him—as the saying goes—my little Thea.

Mrs. Elvsted. So he says himself, at any rate. And he, on his side, has made a real human being of me—taught me to think, and to understand so many things.

Hedda. Did he give you lessons too, then?

Mrs. Elvsted. No, not exactly lessons. But he talked to me—talked about such an infinity of things. And then came the lovely, happy time when I began to share in his work—when he allowed me to help him!

Hedda. Oh, he did, did he?

Mrs. Elvsted. Yes! He never wrote anything without my assistance.

Hedda. You were two good comrades, in fact?

Mrs. Elvsted. [*Eagerly.*] Comrades! Yes, fancy, Hedda—that is the very word he used! Oh, I ought to feel perfectly happy; and yet I cannot; for I don't know how long it will last.

Hedda. Are you no surer of him than that?

Mrs. Elvsted. [*Gloomily.*] A woman's shadow stands between Eilert Lövborg and me.

Hedda. [*Looks at her anxiously.*] Who can that be?

Mrs. Elvsted. I don't know. Some one he knew in his—in his past. Some one he has never been able wholly to forget.

Hedda. What has he told you—about this?

Mrs. Elvsted. He has only once—quite vaguely—alluded to it.

Hedda. Well! And what did he say?

Mrs. Elvsted. He said that when they parted, she threatened to shoot him with a pistol.

Hedda. [*With cold composure.*] Oh, nonsense! No one does that sort of thing here.

Mrs. Elvsted. No. And that is why I think it must have been that red-haired singing woman whom he once—

Hedda. Yes, very likely.

Mrs. Elvsted. For I remember they used to say of her that she carried loaded firearms.

Hedda. Oh—then of course it must have been she.

Mrs. Elvsted. [*Wringing her hands.*] And now just fancy. Hedda—I hear that this singing woman—that she is in town again! Oh, I don't know what to do—

Hedda. [*Glancing towards the inner room.*] Hush! Here comes Tesman. [*Rises and whispers.*] Thea—all this must remain between you and me.

Mrs. Elvsted. [*Springing up.*] Oh, yes, yes! for heaven's sake—!

[GEORGE TESMAN, *with a letter in his hand, comes from the right through the inner room.*]

Tesman. There now—the epistle is finished.

Hedda. That's right. And now Mrs. Elvsted is just going. Wait a moment—I'll go with you to the garden gate.

Tesman. Do you think Berta could post the letter, Hedda dear?

Hedda. [*Takes it.*] I will tell her to.

[BERTA *enters from the hall.*]

Berta. Judge Brack wishes to know if Mrs. Tesman will receive him.

Hedda. Yes, ask Judge Brack to come in. And look here—put this letter in the post.

Berta. [*Taking the letter.*] Yes, ma'am.

[*She opens the door for* JUDGE BRACK *and goes out herself.* BRACK *is a man of forty-five; thickset, but well built and elastic in his movements. His face is roundish with an aristocratic profile. His hair is short, still almost black, and carefully dressed. His eyes are lively and sparkling. His eyebrows thick. His moustaches are also thick, with short-cut ends. He wears a well-cut*

*walking suit, a little too youthful for his age. He uses an eyeglass, which he
now and then lets drop.*]

Judge Brack. [*With his hat in his hand, bowing.*] May one venture to call so
	early in the day?
Hedda. Of course one may.
Tesman. [*Presses his hand.*] You are welcome at any time. [*Introducing
	him.*] Judge Brack—Miss Rysing—
Hedda. Oh—!
Brack. [*Bowing.*] Ah—delighted—
Hedda. [*Looks at him and laughs.*] It's nice to have a look at you by
	daylight, Judge!
Brack. Do you find me—altered?
Hedda. A little younger, I think.
Brack. Thank you so much.
Tesman. But what do you think of Hedda—eh? Doesn't she look
	flourishing? She has actually—
Hedda. Oh, do leave me alone. You haven't thanked Judge Brack for all the
	trouble he has taken—
Brack. Oh, nonsense—it was a pleasure to me—
Hedda. Yes, you are a friend indeed. But here stands Thea all impatience to
	be off—so *au revoir,* Judge. I shall be back again presently. [*Mutual
	salutations.* MRS. ELVSTED *and* HEDDA *go out by the hall door.*]
Brack. Well, is your wife tolerably satisfied—
Tesman. Yes, we can't thank you sufficiently. Of course she talks of a little
	rearrangement here and there; and one or two things are still wanting.
	We shall have to buy some additional trifles.
Brack. Indeed!
Tesman. But we won't trouble you about these things. Hedda says she
	herself will look after what is wanting.—Shan't we sit down? Eh?
Brack. Thanks, for a moment. [*Seats himself beside the table.*] There is
	something I wanted to speak to you about, my dear Tesman.
Tesman. Indeed? Ah, I understand! [*Seating himself.*] I suppose it's the
	serious part of the frolic that is coming now. Eh?
Brack. Oh, the money question is not so very pressing; though, for that
	matter, I wish we had gone a little more economically to work.
Tesman. But that would never have done, you know! Think of Hedda, my
	dear fellow! You who know her so well—I couldn't possibly ask her to
	put up with a shabby style of living!
Brack. No, no—that is just the difficulty.
Tesman. And then—fortunately—it can't be long before I receive my
	appointment.

Brack. Well, you see—such things are often apt to hang fire for a time.

Tesman. Have you heard anything definite? Eh?

Brack. Nothing exactly definite—[*Interrupting himself.*] But, by-the-bye—I have one piece of news for you.

Tesman. Well?

Brack. Your old friend, Eilert Lövborg, has returned to town.

Tesman. I know that already.

Brack. Indeed! How did you learn it?

Tesman. From that lady who went out with Hedda.

Brack. Really? What was her name? I didn't quite catch it.

Tesman. Mrs. Elvsted.

Brack. Aha—Sheriff Elvsted's wife? Of course—he has been living up in their regions.

Tesman. And fancy—I'm delighted to hear that he is quite a reformed character!

Brack. So they say.

Tesman. And then he has published a new book—eh?

Brack. Yes, indeed he has.

Tesman. And I hear it has made some sensation!

Brack. Quite an unusual sensation.

Tesman. Fancy—isn't that good news! A man of such extraordinary talents—I felt so grieved to think that he had gone irretrievably to ruin.

Brack. That was what everybody thought.

Tesman. But I cannot imagine what he will take to now! How in the world will he be able to make his living? Eh?

[*During the last words,* HEDDA *has entered by the hall door.*]

Hedda. [*To* BRACK, *laughing with a touch of scorn.*] Tesman is forever worrying about how people are to make their living.

Tesman. Well, you see, dear—we were talking about poor Eilert Lövborg.

Hedda. [*Glancing at him rapidly.*] Oh, indeed? [*Seats herself in the arm-chair beside the stove and asks indifferently.*] What is the matter with him?

Tesman. Well—no doubt he has run through all his property long ago; and he can scarcely write a new book every year—eh? So I really can't see what is to become of him.

Brack. Perhaps I can give you some information on that point.

Tesman. Indeed!

Brack. You must remember that his relations have a good deal of influence.

Tesman. Oh, his relations, unfortunately, have entirely washed their hands of him.

Brack. At one time they called him the hope of the family.

Tesman. At one time, yes! But he has put an end to all that.

Hedda. Who knows? [*With a slight smile.*] I hear they have reclaimed him up at Sheriff Elvsted's—

Brack. And then this book that he has published—

Tesman. Well, well, I hope to goodness they may find something for him to do. I have just written to him. I asked him to come and see us this evening, Hedda dear.

Brack. But, my dear fellow, you are booked for my bachelors' party this evening. You promised on the pier last night.

Hedda. Had you forgotten, Tesman?

Tesman. Yes, I had utterly forgotten.

Brack. But it doesn't matter, for you may be sure he won't come.

Tesman. What makes you think that? Eh?

Brack. [*With a little hesitation, rising and resting his hands on the back of his chair.*] My dear Tesman—and you too, Mrs. Tesman—I think I ought not to keep you in the dark about something that—that—

Tesman. That concerns Eilert—?

Brack. Both you and him.

Tesman. Well, my dear Judge, out with it.

Brack. You must be prepared to find your appointment deferred longer than you desired or expected.

Tesman. [*Jumping up uneasily.*] Is there some hitch about it? Eh?

Brack. The nomination may perhaps be made conditional on the result of a competition—

Tesman. Competition! Think of that, Hedda!

Hedda. [*Leans farther back in the chair.*] Aha—aha!

Tesman. But who can my competitor be? Surely not—?

Brack. Yes, precisely—Eilert Lövborg.

Tesman. [*Clasping his hands.*] No, no—it's quite inconceivable! Quite impossible! Eh?

Brack. H'm—that is what it may come to, all the same.

Tesman. Well but, Judge Brack—it would show the most incredible lack of consideration for me. [*Gesticulates with his arms.*] For—just think— I'm a married man. We have been married on the strength of these prospects, Hedda and I; and run deep into debt; and borrowed money from Aunt Julia too. Good heavens, they had as good as promised me the appointment. Eh?

Brack. Well, well, well—no doubt you will get it in the end; only after a contest.

Hedda. [*Immovable in her armchair.*] Fancy, Tesman, there will be a sort of sporting interest in that.

Tesman. Why, my dearest Hedda, how can you be so indifferent about it.

Hedda. [*As before.*] I am not at all indifferent. I am most eager to see who wins.

Brack. In any case, Mrs. Tesman, it is best that you should know how matters stand I mean—before you set about the little purchases I hear you are threatening.

Hedda. This can make no difference.

Brack. Indeed! Then I have no more to say. Good-by! [*To* TESMAN.] I shall look in on my way back from my afternoon walk, and take you home with me.

Tesman. Oh yes, yes—your news has quite upset me.

Hedda. [*Reclining, holds out her hand.*] Good-by, Judge; and be sure you call in the afternoon.

Brack. Many thanks. Good-by, good-by!

Tesman. [*Accompanying him to the door.*] Good-by, my dear Judge! You must really excuse me—[JUDGE BRACK *goes out by the hall door.*]

Tesman. [*Crosses the room.*] Oh, Hedda—one should never rush into adventures. Eh?

Hedda. [*Looks at him, smiling.*] Do you do that?

Tesman. Yes, dear—there is no denying—it was adventurous to go and marry and set up house upon mere expectations.

Hedda. Perhaps you are right there.

Tesman. Well—at all events, we have our delightful home, Hedda! Fancy, the home we both dreamed of—the home we were in love with, I may almost say. Eh?

Hedda. [*Rising slowly and wearily.*] It was part of our compact that we were to go into society—to keep open house.

Tesman. Yes, if you only knew how I had been looking forward to it! Fancy—to see you as hostess—in a select circle? Eh? Well, well, well—for the present we shall have to get on without society, Hedda—only to invite Aunt Julia now and then. Oh, I intended you to lead such an utterly different life, dear—!

Hedda. Of course I cannot have my man in livery just yet.

Tesman. Oh no, unfortunately. It would be out of the question for us to keep a footman, you know.

Hedda. And the saddle horse I was to have had—

Tesman. [*Aghast.*] The saddle horse!

Hedda. —I suppose I must not think of that now.

Tesman. Good heavens, no!—that's as clear as daylight.

Hedda. [*Goes up the room.*] Well, I shall have one thing at least to kill time with in the meanwhile.

Tesman. [*Beaming.*] Oh, thank heaven for that! What is it, Hedda? Eh?

Hedda. [*In the middle doorway, looks at him with covert scorn.*] My pistols, George.

Tesman. [*In alarm.*] Your pistols!

Hedda. [*With cold eyes.*] General Gabler's pistols. [*She goes out through the inner room, to the left.*]

Tesman. [*Rushes up to the middle doorway and calls after her.*] No, for heaven's sake, Hedda darling—don't touch those dangerous things! For my sake, Hedda! Eh?

Act II

Scene: *The room at the* TESMANS' *as in the first Act, except that the piano has been removed, and an elegant little writing table with bookshelves put in its place. A smaller table stands near the sofa at the left. Most of the bouquets have been taken away.* MRS. ELVSTED'S *bouquet is upon the large table in front. It is afternoon.*

HEDDA, *dressed to receive callers, is alone in the room. She stands by the open glass door, loading a revolver. The fellow to it lies in an open pistol case on the writing table.*

Hedda. [*Looks down the garden, and calls.*] So you are here again, Judge!

Brack. [*Is heard calling from a distance.*] As you see, Mrs. Tesman!

Hedda. [*Raises the pistol and points.*] Now I'll shoot you, Judge Brack!

Brack. [*Calling unseen.*] No, no, no! Don't stand aiming at me!

Hedda. This is what comes of sneaking in by the back way.[1] [*She fires.*]

Brack. [*Nearer.*] Are you out of your senses—!

Hedda. Dear me—did I happen to hit you?

Brack. [*Still outside.*] I wish you would let these pranks alone!

Hedda. Come in then, Judge.

[JUDGE BRACK, *dressed as though for a men's party, enters by the glass door. He carries a light overcoat over his arm.*]

Brack. What the deuce—haven't you tired of that sport, yet? What are you shooting at?

Hedda. Oh, I am only firing in the air.

Brack. [*Gently takes the pistol out of her hand.*] Allow me, madam! [*Looks at it.*] Ah—I know this pistol well! [*Looks around.*] Where is the case? Ah, here it is. [*Lays the pistol in it, and shuts it.*] Now we won't play at that game any more today.

Hedda. Then what in heaven's name would you have me do with myself?

Brack. Have you had no visitors?

Hedda. [*Closing the glass door.*] Not one. I suppose all our set are still out of town.

Brack. And is Tesman not at home either?

Hedda. [*At the writing table, putting the pistol case in a drawer which she*

[1]"Bagveje" means both "back ways" and "underhand courses."

shuts.] No. He rushed off to his aunt's directly after lunch; he didn't expect you so early.

Brack. H'm—how stupid of me not to have thought of that!

Hedda. [*Turning her head to look at him.*] Why stupid?

Brack. Because if I had tought of it I should have come a little—earlier.

Hedda. [*Crossing the room.*] Then you would have found no one to receive you; for I have been in my room changing my dress ever since lunch.

Brack. And is there no sort of little chink that we could hold a parley through?

Hedda. You have forgotten to arrange one.

Brack. That was another piece of stupidity.

Hedda. Well, we must just settle down here—and wait. Tesman is not likely to be back for some time yet.

Brack. Never mind; I shall not be impatient.

[HEDDA *seats herself in the corner of the sofa.* BRACK *lays his overcoat over the back of the nearest chair, and sits down, but keeps his hat in his hand. A short silence. They look at each other.*]

Hedda. Well?

Brack. [*In the same tone.*] Well?

Hedda. I spoke first.

Brack. [*Bending a little forward.*] Come, let us have a cosy little chat, Mrs. Hedda.

Hedda. [*Leaning further back in the sofa.*] Does it not seem like a whole eternity since our last talk? Of course I don't count those few words yesterday evening and this morning.

Brack. You mean since our last confidential talk? Our last tête-à-tête?

Hedda. Well, yes—since you put it so.

Brack. Not a day has passed but I have wished that you were home again.

Hedda. And I have done nothing but wish the same thing.

Brack. You? Really, Mrs. Hedda? And I thought you had been enjoying your tour so much!

Hedda. Oh, yes, you may be sure of that!

Brack. But Tesman's letters spoke of nothing but happiness.

Hedda. Oh, Tesman! You see, he thinks nothing so delightful as grubbing in libraries and making copies of old parchments, or whatever you call them.

Brack. [*With a spice of malice.*] Well, that is his vocation in life—or part of it at any rate.

Hedda. Yes, of course; and no doubt when it's your vocation—But *I!* Oh, my dear Mr. Brack, how mortally bored I have been.

Brack. [*Sympathetically.*] Do you really say so? In downright earnest?

Hedda. Yes, you can surely understand it—! To go for six whole months without meeting a soul that knew anything of our circle, or could talk about the things we are interested in.

Brack. Yes, yes—I too should feel that a deprivation.

Hedda. And then, what I found most intolerable of all—

Brack. Well?

Hedda. —was being everlastingly in the company of—one and the same person—

Brack. [*With a nod of assent.*] Morning, noon, and night, yes—at all possible times and seasons.

Hedda. I said "everlastingly."

Brack. Just so. But I should have thought, with our excellent Tesman, one could—

Hedda. Tesman is—a specialist, my dear Judge.

Brack. Undeniably.

Hedda. And specialists are not at all amusing to travel with. Not in the long run at any rate.

Brack. Not even—the specialist one happens to love?

Hedda. Faugh—don't use that sickening word!

Brack. [*Taken aback.*] What do you say, Mrs. Hedda?

Hedda. [*Half laughing, half irritated.*] You should just try it! To hear of nothing but the history of civilization, morning, noon, and night—

Brack. Everlastingly.

Hedda. Yes, yes, yes! And then all this about the domestic industry of the middle ages—! That's the most disgusting part of it!

Brack. [*Looks searchingly at her.*] But tell me—in that case, how am I to understand your—? H'm—

Hedda. My accepting George Tesman, you mean?

Brack. Well, let us put it so.

Hedda. Good heavens, do you see anything so wonderful in that?

Brack. Yes and no—Mrs. Hedda.

Hedda. I had positively danced myself tired, my dear Judge. My day was done—[*With a slight shudder.*] Oh no—I won't say that; nor think it either!

Brack. You have assuredly no reason to.

Hedda. Oh, reasons—[*Watching him closely.*] George Tesman—after all, you must admit that he is correctness itself.

Brack. His correctness and respectability are beyond all question.

Hedda. And I don't see anything absolutely ridiculous about him. Do you?

Brack. Ridiculous? N—no—I shouldn't exactly say so—

Hedda. Well—and his powers of research, at all events, are untiring. I see no reason why he should not one day come to the front, after all.

Brack. [*Looks at her hesitatingly.*] I thought that you, like every one else, expected him to attain the highest distinction.

Hedda. [*With an expression of fatigue.*] Yes, so I did.—And then, since he was bent, at all hazards, on being allowed to provide for me—I really don't know why I should not have accepted his offer?

Brack. No—if you look at it in that light—

Hedda. It was more than my other adorers were prepared to do for me, my dear Judge.

Brack. [*Laughing.*] Well, I can't answer for all the rest; but as for myself, you know quite well that I have always entertained a—a certain respect for the marriage tie—for marriage as an institution, Mrs. Hedda.

Hedda. [*Jestingly.*] Oh, I assure you I have never cherished any hopes with respect to you.

Brack. All I require is a pleasant and intimate interior, where I can make myself useful in every way, and am free to come and go as—as a trusted friend—

Hedda. Of the master of the house, do you mean?

Brack. [*Bowing.*] Frankly—of the mistress first of all; but of course of the master, too, in the second place. Such a triangular friendship—if I may call it so—is really a great convenience for all parties, let me tell you.

Hedda. Yes, I have many a time longed for some one to make a third on our travels. Oh—those railway-carriage tête-à-têtes—!

Brack. Fortunately your wedding journey is over now.

Hedda. [*Shaking her head.*] Not by a long—long way. I have only arrived at a station on the line.

Brack. Well, then the passengers jump out and move about a little, Mrs. Hedda.

Hedda. I never jump out.

Brack. Really?

Hedda. No—because there is always some one standing by to—

Brack. [*Laughing.*] To look at your ankles, do you mean?

Hedda. Precisely.

Brack. Well but, dear me—

Hedda. [*With a gesture of repulsion.*] I won't have it. I would rather keep my seat where I happen to be—and continue the tête-à-tête.

Brack. But suppose a third person were to jump in and join the couple.

Hedda. Ah—that is quite another matter!

Brack. A trusted, sympathetic friend—

Hedda. —with a fund of conversation on all sorts of lively topics—

Brack. —and not the least bit of a specialist!

Hedda. [*With an audible sigh.*] Yes, that would be a relief indeed.

Brack. [*Hears the front door open, and glances in that direction.*] The triangle is completed.

Hedda. [*Half aloud.*] And on goes the train.

[GEORGE TESMAN, *in a gray walking suit, with a soft felt hat, enters from the hall. He has a number of unbound books under his arm and in his pockets.*]

Tesman. [*Goes up to the table beside the corner settee.*] Ouf—what a load for a warm day—all these books. [*Lays them on the table.*] I'm positively perspiring, Hedda. Hallo—are you there already, my dear Judge? Eh? Berta didn't tell me.

Brack. [*Rising.*] I came in through the garden.

Hedda. What books have you got there?

Tesman. [*Stands looking them through.*] Some new books on my special subjects—quite indispensable to me.

Hedda. Your special subjects?

Brack. Yes, books on his special subjects, Mrs. Tesman. [BRACK *and* HEDDA *exchange a confidential smile.*]

Hedda. Do you need still more books on your special subjects?

Tesman. Yes, my dear Hedda, one can never have too many of them. Of course one must keep up with all that is written and published.

Hedda. Yes, I suppose one must.

Tesman. [*Searching among his books.*] And look here—I have got hold of Eilert Lövborg's new book too. [*Offering it to her.*] Perhaps you would like to glance through it, Hedda? Eh?

Hedda. No, thank you. Or rather—afterwards perhaps.

Tesman. I looked into it a little on the way home.

Brack. Well, what do you think of it—as a specialist?

Tesman. I think it shows quite remarkable soundness of judgment. He never wrote like that before. [*Putting the books together.*] Now I shall take all these into my study. I'm longing to cut the leaves—! And then I must change my clothes. [*To* BRACK.] I suppose we needn't start just yet? Eh?

Brack. Oh, dear no—there is not the slightest hurry.

Tesman. Well then, I will take my time. [*Is going with his books, but stops in the doorway and turns.*] By-the-bye, Hedda—Aunt Julia is not coming this evening.

Hedda. Not coming? Is it that affair of the bonnet that keeps her away?

Tesman. Oh, not at all. How could you think such a thing of Aunt Julia? Just fancy—! The fact is, Aunt Rina is very ill.

Hedda. She always is.

Tesman. Yes, but today she is much worse than usual, poor dear.

Hedda. Oh, then it's only natural that her sister should remain with her. I must bear my disappointment.

Tesman. And you can't imagine, dear, how delighted Aunt Julia seemed to be—because you had come home looking so flourishing!

Hedda. [*Half aloud, rising.*] Oh, those everlasting aunts!

Tesman. What?

Hedda. [*Going to the glass door.*] Nothing.

Tesman. Oh, all right. [*He goes through the inner room, out to the right.*]

Brack. What bonnet were you talking about?

Hedda. Oh, it was a little episode with Miss Tesman this morning. She had laid down her bonnet on the chair there—[*Looks at him and smiles.*] — and I pretended to think it was the servant's.

Brack. [*Shaking his head.*] Now my dear Mrs. Hedda how could you do such a thing? To that excellent old lady, too!

Hedda. [*Nervously crossing the room.*] Well, you see—these impulses come over me all of a sudden; and I cannot resist them. [*Throws herself down in the easy chair by the stove.*] Oh, I don't know how to explain it.

Brack. [*Behind the easy chair.*] You are not really happy—that is at the bottom of it.

Hedda. [*Looking straight before her.*] I know of no reason why I should be—happy. Perhaps you can give me one?

Brack. Well—amongst other things, because you have got exactly the home you had set your heart on.

Hedda. [*Looks up at him and laughs.*] Do you too believe in that legend?

Brack. Is there nothing in it, then?

Hedda. Oh, yes, there is something in it.

Brack. Well?

Hedda. There is this in it, that I made use of Tesman to see me home from evening parties last summer—

Brack. I, unfortunately, had to go quite a different way.

Hedda. That's true. I know you were going a different way last summer.

Brack. [*Laughing.*] Oh fie, Mrs. Hedda! Well, then—you and Tesman—?

Hedda. Well, we happened to pass here one evening; Tesman, poor fellow, was writhing in the agony of having to find conversation; so I took pity on the learned man—

Brack. [*Smiles doubtfully.*] You took pity? H'm—

Hedda. Yes, I really did. And so—to help him out of his torment—I happened to say, in pure thoughtlessness, that I should like to live in this villa.

Brack. No more than that?

Hedda. Not that evening.

Brack. But afterwards?

Hedda. Yes, my thoughtlessness had consequences, my dear Judge.

Brack. Unfortunately that too often happens, Mrs. Hedda.

Hedda. Thanks! So you see it was this enthusiasm for Secretary Falk's villa that first constituted a bond of sympathy between George Tesman and me. From that came our engagement and our marriage, and our wedding journey, and all the rest of it. Well, well, my dear Judge—as you make your bed so you must lie, I could almost say.

Brack. This is exquisite! And you really cared not a rap about it all the time.

Hedda. No, heaven knows I didn't.

Brack. But now? Now that we have made it so homelike for you?

Hedda. Uh—the rooms all seem to smell of lavender and dried rose leaves.—But perhaps it's Aunt Julia that has brought that scent with her.

Brack. [*Laughing.*] No, I think it must be a legacy from the late Mrs. Secretary Falk.

Hedda. Yes, there is an odor of mortality about it. It reminds me of a bouquet—the day after the ball. [*Clasps her hands behind her head, leans back in her chair and looks at him.*] Oh, my dear Judge—you cannot imagine how horribly I shall bore myself here.

Brack. Why should not you, too, find some sort of vocation in life, Mrs. Hedda?

Hedda. A vocation—that should attract me?

Brack. If possible, of course.

Hedda. Heaven knows what sort of a vocation that could be. I often wonder whether—[*Breaking off.*] But that would never do either.

Brack. Who can tell? Let me hear what it is.

Hedda. Whether I might not get Tesman to go into politics, I mean.

Brack. [*Laughing.*] Tesman? No, really now, political life is not the thing for him—not at all in his line.

Hedda. No, I daresay not. But if I could get him into it all the same?

Brack. Why—what satisfaction could you find in that? If he is not fitted for that sort of thing, why should you want to drive him into it?

Hedda. Because I am bored, I tell you! [*After a pause.*] So you think it quite out of the question that Tesman should ever get into the ministry?

Brack. H'm—you see, my dear Mrs. Hedda—to get into the ministry, he would have to be a tolerably rich man.

Hedda. [*Rising impatiently.*] Yes, there we have it! It is this genteel poverty I have managed to drop into—! [*Crosses the room.*] That is what makes life so pitiable! So utterly ludicrous! For that's what it is.

Brack. Now *I* should say the fault lay elsewhere.

Hedda. Where, then?

Brack. You have never gone through any really stimulating experience.

Hedda. Anything serious, you mean?

Brack. Yes, you may call it so. But now you may perhaps have one in store.

Hedda. [*Tossing her head.*] Oh, you're thinking of the annoyances about this wretched professorship! But that must be Tesman's own affair. I assure you I shall not waste a thought upon it.

Brack. No, no, I daresay not. But suppose now that what people call—in elegant language—a solemn responsibility were to come upon you? [*Smiling.*] A new responsibility, Mrs. Hedda?

Hedda. [*Angrily.*] Be quiet! Nothing of that sort will ever happen!

Brack. [*Warily.*] We will speak of this again a year hence—at the very
outside.

Hedda. [*Curtly.*] I have no turn for anything of the sort, Judge Brack. No
responsibilities for me!

Brack. Are you so unlike the generality of women as to have no turn for
duties which—?

Hedda. [*Beside the glass door.*] Oh, be quiet, I tell you! I often think there
is only one thing in the world I have any turn for.

Brack. [*Drawing near to her.*] And what is that, if I may ask?

Hedda. [*Stands looking out.*] Boring myself to death. Now you know it.
[*Turns, looks towards the inner room, and laughs.*] Yes, as I thought!
Here comes the Professor.

Brack. [*Softly, in a tone of warning.*] Come, come, come, Mrs. Hedda!

[GEORGE TESMAN, *dressed for the party, with his gloves and hat in his hand,
enters from the right through the inner room.*]

Tesman. Hedda, has no message come from Eilert Lövborg? Eh?

Hedda. No.

Tesman. Then you'll see he'll be here presently.

Brack. Do you really think he will come?

Tesman. Yes, I am almost sure of it. For what you were telling us this
morning must have been a mere floating rumor.

Brack. You think so?

Tesman. At any rate, Aunt Julia said she did not believe for a moment that
he would ever stand in my way again. Fancy that!

Brack. Well then, that's all right.

Tesman. [*Placing his hat and gloves on a chair on the right.*] Yes, but you
must really let me wait for him as long as possible.

Brack. We have plenty of time yet. None of my guests will arrive before
seven or half-past.

Tesman. Then meanwhile we can keep Hedda company, and see what
happens. Eh?

Hedda. [*Placing* BRACK'S *hat and overcoat upon the corner settee.*] And at
the worst Mr. Lövborg can remain here with me.

Brack. [*Offering to take his things.*] Oh, allow me, Mrs. Tesman! What do
you mean by "At the worst"?

Hedda. If he won't go with you and Tesman.

Tesman. [*Looks dubiously at her.*] But, Hedda dear—do you think it would
quite do for him to remain with you? Eh? Remember, Aunt Julia can't
come.

Hedda. No, but Mrs. Elvsted is coming. We three can have a cup of tea together.

Tesman. Oh, yes, that will be all right.

Brack. [*Smiling.*] And that would perhaps be the safest plan for him.

Hedda. Why so?

Brack. Well, you know, Mrs. Tesman, how you used to gird at my little bachelor parties. You declared they were adapted only for men of the strictest principles.

Hedda. But no doubt Mr. Lövborg's principles are strict enough now. A converted sinner—[BERTA *appears at the hall door.*]

Berta. There's a gentleman asking if you are at home, ma'am—

Hedda. Well, show him in.

Tesman. [*Softly.*] I'm sure it is he! Fancy that!

[EILERT LÖVBORG *enters from the hall. He is slim and lean; of the same age as* TESMAN, *but looks older and somewhat worn-out. His hair and beard are of a blackish brown, his face long and pale, but with patches of color on the cheekbones. He is dressed in a well-cut black visiting suit, quite new. He has dark gloves and a silk hat. He stops near the door, and makes a rapid bow, seeming somewhat embarrassed.*]

Tesman. [*Goes up to him and shakes him warmly by the hand.*] Well, my dear Eilert—so at last we meet again!

Lövborg. [*Speaks in a subdued voice.*] Thanks for your letter, Tesman. [*Approaching* HEDDA.] Will you too shake hands with me, Mrs. Tesman?

Hedda. [*Taking his hand.*] I am glad to see you, Mr. Lövborg. [*With a motion of her hand.*] I don't know whether you two gentlemen—?

Lövborg. [*Bowing slightly.*] Judge Brack, I think.

Brack. [*Doing likewise.*] Oh, yes, in the old days—

Tesman. [*To* LÖVBORG, *with his hands on his shoulders.*] And now you must make yourself entirely at home, Eilert! Mustn't he, Hedda? For I hear you are going to settle in town again? Eh?

Lövborg. Yes, I am.

Tesman. Quite right, quite right. Let me tell you, I have got hold of your new book; but I haven't had time to read it yet.

Lövborg. You may spare yourself the trouble.

Tesman. Why so?

Lövborg. Because there is very little in it.

Tesman. Just fancy—how can you say so?

Brack. But it has been very much praised, I hear.

Lövborg. That was what I wanted; so I put nothing into the book but what every one would agree with.

Brack. Very wise of you.

Tesman. Well but, my dear Eilert—!

Lövborg. For now I mean to win myself a position again—to make a fresh start.

Tesman. [*A little embarrassed.*] Ah, that is what you wish to do? Eh?

Lövborg. [*Smiling, lays down his hat, and draws a packet, wrapped in paper, from his coat pocket.*] But when this one appears, George Tesman, you will have to read it. For this is the real book—the book I have put my true self into.

Tesman. Indeed? And what is it?

Lövborg. It is the continuation.

Tesman. The continuation? Of what?

Lövborg. Of the book.

Tesman. Of the new book?

Lövborg. Of course.

Tesman. Why, my dear Eilert—does it not come down to our own days?

Lövborg. Yes, it does; and this one deals with the future.

Tesman. With the future! But, good heavens, we know nothing of the future!

Lövborg. No; but there is a thing or two to be said about it all the same. [*Opens the packet.*] Look here—

Tesman. Why, that's not your handwriting.

Lövborg. I dictated it. [*Turning over the pages.*] It falls into two sections. The first deals with the civilizing forces of the future. And here is the second—[*Running through the pages towards the end.*] —forecasting the probable line of development.

Tesman. How odd now! I should never have thought of writing anything of that sort.

Hedda. [*At the glass door, drumming on the pane.*] H'm—I daresay not.

Lövborg. [*Replacing the manuscript in its paper and laying the packet on the table.*] I brought it, thinking I might read you a little of it this evening.

Tesman. That was very good of you, Eilert. But this evening—? [*Looking at* BRACK.] I don't quite see how we can manage it—

Lövborg. Well then, some other time. There is no hurry.

Brack. I must tell you, Mr. Lövborg—there is a little gathering at my house this evening—mainly in honor of Tesman, you know—

Lövborg. [*Looking for his hat.*] Oh—then I won't detain you—

Brack. No, but listen—will you not do me the favor of joining us?

Lövborg. [*Curtly and decidedly.*] No, I can't—thank you very much.

Brack. Oh, nonsense—do! We shall be quite a select little circle. And I assure you we shall have a "lively time," as Mrs. Hed—as Mrs. Tesman says.

Lövborg. I have no doubt of it. But nevertheless—

Brack. And then you might bring your manuscript with you, and read it to Tesman at my house. I could give you a room to yourselves.

Tesman. Yes, think of that, Eilert,—why shouldn't you? Eh?

Hedda. [*Interposing.*] But, Tesman, if Mr. Lövborg would really rather not! I am sure Mr. Lövborg is much more inclined to remain here and have supper with me.

Lövborg. [*Looking at her.*] With you, Mrs. Tesman?

Hedda. And with Mrs. Elvsted.

Lövborg. Ah—[*Lightly.*] I saw her for a moment this morning.

Hedda. Did you? Well, she is coming this evening. So you see you are almost bound to remain, Mr. Lövborg, or she will have no one to see her home.

Lövborg. That's true. Many thanks, Mrs. Tesman—in that case I will remain.

Hedda. Then I have one or two orders to give the servant—

[*She goes to the hall door and rings.* BERTA *enters.* HEDDA *talks to her in a whisper, and points toward the inner room.* BERTA *nods and goes out again.*]

Tesman. [*At the same time, to* LÖVBORG.] Tell me, Eilert—is it this new subject—the future—that you are going to lecture about?

Lövborg. Yes.

Tesman. They told me at the bookseller's, that you are going to deliver a course of lectures this autumn.

Lövborg. That is my intention. I hope you won't take it ill, Tesman.

Tesman. Oh no, not in the least! But—?

Lövborg. I can quite understand that it must be disagreeable to you.

Tesman. [*Cast down.*] Oh, I can't expect you, out of consideration for me, to—

Lövborg. But I shall wait till you have received your appointment.

Tesman. Will you wait? Yes, but—yes, but—are you not going to compete with me? Eh?

Lövborg. No; it is only the moral victory I care for.

Tesman. Why, bless me—then Aunt Julia was right after all! Oh yes—I knew it! Hedda! Just fancy—Eilert Lövborg is not going to stand in our way!

Hedda. [*Curtly.*] Our way? Pray leave me out of the question.

[*She goes up towards the inner room, where* BERTA *is placing a tray with decanters and glasses on the table.* HEDDA *nods approval, and comes forward again.* BERTA *goes out.*]

Tesman. [*At the same time.*] And you, Judge Brack—what do you say to this? Eh?

Brack. Well, I say that a moral victory—h'm—may be all very fine—

Tesman. Yes, certainly. But all the same—

Hedda. [*Looking at* TESMAN *with a cold smile.*] You stand there looking as if
you were thunderstruck—

Tesman. Yes—so I am—I almost think—

Brack. Don't you see, Mrs. Tesman, a thunderstorm has just passed over?

Hedda. [*Pointing towards the inner room.*] Will you not take a glass of cold
punch, gentlemen?

Brack. [*Looking at his watch.*] A stirrup cup? Yes, it wouldn't come amiss.

Tesman. A capital idea, Hedda! Just the thing? Now that the weight has
been taken off my mind—

Hedda. Will you not join them, Mr. Lövborg?

Lövborg. [*With a gesture of refusal.*] No, thank you. Nothing for me.

Brack. Why, bless me—cold punch is surely not poison.

Lövborg. Perhaps not for every one.

Hedda. I will keep Mr. Lövborg company in the meantime.

Tesman. Yes, yes, Hedda dear, do.

[*He and* BRACK *go into the inner room, seat themselves, drink punch, smoke
cigarettes, and carry on a lively conversation during what follows.* EILERT
LÖVBORG *remains beside the stove.* HEDDA *goes to the writing table.*]

Hedda. [*Raising her voice a little.*] Do you care to look at some photographs, Mr. Lövborg? You know Tesman and I made a tour in the
Tyrol on our way home?

[*She takes up an album, and places it on the table beside the sofa, in the
further corner of which she seats herself.* EILERT LÖVBORG *approaches,
stops, and looks at her. Then he takes a chair and seats himself at her left,
with his back towards the inner room.*]

Hedda. [*Opening the album.*] Do you see this range of mountains, Mr.
Lövborg? It's the Ortler group. Tesman has written the name under-
neath. Here it is: "The Ortler group near Meran."

Lövborg. [*Who has never taken his eyes off her, says softly and slowly.*]
Hedda—Gabler!

Hedda. [*Glancing hastily at him.*] Ah! Hush!

Lövborg. [*Repeats softly.*] Hedda Gabler!

Hedda. [*Looking at the album.*] That was my name in the old days—when
we two knew each other.

Lövborg. And I must teach myself never to say Hedda Gabler again—never,
as long as I live.

Hedda. [*Still turning over the pages.*] Yes, you must. And I think you ought
to practice in time. The sooner the better, I should say.

Lövborg. [*In a tone of indignation.*] Hedda Gabler married? And married
to—George Tesman!

Hedda. Yes—so the world goes.

Lövborg. Oh, Hedda, Hedda—how could you[2] throw yourself away!

Hedda. [*Looks sharply at him.*] What? I can't allow this!

Lövborg. What do you mean? [TESMAN *comes into the room and goes toward the sofa.*]

Hedda. [*Hears him coming and says in an indifferent tone.*] And this is a view from the Val d'Ampezzo, Mr. Lövborg. Just look at these peaks! [*Looks affectionately up at* TESMAN,] What's the name of these curious peaks, dear?

Tesman. Let me see? Oh, those are the Dolomites.

Hedda. Yes, that's it! Those are the Dolomites, Mr. Lövborg.

Tesman. Hedda dear, I only wanted to ask whether I shouldn't bring you a little punch after all? For yourself at any rate—eh?

Hedda. Yes, do, please; and perhaps a few biscuits.

Tesman. No cigarettes?

Hedda. No.

Tesman. Very well.

[*He goes into the inner room and out to the right.* BRACK *sits in the inner room, and keeps an eye from time to time on* HEDDA *and* LÖVBORG.]

Lövborg. [*Softly, as before.*] Answer me, Hedda—how could you go and do this?

Hedda. [*Apparently absorbed in the album.*] If you continue to say *du* to me I won't talk to you.

Lövborg. May I say *du* when we are alone?

Hedda. No. You may think it; but you mustn't say it.

Lövborg. Ah, I understand. It is an offense against George Tesman, whom you[3]—love.

Hedda. [*Glances at him and smiles.*] Love? What an idea!

Lövborg. You don't love him then!

Hedda. But I won't hear of any sort of unfaithfulness! Remember that.

Lövborg. Hedda—answer me one thing—

Hedda. Hush! [TESMAN *enters with a small tray from the inner room.*]

Tesman. Here you are! Isn't this tempting? [*He puts the tray on the table.*]

Hedda. Why do you bring it yourself?

Tesman. [*Filling the glasses.*] Because I think it's such fun to wait upon you, Hedda.

---

[2] He uses the familiar *du.*

[3] From this point onward Lövborg uses the formal *De.*

Hedda. But you have poured out two glasses. Mr. Lövborg said he wouldn't have any—

Tesman. No, but Mrs. Elvsted will soon be here, won't she?

Hedda. Yes, by-the-bye—Mrs. Elvsted—

Tesman. Had you forgotten her? Eh?

Hedda. We were so absorbed in these photographs. [*Shows him a picture.*] Do you remember this little village?

Tesman. Oh, it's that one just below the Brenner Pass. It was there we passed the night—

Hedda. —and met that lively party of tourists.

Tesman. Yes, that was the place. Fancy—if we could only have had you with us, Eilert! Eh? [*He returns to the inner room and sits beside* BRACK.]

Lövborg. Answer me this one thing, Hedda—

Hedda. Well?

Lövborg. Was there no love in your friendship for me either? Not a spark—not a tinge of love in it?

Hedda. I wonder if there was? To me it seems as though we were two good comrades—two thoroughly intimate friends. [*Smilingly.*] You especially were frankness itself.

Lövborg. It was you that made me so.

Hedda. As I look back upon it all, I think there was really something beautiful, something fascinating—something daring—in—in that secret intimacy—that comradeship which no living creature so much as dreamed of.

Lövborg. Yes, yes, Hedda! Was there not? When I used to come to your father's in the afternoon—and the General sat over at the window reading his papers—with his back towards us—

Hedda. And we two on the corner sofa—

Lövborg. Always with the same illustrated paper before us—

Hedda. For want of an album, yes.

Lövborg. Yes, Hedda, and when I made my confessions to you—told you about myself, things that at that time no one else knew! There I would sit and tell you of my escapades—my days and nights of devilment. Oh, Hedda—what was the power in you that forced me to confess these things?

Hedda. Do you think it was any power in me?

Lövborg. How else can I explain it? And all those—those roundabout questions you used to put to me—

Hedda. Which you understood so particularly well—

Lövborg. How could you sit and question me like that? Question me quite frankly—

Hedda. In roundabout terms, please observe.

Lövborg. Yes, but frankly nevertheless. Cross-question me about—all that sort of thing?

Hedda. And how could you answer, Mr. Lövborg?

Lövborg. Yes, that is just what I can't understand—in looking back upon it. But tell me now, Hedda—was there not love at the bottom of our friendship? On your side, did you not feel as though you might purge my stains away if I made you my confessor? Was it not so?

Hedda. No, not quite.

Lövborg. What was your motive, then?

Hedda. Do you think it quite incomprehensible that a young girl—when it can be done—without any one knowing—

Lövborg. Well?

Hedda. —should be glad to have a peep, now and then, into a world which—

Lövborg. Which—?

Hedda. —which she is forbidden to know anything about?

Lövborg. So that was it?

Hedda. Partly. Partly—I almost think.

Lövborg. Comradeship in the thirst for life. But why should not that, at any rate, have continued?

Hedda. The fault was yours.

Lövborg. It was you that broke with me.

Hedda. Yes, when our friendship threatened to develop into something more serious. Shame upon you, Eilert Lövborg! How could you think of wronging your—frank comrade?

Lövborg. [*Clenching his hands.*] Oh, why did you not carry out your threat? Why did you not shoot me down?

Hedda. Because I have such a dread of scandal.

Lövborg. Yes, Hedda, you are a coward at heart.

Hedda. A terrible coward. [*Changing her tone.*] But it was a lucky thing for you. And now you have found ample consolation at the Elvsteds'.

Lövborg. I know what Thea has confided to you.

Hedda. And perhaps you have confided to her something about us?

Lövborg. Not a word. She is too stupid to understand anything of that sort.

Hedda. Stupid?

Lövborg. She is stupid about matters of that sort.

Hedda. And I am cowardly. [*Bends over towards him, without looking him in the face, and says more softly.*] But now I will confide something to you.

Lövborg. [*Eagerly.*] Well?

Hedda. The fact that I dared not shoot you down—

Lövborg. Yes!
Hedda. —that was not my most arrant cowardice—that evening.
Lövborg. [*Looks at her a moment, understands, and whispers passionately.*]
Oh, Hedda! Hedda Gabler! Now I begin to see a hidden reason
beneath our comradeship! You[4] and I—! After all, then, it was your
craving for life—
Hedda. [*Softly, with a sharp glance.*] Take care! Believe nothing of the sort!

[*Twilight has begun to fall. The hall door is opened from without by* BERTA.]

Hedda. [*Closes the album with a bang and calls smilingly.*] Ah, at last! My
darling Thea, come along!

[MRS. ELVSTED *enters from the hall. She is in evening dress. The door is
closed behind her.*]

Hedda. [*On the sofa, stretches out her arms towards her.*] My sweet Thea—
you can't think how I have been longing for you!

[MRS. ELVSTED, *in passing, exchanges slight salutations with the gentlemen
in the inner room, then goes up to the table and gives* HEDDA *her hands.*
EILERT LÖVBORG *has risen. He and* MRS. ELVSTED *greet each other with a
silent nod.*]

Mrs. Elvsted. Ought I to go in and talk to your husband for a moment?
Hedda. Oh, not at all. Leave those two alone. They will soon be going.
Mrs. Elvsted. Are they going out?
Hedda. Yes, to a supper party.
Mrs. Elvsted. [*Quickly, to* LÖVBORG.] Not you?
Lövborg. No.
Hedda. Mr. Lövborg remains with us.
Mrs. Elvsted. [*Takes a chair and is about to seat herself at his side.*] Oh,
how nice it is here!
Hedda. No, thank you, my little Thea! Not there! You'll be good enough to
come over here to me. I will sit between you.
Mrs. Elvsted. Yes, just as you please.

[*She goes round the table and seats herself on the sofa on* HEDDA'S *right.*
LÖVBORG *reseats himself on his chair.*]

Lövborg. [*After a short pause, to* HEDDA.] Is not she lovely to look at?
Hedda. [*Lightly stroking her hair.*] Only to look at?
Lövborg. Yes. For we two—she and I—we are two real comrades. We have

---

[4] In this speech he once more says *du*. Hedda addresses him throughout as *De*.

absolute faith in each other; so we can sit and talk with perfect
frankness—

Hedda. Not round about, Mr. Lövborg?

Lövborg. Well—

Mrs. Elvsted. [*Softly clinging close to* HEDDA.] Oh, how happy I am, Hedda;
for, only think, he says I have inspired him too.

Hedda. [*Looks at her with a smile.*] Ah! Does he say that, dear?

Lövborg. And then she is so brave, Mrs. Tesman!

Mrs. Elvsted. Good heavens—am I brave?

Lövborg. Exceedingly—where your comrade is concerned.

Hedda. Ah, yes—courage! If one only had that!

Lövborg. What then? What do you mean?

Hedda. Then life would perhaps be liveable, after all. [*With a sudden change
of tone.*] But now, my dearest Thea, you really must have a glass of
cold punch.

Mrs. Elvsted. No, thanks—I never take anything of that kind.

Hedda. Well then, you Mr. Lövborg.

Lövborg. Nor I, thank you.

Mrs. Elvsted. No, he doesn't either.

Hedda. [*Looks fixedly at him.*] But if I say you shall?

Lövborg. It would be no use.

Hedda. [*Laughing.*] Then I, poor creature, have no sort of power over you?

Lövborg. Not in that respect.

Hedda. But seriously, I think you ought to—for your own sake.

Mrs. Elvsted. Why, Hedda—!

Lövborg. How so?

Hedda. Or rather on account of other people.

Lövborg. Indeed?

Hedda. Otherwise people might be apt to suspect that—in your heart of
hearts—you did not feel quite secure—quite confident of yourself.

Mrs. Elvsted. [*Softly.*] Oh please, Hedda—

Lövborg. People may suspect what they like—for the present.

Mrs. Elvsted. [*Joyfully.*] Yes, let them!

Hedda. I saw it plainly in Judge Brack's face a moment ago.

Lövborg. What did you see?

Hedda. His contemptuous smile, when you dared not go with them into the
inner room.

Lövborg. Dared not? Of course I preferred to stop here and talk to you.

Mrs. Elvsted. What could be more natural, Hedda?

Hedda. But the Judge could not guess that. And I saw, too, the way he
smiled and glanced at Tesman when you dared not accept his invitation
to this wretched little supper party of his.

Lövborg. Dared not! Do you say I dared not?

Hedda. I don't say so. But that was how Judge Brack understood it.

Lövborg. Well, let him.

Hedda. Then you are not going with them?

Lövborg. I will stay here with you and Thea.

Mrs. Elvsted. Yes, Hedda—how can you doubt that?

Hedda. [*Smiles and nods approvingly to* LÖVBORG,] Firm as a rock! Faithful to your principles, now and forever! Ah, that is how a man should be! [*Turns to* MRS. ELVSTED *and caresses her.*] Well now, what did I tell you, when you came to us this morning in such a state of distraction—

Lövborg. [*Surprised.*] Distraction!

Mrs. Elvsted. [*Terrified.*] Hedda—oh Hedda—!

Hedda. You can see for yourself; you haven't the slightest reason to be in such mortal terror— [*Interrupting herself.*] There! Now we can all three enjoy ourselves!

Lövborg. [*Who has given a start.*] Ah—what is all this, Mrs. Tesman?

Mrs. Elvsted. Oh my God, Hedda! What are you saying? What are you doing?

Hedda. Don't get excited! That horrid Judge Brack is sitting watching you.

Lövborg. So she was in mortal terror! On my account!

Mrs. Elvsted. [*Softly and piteously.*] Oh, Hedda—now you have ruined everything!

Lövborg. [*Looks fixedly at her for a moment. His face is distorted.*] So that was my comrade's frank confidence in me?

Mrs. Elvsted [*Imploringly.*] Oh, my dearest friend—only let me tell you—

Lövborg. [*Takes one of the glasses of punch, raises it to his lips, and says in a low, husky voice.*] Your health, Thea!

[*He empties the glass, puts it down, and takes the second.*]

Mrs. Elvsted. [*Softly.*] Oh, Hedda, Hedda—how could you do this?

Hedda. I do it? I? Are you crazy?

Lövborg. Here's to your health too, Mrs. Tesman. Thanks for the truth. Hurrah for the truth!

[*He empties the glass and is about to refill it.*]

Hedda. [*Lays her hand on his arm.*] Come, come—no more for the present. Remember you are going out to supper.

Mrs. Elvsted. No, no, no!

Hedda. Hush! They are sitting watching you.

Lövborg. [*Putting down the glass.*] Now, Thea—tell me the truth—

Mrs. Elvsted. Yes.

Lövborg. Did your husband know that you had come after me?

Mrs. Elvsted. [*Wringing her hands.*] Oh, Hedda—do you hear what he is asking?

Lövborg. Was it arranged between you and him that you were to come to town and look after me? Perhaps it was the Sheriff himself that urged you to come? Aha, my dear—no doubt he wanted my help in his office! Or was it at the card table that he missed me?

Mrs. Elvsted. [*Softly, in agony.*] Oh, Lövborg, Lövborg—!

Lövborg. [*Seizes a glass and is on the point of filling it.*] Here's a glass for the old Sheriff too!

Hedda. [*Preventing him.*] No more just now. Remember you have to read your manuscript to Tesman.

Lövborg. [*Calmly, putting down the glass.*] It was stupid of me all this, Thea—to take it in this way, I mean. Don't be angry with me, my dear, dear comrade. You shall see—both you and the others—that if I was fallen once—now I have risen again! Thanks to you, Thea.

Mrs. Elvsted. [*Radiant with joy.*] Oh, heaven be praised—!

[BRACK *has in the meantime looked at his watch. He and* TESMAN *rise and come into the drawing room.*]

Brack. [*Takes his hat and overcoat.*] Well, Mrs. Tesman, our time has come.

Hedda. I suppose it has.

Lövborg. [*Rising.*] Mine too, Judge Brack.

Mrs. Elvsted. [*Softly and imploringly.*] Oh, Lövborg, don't do it!

Hedda. [*Pinching her arm.*] They can hear you!

Mrs. Elvsted. [*With a suppressed shriek.*] Ow!

Lövborg. [*To* BRACK.] You were good enough to invite me.

Brack. Well, are you coming after all?

Lövborg. Yes, many thanks.

Brack. I'm delighted—

Lövborg. [*To* TESMAN, *putting the parcel of MS. in his pocket.*] I should like to show you one or two things before I send it to the printer's.

Tesman. Fancy—that will be delightful. But, Hedda dear, how is Mrs. Elvsted to get home? Eh?

Hedda. Oh, that can be managed somehow.

Lövborg. [*Looking towards the ladies.*] Mrs. Elvsted? Of course, I'll come again and fetch her. [*Approaching.*] At ten or thereabouts, Mrs. Tesman? Will that do?

Hedda. Certainly. That will do capitally.

Tesman. Well, then, that's all right. But you must not expect me so early, Hedda.

Hedda. Oh, you may stop as long—as long as ever you please.

Mrs. Elvsted. [*Trying to conceal her anxiety.*] Well then, Mr. Lövborg—I shall remain here until you come.

Lövborg. [*With his hat in his hand.*] Pray do, Mrs. Elvsted.

Brack. And now off goes the excursion train, gentlemen! I hope we shall have a lively time, as a certain fair lady puts it.

Hedda. Ah, if only the fair lady could be present unseen—!

Brack. Why unseen?

Hedda. In order to hear a little of your liveliness at first hand, Judge Brack.

Brack. [*Laughing.*] I should not advise the fair lady to try it.

Tesman. [*Also laughing.*] Come, you're a nice one, Hedda! Fancy that!

Brack. Well, good-by, good-by, ladies.

Lövborg. [*Bowing.*] About ten o'clock, then.

[BRACK, LÖVBORG, *and* TESMAN *go out by the hall door. At the same time* BERTA *enters from the inner room with a lighted lamp, which she places on the dining room table; she goes out by the way she came.*]

Mrs. Elvsted. [*Who has risen and is wandering restlessly about the room.*] Hedda—Hedda—what will come of all this?

Hedda. At ten o'clock—he will be here. I can see him already—with vine leaves in his hair—flushed and fearless—

Mrs. Elvsted. Oh, I hope he may.

Hedda. And then, you see—then he will have regained control over himself. Then he will be a free man for all his days.

Mrs. Elvsted. Oh God!—if he would only come as you see him now!

Hedda. He will come as I see him—so, and not otherwise! [*Rises and approaches* THEA.] You may doubt him as long as you please; I believe in him. And now we will try—

Mrs. Elvsted. You have some hidden motive in this, Hedda!

Hedda. Yes, I have. I want for once in my life to have power to mold a human destiny.

Mrs. Elvsted. Have you not the power?

Hedda. I have not—and have never had it.

Mrs. Elvsted. Not your husband's?

Hedda. Do you think that is worth the trouble? Oh, if you could only understand how poor I am. And fate has made you so rich! [*Clasps her passionately in her arms.*] I think I must burn your hair off, after all.

Mrs. Elvsted. Let me go! Let me go! I am afraid of you, Hedda!

Berta. [*In the middle doorway.*] Tea is laid in the dining room, ma'am.

Hedda. Very well. We are coming.

Mrs. Elvsted. No, no, no! I would rather go home alone! At once!

Hedda. Nonsense! First you shall have a cup of tea, you little stupid. And then—at ten o'clock—Eilert Lövborg will be here—with vine leaves in his hair. [*She drags* MRS. ELVSTED *almost by force towards the middle doorway.*]

Act III

Scene: *The room at the* TESMANS'. *The curtains are drawn over the middle doorway, and also over the glass door. The lamp, half turned down, and with a shade over it, is burning on the table. In the stove, the door of which stands open, there has been a fire, which is now nearly burnt out.*

MRS. ELVSTED, *wrapped in a large shawl, and with her feet upon a footrest, sits close to the stove, sunk back in the armchair.* HEDDA, *fully dressed, lies sleeping upon the sofa, with a sofa blanket over her.*

Mrs. Elvsted. [*After a pause, suddenly sits up in her chair, and listens eagerly. Then she sinks back again wearily, moaning to herself.*] Not yet!—Oh God—oh God—not yet!

[BERTA *slips in by the hall door. She has a letter in her hand.*]

Mrs. Elvsted. [*Turns and whispers eagerly.*] Well—has any one come?
Berta. [*Softly.*] Yes, a girl has brought this letter.
Mrs. Elvsted. [*Quickly, holding out her hand.*] A letter! Give it to me!
Berta. No, it's for Dr. Tesman, ma'am.
Mrs. Elvsted. Oh, indeed.
Berta. It was Miss Tesman's servant that brought it. I'll lay it here on the table.
Mrs. Elvsted. Yes, do.
Berta. [*Laying down the letter.*] I think I had better put out the lamp. It's smoking.
Mrs. Elvsted. Yes, put it out. It must soon be daylight now.
Berta. [*Putting out the lamp.*] It is daylight already, ma'am.
Mrs. Elvsted. Yes, broad day! And no one come back yet—!
Berta. Lord bless you, ma'am! I guessed how it would be.
Mrs. Elvsted. You guessed?
Berta. Yes, when I saw that a certain person had come back to town—and that he went off with them. For we've heard enough about that gentleman before now.
Mrs. Elvsted. Don't speak so loud. You will waken Mrs. Tesman.
Berta. [*Looks towards the sofa and sighs.*] No, no—let her sleep, poor thing. Shan't I put some wood on the fire?
Mrs. Elvsted. Thanks, not for me.
Berta. Oh, very well. [*She goes softly out by the hall door.*]

Hedda. [*Is awakened by the shutting of the door, and looks up.*] What's that—?

Mrs. Elvsted. It was only the servant—

Hedda. [*Looking about her.*] Oh, we're here—! Yes, now I remember. [*Sits erect upon the sofa, stretches herself, and rubs her eyes.*] What o'clock is it, Thea?.

Mrs. Elvsted. [*Looks at her watch.*] It's past seven.

Hedda. When did Tesman come home?

Mrs. Elvsted. He has not come.

Hedda. Not come home yet?

Mrs. Elvsted. [*Rising.*] No one has come.

Hedda. Think of our watching and waiting here till four in the morning—

Mrs. Elvsted. [*Wringing her hands.*] And how I watched and waited for him!

Hedda. [*Yawns, and says with her hand before her mouth.*] Well, well—we might have spared ourselves the trouble.

Mrs. Elvsted. Did you get a little sleep?

Hedda. Oh yes; I believe I have slept pretty well. Have you not?

Mrs. Elvsted. Not for a moment. I couldn't, Hedda—not to save my life.

Hedda. [*Rises and goes towards her.*] There, there, there! There's nothing to be so alarmed about. I understand quite well what has happened.

Mrs. Elvsted. Well, what do you think? Won't you tell me?

Hedda. Why, of course it has been a very late affair at Judge Brack's—

Mrs. Elvsted. Yes, yes, that is clear enough. But all the same—

Hedda. And then, you see, Tesman hasn't cared to come home and ring us up in the middle of the night. [*Laughing.*] Perhaps he wasn't inclined to show himself either—immediately after a jollification.

Mrs. Elvsted. But in that case—where can he have gone?

Hedda. Of course he has gone to his aunts' and slept there. They have his old room ready for him.

Mrs. Elvsted. No, he can't be with them; for a letter has just come for him from Miss Tesman. There it lies.

Hedda. Indeed? [*Looks at the address.*] Why yes, it's addressed in Aunt Julia's own hand. Well then, he has remained at Judge Brack's. And as for Eilert Lövborg—he is sitting, with vine leaves in his hair, reading his manuscript.

Mrs. Elvsted. Oh Hedda, you are just saying things you don't believe a bit.

Hedda. You really are a little blockhead, Thea.

Mrs. Elvsted. Oh yes, I suppose I am.

Hedda. And how mortally tired you look.

Mrs. Elvsted. Yes, I am mortally tired.

Hedda. Well then, you must do as I tell you. You must go into my room and lie down for a little while.

Mrs. Elvsted. Oh no, no—I shouldn't be able to sleep.

Hedda. I am sure you would.

Mrs. Elvsted. Well, but your husband is certain to come soon now; and then I want to know at once—

Hedda. I shall take care to let you know when he comes.

Mrs. Elvsted. Do you promise me, Hedda?

Hedda. Yes, rely upon me. Just you go in and have a sleep in the meantime.

Mrs. Elvsted. Thanks; then I'll try to. [*She goes off through the inner room.*]

[HEDDA *goes up to the glass door and draws back the curtains. The broad daylight streams into the room. Then she takes a little hand glass from the writing table, looks at herself in it, and arranges her hair. Next she goes to the hall door and presses the bell button.*]

[BERTA *presently appears at the hall door.*]

Berta. Did you want anything, ma'am?

Hedda. Yes; you must put some more wood in the stove. I am shivering.

Berta. Bless me—I'll make up the fire at once. [*She rakes the embers together and lays a piece of wood upon them; then stops and listens.*] That was a ring at the front door, ma'am.

Hedda. Then go to the door. I will look after the fire.

Berta. It'll soon burn up. [*She goes out by the hall door.*]

[HEDDA *kneels on the footrest and lays some more pieces of wood in the stove.*]

[*After a short pause,* GEORGE TESMAN *enters from the hall. He looks tired and rather serious. He steals on tiptoe towards the middle doorway and is about to slip through the curtains.*]

Hedda. [*at the stove, without looking up.*] Good morning.

Tesman. [*Turns.*] Hedda! [*Approaching her.*] Good heavens—are you up so early? Eh?

Hedda. Yes, I am up very early this morning.

Tesman. And I never doubted you were still sound asleep! Fancy that, Hedda!

Hedda. Don't speak so loud. Mrs. Elvsted is resting in my room.

Tesman. Has Mrs. Elvsted been here all night?

Hedda. Yes, since no one came to fetch her.

Tesman. Ah, to be sure.

Hedda. [*Closes the door of the stove and rises.*] Well, did you enjoy yourself at Judge Brack's?

Tesman. Have you been anxious about me? Eh?

Hedda. No, I should never think of being anxious. But I asked if you had enjoyed yourself.

Tesman. Oh yes—for once in a way. Especially the beginning of the evening; for then Eilert read me part of his book. We arrived more than an hour too early—fancy that! And Brack had all sorts of arrangements to make—so Eilert read to me.

Hedda. [*Seating herself by the table on the right.*] Well? Tell me, then—

Tesman. [*Sitting on a footstool near the stove.*] Oh Hedda, you can't conceive what a book that is going to be! I believe it is one of the most remarkable things that have ever been written. Fancy that!

Hedda. Yes, yes; I don't care about that—

Tesman. I must make a confession to you, Hedda. When he had finished reading—a horrid feeling came over me.

Hedda. A horrid feeling?

Tesman. I felt jealous of Eilert for having had it in him to write such a book. Only think, Hedda!

Hedda. Yes, yes, I am thinking!

Tesman. And then how pitiful to think that he—with all his gifts—should be irreclaimable after all.

Hedda. I suppose you mean that he has more courage than the rest?

Tesman. No, not at all—I mean that he is incapable of taking his pleasures in moderation.

Hedda. And what came of it all—in the end?

Tesman. Well to tell the truth, I think it might best be described as an orgy, Hedda.

Hedda. Had he vine leaves in his hair?

Tesman. Vine leaves? No, I saw nothing of the sort. But he made a long, rambling speech in honor of the woman who had inspired him in his work—that was the phrase he used.

Hedda. Did he name her?

Tesman. No, he didn't; but I can't help thinking he meant Mrs. Elvsted. You may be sure he did.

Hedda. Well—where did you part from him?

Tesman. On the way to town. We broke up—the last of us at any rate—all together; and Brack came with us to get a breath of fresh air. And then, you see, we agreed to take Eilert home; for he had had far more than was good for him.

Hedda. I daresay.

Tesman. But now comes the strange part of it, Hedda; or, I should rather say, the melancholy part of it. I declare I am almost ashamed—on Eilert's account—to tell you—

Hedda. Oh, go on—

Tesman. Well, as we were getting near town, you see, I happened to drop a little behind the others. Only for a minute or two—fancy that!

Hedda. Yes, yes, yes, but—?

Tesman. And then, as I hurried after them—what do you think I found by the wayside? Eh?

Hedda. Oh, how should I know!

Tesman. You mustn't speak of it to a soul, Hedda! Do you hear! Promise me, for Eilert's sake. [*Draws a parcel, wrapped in paper, from his coat pocket.*] Fancy, dear—I found this.

Hedda. Is not that the parcel he had with him yesterday?

Tesman. Yes, it is the whole of his precious, irreplaceable manuscript! And he had gone and lost it, and knew nothing about it. Only fancy, Hedda! So deplorably—

Hedda. But why did you not give him back the parcel at once?

Tesman. I didn't dare to—in the state he was then in—

Hedda. Did you not tell any of the others that you had found it?

Tesman. Oh, far from it! You can surely understand that, for Eilert's sake, I wouldn't do that.

Hedda. So no one knows that Eilert Lövborg's manuscript is in your possession?

Tesman. No. And no one must know it.

Hedda. Then what did you say to him afterwards?

Tesman. I didn't talk to him again at all; for when we got in among the streets, he and two or three of the others gave us the slip and disappeared. Fancy that!

Hedda. Indeed! They must have taken him home then.

Tesman. Yes, so it would appear. And Brack, too, left us.

Hedda. And what have you been doing with yourself since?

Tesman. Well, I and some of the others went home with one of the party, a jolly fellow, and took our morning coffee with him; or perhaps I should rather call it our night coffee—eh? But now, when I have rested a little, and given Eilert, poor fellow, time to have his sleep out, I must take this back to him.

Hedda [*Holds out her hand for the packet.*] No—don't give it to him! Not in such a hurry, I mean. Let me read it first.

Tesman. No, my dearest Hedda, I mustn't, I really mustn't.

Hedda. You must not?

Tesman. No—for you can imagine what a state of despair he will be in when he awakens and misses the manuscript. He has no copy of it, you must know! He told me so.

Hedda [*Looking searchingly at him.*] Can such a thing not be reproduced? Written over again?

Tesman. No, I don't think that would be possible. For the inspiration, you see—

Hedda. Yes, yes—I suppose it depends on that. [*Lightly.*] But, by-the-bye—
here is a letter for you.

Tesman. Fancy—!

Hedda. [*Handing it to him.*] It came early this morning.

Tesman. It's from Aunt Julia! What can it be? [*He lays the packet on the other footstool, opens the letter, runs his eye through it, and jumps up.*] Oh, Hedda—she says that poor Aunt Rina is dying!

Hedda. Well, we were prepared for that.

Tesman. And that if I want to see her again, I must make haste. I'll run in to them at once.

Hedda [*Suppressing a smile.*] Will you run?

Tesman. Oh, dearest Hedda—if you could only make up your mind to come with me! Just think!

Hedda. [*Rises and says wearily, repelling the idea.*] No, no, don't ask me. I will not look upon sickness and death. I loathe all sorts of ugliness.

Tesman. Well, well, then—! [*Bustling around.*] My hat—my overcoat—? Oh, in the hall—I do hope I mayn't come too late, Hedda! Eh?

Hedda. Oh, if you run—

[BERTA *appears at the hall door.*]

Berta. Judge Brack is at the door, and wishes to know if he may come in.

Tesman. At this time! No, I can't possibly see him.

Hedda. But I can. [*To* BERTA.] Ask Judge Brack to come in. [BERTA *goes out.*]

Hedda. [*Quickly whispering.*] The parcel, Tesman! [*She snatches it up from the stool.*]

Tesman. Yes, give it to me!

Hedda. No, no, I will keep it till you come back.

[*She goes to the writing table and places it in the bookcase.* TESMAN *stands in a flurry of haste and cannot get his gloves on.*]

[JUDGE BRACK *enters from the hall.*]

Hedda. [*Nodding to him.*] You are an early bird, I must say.

Brack. Yes, don't you think so? [*To* TESMAN.] Are you on the move, too?

Tesman. Yes, I must rush off to my aunts'. Fancy—the invalid one is lying at death's door, poor creature.

Brack. Dear me, is she indeed? Then on no account let me detain you. At such a critical moment—

Tesman. Yes, I must really rush—Good-by! Good-by! [*He hastens out by the hall door.*]

Hedda. [*Approaching.*] You seem to have made a particularly lively night of it at your rooms, Judge Brack.

Brack. I assure you I have not had my clothes off, Mrs. Hedda.

Hedda. Not you, either?

Brack. No, as you may see. But what has Tesman been telling you of the night's adventures?

Hedda. Oh, some tiresome story. Only that they went and had coffee somewhere or other.

Brack. I have heard about that coffee-party already. Eilert Lövborg was not with them, I fancy?

Hedda. No, they had taken him home before that.

Brack. Tesman, too?

Hedda. No, but some of the others, he said.

Brack. [*Smiling.*] George Tesman is really an ingenuous creature, Mrs. Hedda.

Hedda. Yes, heaven knows he is. Then is there something behind all this?

Brack. Yes, perhaps there may be.

Hedda. Well then, sit down, my dear Judge, and tell your story in comfort.

[*She seats herself to the left of the table.* BRACK *sits near her, at the long side of the table.*]

Hedda. Now then?

Brack. I had special reasons for keeping track of my guests—or rather of some of my guests—last night.

Hedda. Of Eilert Lövborg among the rest, perhaps?

Brack. Frankly, yes.

Hedda. Now you make me really curious—

Brack. Do you know where he and one or two of the others finished the night, Mrs. Hedda?

Hedda. If it is not quite unmentionable, tell me.

Brack. Oh no, it's not at all unmentionable. Well, they put in an appearance at a particularly animated soirée.

Hedda. Of the lively kind?

Brack. Of the very liveliest—

Hedda. Tell me more of this, Judge Brack—

Brack. Lövborg, as well as the others, had been invited in advance. I knew all about it. But he had declined the invitation; for now, as you know, he has become a new man.

Hedda. Up at the Elvsteds', yes. But he went after all, then?

Brack. Well, you see, Mrs. Hedda—unhappily the spirit moved him at my rooms last evening—

Hedda. Yes, I hear he found inspiration.

Brack. Pretty violent inspiration. Well, I fancy that altered his purpose; for we men folk are unfortunately not always so firm in our principles as we ought to be.

Hedda. Oh, I am sure you are an exception, Judge Brack. But as to Lövborg—?

Brack. To make a long story short—he landed at last in Mademoiselle Diana's rooms.

Hedda. Mademoiselle Diana's?

Brack. It was Mademoiselle Diana that was giving the soirée, to a select circle of her admirers and her lady friends.

Hedda. Is she a red-haired woman?

Brack. Precisely.

Hedda. A sort of a—singer?

Brack. Oh yes—in her leisure moments. And moreover a mighty huntress—of men—Mrs. Hedda. You have no doubt heard of her. Eilert Lövborg was one of her most enthusiastic protectors—in the days of his glory.

Hedda. And how did all this end?

Brack. Far from amicably, it appears. After a most tender meeting, they seem to have come to blows—

Hedda. Lövborg and she?

Brack. Yes. He accused her or her friends of having robbed him. He declared that his pocketbook had disappeared—and other things as well. In short, he seems to have made a furious disturbance.

Hedda. And what came of it all?

Brack. It came to a general scrimmage, in which the ladies as well as the gentlemen took part. Fortunately the police at last appeared on the scene.

Hedda. The police too?

Brack. Yes. I fancy it will prove a costly frolic for Eilert Lövborg, crazy being that he is.

Hedda. How so?

Brack. He seems to have made a violent resistance—to have hit one of the constables on the head and torn the coat off his back. So they had to march him off to the police station with the rest.

Hedda. How have you learnt all this?

Brack. From the police themselves.

Hedda. [*Gazing straight before her.*] So that is what happened. Then he had no vine leaves in his hair.

Brack. Vine leaves, Mrs. Hedda?

Hedda. [*Changing her tone.*] But tell me now, Judge—what is your real reason for tracking out Eilert Lövborg's movements so carefully?

Brack. In the first place, it could not be entirely indifferent to me if it should appear in the police court that he came straight from my house.

Hedda. Will the matter come into court, then?

Brack. Of course. However, I should scarcely have troubled so much about that. But I thought that, as a friend of the family, it was my duty to supply you and Tesman with a full account of his nocturnal exploits.

Hedda. Why so, Judge Brack?

Brack. Why, because I have a shrewd suspicion that he intends to use you as a sort of blind.

Hedda. Oh, how can you think such a thing!

Brack. Good heavens, Mrs. Hedda—we have eyes in our head. Mark my words! This Mrs. Elvsted will be in no hurry to leave town again.

Hedda. Well, even if there should be anything between them, I suppose there are plenty of other places where they could meet.

Brack. Not a single home. Henceforth, as before, every respectable house will be closed against Eilert Lövborg.

Hedda. And so ought mine to be, you mean?

Brack. Yes. I confess it would be more than painful to me if this personage were to be made free of your house. How superfluous, how intrusive, he would be, if he were to force his way into—

Hedda. —into the triangle?

Brack. Precisely. It would simply mean that I should find myself homeless.

Hedda. [*Looks at him with a smile.*] So you want to be the one cock in the basket—that is your aim.

Brack. [*Nods slowly and lowers his voice.*] Yes, that is my aim. And for that I will fight—with every weapon I can command.

Hedda. [*Her smile vanishing.*] I see you are a dangerous person—when it comes to the point.

Brack. Do you think so?

Hedda. I am beginning to think so. And I am exceedingly glad to think— that you have no sort of hold over me.

Brack. [*Laughing equivocally.*] Well, well Mrs. Hedda—perhaps you are right there. If I had, who knows what I might be capable of?

Hedda. Come, come now, Judge Brack. That sounds almost like a threat.

Brack. [*Rising.*] Oh, not at all! The triangle, you know, ought, if possible, to be spontaneously constructed.

Hedda. There I agree with you.

Brack. Well, now I have said all I had to say; and I had better be getting back to town. Good-by, Mrs. Hedda. [*He goes towards the glass door.*]

Hedda. [*Rising.*] Are you going through the garden?

Brack. Yes, it's a short cut for me.

Hedda. And then it is the back way, too.

Brack. Quite so. I have no objection to back ways. They may be piquant enough at times.

Hedda. When there is ball practice going on, you mean?

Brack [*In the doorway, laughing to her.*] Oh, people don't shoot their tame poultry, I fancy.

Hedda [*Also laughing.*] Oh no, when there is only one cock in the basket—

[*They exchange laughing nods of farewell. He goes. She closes the door behind him.*]

HEDDA, *who has become quite serious, stands for a moment looking out. Presently she goes and peeps through the curtain over the middle doorway. Then she goes to the writing table, takes* LÖVBORG'S *packet out of the bookcase, and is on the point of looking through its contents.* BERTA *is heard speaking loudly in the hall.* HEDDA *turns and listens. Then she hastily locks up the packet in the drawer, and lays the key on the inkstand.*

[EILERT LÖVBORG, *with his great coat on and his hat in his hand, tears open the hall door. He looks somewhat confused and irritated.*]

Lövborg. [*Looking towards the hall.*] And I tell you I must and will come in! There!

[*He closes the door, turns and sees* HEDDA, *at once regains his self-control, and bows.*]

Hedda. [*At the writing table.*] Well Mr. Lövborg, this is rather a late hour to call for Thea.

Lövborg. You mean rather an early hour to call on you. Pray pardon me.

Hedda. How do you know that she is still here?

Lövborg. They told me at her lodgings that she had been out all night.

Hedda. [*Going to the oval table.*] Did you notice anything about the people of the house when they said that?

Lövborg. [*Looks inquiringly at her.*] Notice anything about them?

Hedda. I mean, did they seem to think it odd?

Lövborg. [*Suddenly understanding.*] Oh yes, of course! I am dragging her down with me! However, I didn't notice anything—I suppose Tesman is not up yet?

Hedda. No—I think not—

Lövborg. When did he come home?

Hedda. Very late.

Lövborg. Did he tell you anything?

Hedda. Yes, I gathered that you had had an exceedingly jolly evening at Judge Brack's.

Lövborg. Nothing more?

Hedda. I don't think so. However, I was so dreadfully sleepy—

[MRS. ELVSTED *enters through the curtains of the middle doorway.*]

Mrs. Elvsted. [*Going towards him.*] Ah, Lövborg! At last—!

Lövborg. Yes, at last. And too late!

Mrs. Elvsted. [*Looks anxiously at him.*] What is too late?

Lövborg. Everything is too late now. It is all over with me.

Mrs. Elvsted. Oh no, no—don't say that!

Lövborg. You will say the same when you hear—

Mrs. Elvsted. I won't hear anything!

Hedda. Perhaps you would prefer to talk to her alone! If so, I will leave you.

Lövborg. No, stay—you too. I beg you to stay.

Mrs. Elvsted. Yes, but I won't hear anything, I tell you.

Lövborg. It is not last night's adventures that I want to talk about.

Mrs. Elvsted. What is it then—?

Lövborg. I want to say that now our ways must part.

Mrs. Elvsted. Part!

Hedda. [*Involuntarily.*] I knew it!

Lövborg. You can be of no more service to me, Thea.

Mrs. Elvsted. How can you stand there and say that! No more service to you! Am I not to help you now, as before? Are we not to go on working together?

Lövborg. Henceforward I shall do no work.

Mrs. Elvsted. [*Despairingly.*] Then what am I to do with my life?

Lövborg. You must try to live your life as if you had never known me.

Mrs. Elvsted. But you know I cannot do that!

Lövborg. Try if you cannot, Thea. You must go home again—

Mrs. Elvsted. [*In vehement protest.*] Never in this world! Where you are, there will I be also! I will not let myself be driven away like this! I will remain here! I will be with you when the book appears.

Hedda. [*Half aloud, in suspense.*] Ah yes—the book!

Lövborg. [*Looks at her.*] My book and Thea's; for that is what it is.

Mrs. Elvsted. Yes, I feel that it is. And that is why I have a right to be with you when it appears! I will see with my own eyes how respect and honor pour in upon you afresh. And the happiness—the happiness—oh, I must share it with you!

Lövborg. Thea—our book will never appear.

Hedda. Ah!

Mrs. Elvsted. Never appear!

Lövborg. Can never appear.

Mrs. Elvsted. [*In agonized foreboding.*] Lövborg—what have you done with the manuscript?

Hedda. [*Looks anxiously at him.*] Yes, the manuscript—?

Mrs. Elvsted. Where is it?

Lövborg. Oh Thea—don't ask me about it!

Mrs. Elvsted. Yes, yes, I will know. I demand to be told at once.

Lövborg. The manuscript—Well then—I have torn the manuscript into a thousand pieces.

Mrs. Elvsted. [*Shrieks.*] Oh no, no—!

Hedda. [*Involuntarily.*] But that's not—

Lövborg. [*Looks at her.*] Not true, you think?

Hedda. [*Collecting herself.*] Oh well, of course—since you say so. But it sounded so improbable—

Lövborg. It is true, all the same.

Mrs. Elvsted. [*Wringing her hands.*] Oh God—oh God, Hedda—torn his own work to pieces!

Lövborg. I have torn my own life to pieces. So why should I not tear my lifework too—?

Mrs. Elvsted. And you did this last night?

Lövborg. Yes, I tell you! Tore it into a thousand pieces and scattered them on the fiord—far out. There there is cool sea water at any rate—let them drift upon it—drift with the current and the wind. And then presently they will sink—deeper and deeper—as I shall, Thea.

Mrs. Elvsted. Do you know, Lövborg, that what you have done with the book—I shall think of it to my dying day as though you had killed a little child.

Lövborg. Yes, you are right. It is a sort of child murder.

Mrs. Elvsted. How could you, then—! Did not the child belong to me too?

Hedda [*Almost inaudibly.*] Ah, the child—

Mrs. Elvsted. [*Breathing heavily.*] It is all over then. Well, well, now I will go, Hedda.

Hedda. But you are not going away from town?

Mrs. Elvsted. Oh, I don't know what I shall do. I see nothing but darkness before me. [*She goes out by the hall door.*]

Hedda. [*Stands waiting for a moment.*] So you are not going to see her home, Mr. Lövborg?

Lövborg. I? Through the streets? Would you have people see her walking with me?

Hedda. Of course I don't know what else may have happened last night. But is it so utterly irretrievable?

Lövborg. It will not end with last night—I know that perfectly well. And the thing is that now I have no taste for that sort of life either. I won't begin it anew. She has broken my courage and my power of braving life out.

Hedda. [*Looking straight before her.*] So that pretty little fool has had her fingers in a man's destiny. [*Looks at him.*] But all the same, how could you treat her so heartlessly?

Lövborg. Oh, don't say that it was heartless!

Hedda. To go and destroy what has filled her whole soul for months and years! You do not call that heartless!

Lövborg. To you I can tell the truth, Hedda.

Hedda. The truth?

Lövborg. First promise me—give me your word—that what I now confide to you Thea shall never know.

Hedda. I give you my word.

Lövborg. Good. Then let me tell you that what I said just now was untrue.

Hedda. About the manuscript?

Lövborg. Yes. I have not torn it to pieces—nor thrown it into the fiord.

Hedda. No, n—But—where is it then!

Lövborg. I have destroyed it none the less—utterly destroyed it, Hedda!

Hedda. I don't understand.

Lövborg. Thea said that what I had done seemed to her like a child murder.

Hedda. Yes, so she said.

Lövborg. But to kill his child—that is not the worst thing a father can do to it.

Hedda. Not the worst?

Lövborg. No. I wanted to spare Thea from hearing the worst.

Hedda. Then what is the worst?

Lövborg. Suppose now, Hedda, that a man—in the small hours of the morning—came home to his child's mother after a night of riot and debauchery, and said: "Listen—I have been here and there—in this place and in that. And I have taken our child with me—to this place and to that. And I have lost the child—utterly lost it. The devil knows into what hands it may have fallen—who may have had their clutches on it."

Hedda. Well—but when all is said and done, you know—that was only a book—

Lövborg. Thea's pure soul was in that book.

Hedda. Yes, so I understand.

Lövborg. And you can understand, too, that for her and me together no future is possible.

Hedda. What path do you mean to take then?

Lövborg. None. I will only try to make an end of it all—the sooner the better.

Hedda. [*A step nearer to him.*] Eilert Lövborg—listen to me. Will you not try to—to do it beautifully?

Lövborg. Beautifully? [*Smiling.*] With vine leaves in my hair, as you used to dream in the old days—?

Hedda. No, no. I have lost my faith in the vine leaves. But beautifully, nevertheless! For once in a way!—Good-by! You must go now—and do not come here any more.

Lövborg. Good-by, Mrs. Tesman. And give George Tesman my love. [*He is on the point of going.*]

Hedda. No, wait! I must give you a memento to take with you.

[*She goes to the writing table and opens the drawer and the pistol case; then returns to* LÖVBORG *with one of the pistols.*]

Lövborg. [*Looks at her.*] This? Is this the token?

Hedda. [*Nodding slowly.*] Do you recognize it? It was aimed at you once.

Lövborg. You should have used it then.

Hedda. Take it—and do you use it now.

Lövborg. [*Puts the pistol in his breast pocket.*] Thanks!

Hedda. And beautifully, Eilert Lövborg. Promise me that!

Lövborg. Good-by, Hedda Gabler. [*He goes out by the hall door.*]

[HEDDA *listens for a moment at the door. Then she goes up to the writing table, takes out the packet of manuscript, peeps under the cover, draws a few of the sheets half out, and looks at them. Next she goes over and seats herself in the armchair beside the stove, with the packet in her lap. Presently she opens the stove door, and then the packet.*]

Hedda. [*Throws one of the quires into the fire and whispers to herself.*] Now I am burning your child, Thea!—Burning it, curlylocks! [*Throwing one or two more quires into the stove.*] Your child and Eilert Lövborg's. [*Throws the rest in.*] I am burning—I am burning your child.

Act IV

Scene: *The same rooms at the* TESMANS'. *It is evening. The drawing room is in darkness. The back room is lighted by the hanging lamp over the table. The curtains over the glass door are drawn close.*

HEDDA, *dressed in black, walks to and fro in the dark room. Then she goes into the back room and disappears, for a moment to the left. She is heard to strike a few chords on the piano. Presently she comes in sight again, and returns to the drawing room.*

BERTA *enters from the right, through the inner room, with a lighted lamp, which she places on the table in front of the corner settee in the drawing room. Her eyes are red with weeping, and she has black ribbons in her cap. She goes quietly and circumspectly out to the right.*

HEDDA, *goes up to the glass door, lifts the curtain a little aside, and looks out into the darkness.*

Shortly afterwards, MISS TESMAN, *in mourning, with a bonnet and veil on, comes in from the hall.* HEDDA *goes towards her and holds out her hand.*

Miss Tesman. Yes, Hedda, here I am, in mourning and forlorn; for now my poor sister has at last found peace.

Hedda. I have heard the news already, as you see. Tesman sent me a card.

Miss Tesman. Yes, he promised me he would. But nevertheless I thought that to Hedda—here in the house of life—I ought myself to bring the tidings of death.

Hedda. That was very kind of you.

Miss Tesman. Ah, Rina ought not to have left us just now. This is not the time for Hedda's house to be a house of mourning.

Hedda. [*Changing the subject.*] She died quite peacefully, did she not, Miss Tesman?

Miss Tesman. Oh, her end was so calm, so beautiful. And then she had the unspeakable happiness of seeing George once more—and bidding him good-bye. Has he come home yet?

Hedda. No. He wrote that he might be detained. But won't you sit down?

Miss Tesman. No thank you, my dear, dear Hedda. I should like to, but I have so much to do. I must prepare my dear one for her rest as well as I can. She shall go to her grave looking her best.

Hedda. Can I not help you in any way?

Miss Tesman. Oh, you must not think of it! Hedda Tesman must have no hand in such mournful work. Nor let her thoughts dwell on it either— not at this time.

Hedda. One is not always mistress of one's thoughts—

Miss Tesman. [*Continuing.*] Ah yes, it is the way of the world. At home we shall be sewing a shroud; and here there will soon be sewing too, I suppose—but of another sort, thank God!

[GEORGE TESMAN *enters by the hall door.*]

Hedda. Ah, you have come at last!

Tesman. You here, Aunt Julia? With Hedda? Fancy that!

Miss Tesman. I was just going, my dear boy. Well, have you done all you promised?

Tesman. No; I'm really afraid I have forgotten half of it. I must come to you again tomorrow. Today my brain is all in a whirl. I can't keep my thoughts together.

Miss Tesman. Why, my dear George, you mustn't take it in this way.

Tesman. Mustn't—? How do you mean?

Miss Tesman. Even in your sorrow you must rejoice, as I do—rejoice that she is at rest.

Tesman. Oh yes, yes—you are thinking of Aunt Rina.

Hedda. You will feel lonely now, Miss Tesman.

Miss Tesman. Just at first, yes. But that will not last very long, I hope. I daresay I shall soon find an occupant for poor Rina's little room.

Tesman. Indeed? Who do you think will take it? Eh?

Miss Tesman. Oh, there's always some poor invalid or other in want of nursing, unfortunately.

Hedda. Would you really take such a burden upon you again?

Miss Tesman. A burden! Heaven forgive you, child—it has been no burden to me.

Hedda. But suppose you had a total stranger on your hands—

Miss Tesman. Oh, one soon makes friends with sick folk; and it's such an absolute necessity for me to have some one to live for. Well, heaven be praised, there may soon be something in this house, too, to keep an old aunt busy.

Hedda. Oh, don't trouble about anything here.

Tesman. Yes, just fancy what a nice time we three might have together, if—?

Hedda. If—?

Tesman. [*Uneasily.*] Oh, nothing. It will all come right. Let us hope so—eh?

Miss Tesman. Well, well, I daresay you two want to talk to each other. [*Smiling.*] And perhaps Hedda may have something to tell you too, George. Good-by! I must go home to Rina. [*Turning at the door.*] How strange it is to think that now Rina is with me and with my poor brother as well!

Tesman. Yes, fancy that, Aunt Julia! Eh?

[MISS TESMAN *goes out by the hall door.*]

Hedda. [*Follows* TESMAN *coldly and searchingly with her eyes.*] I almost believe your Aunt Rina's death affects you more than it does your Aunt Julia.

Tesman. Oh, it's not that alone. It's Eilert I am so terribly uneasy about.

Hedda. [*Quickly.*] Is there anything new about him?

Tesman. I looked in at his rooms this afternoon, intending to tell him the manuscript was in safe keeping.

Hedda. Well, did you not find him?

Tesman. No. He wasn't at home. But afterwards I met Mrs. Elvsted, and she told me that he had been here early this morning.

Hedda. Yes, directly after you had gone.

Tesman. And he said that he had torn his manuscript to pieces—eh?

Hedda. Yes, so he declared.

Tesman. Why, good heavens, he must have been completely out of his mind! And I suppose you thought it best not to give it back to him, Hedda?

Hedda. No, he did not get it.

Tesman. But of course you told him that we had it?

Hedda. No. [*Quickly.*] Did you tell Mrs. Elvsted?

Tesman. No, I thought I had better not. But you ought to have told him. Fancy, if, in desperation, he should go and do himself some injury! Let me have the manuscript, Hedda! I will take it to him at once. Where is it?

Hedda. [*Cold and immovable, leaning on the armchair.*] I have not got it.

Tesman. Have not got it? What in the world do you mean?

Hedda. I have burnt it—every line of it.

Tesman. [*With a violent movement of terror.*] Burnt! Burnt Eilert's manuscript!

Hedda. Don't scream so. The servant might hear you.

Tesman. Burnt! Why, good God—! No, no, no! It's impossible!

Hedda. It is so, nevertheless.

Tesman. Do you know what you have done, Hedda? It's unlawful appropriation of lost property. Fancy that! Just ask Judge Brack, and he'll tell you what it is.

Hedda. I advise you not to speak of it—either to Judge Brack, or to any one else.

Tesman. But how could you do anything so unheard-of? What put it into your head? What possessed you? Answer me that—eh?

Hedda. [*Suppressing an almost imperceptible smile.*] I did it for your sake, George.

Tesman. For my sake!

Hedda. This morning, when you told me about what he had read to you—

Tesman. Yes, yes—what then?

Hedda. You acknowledged that you envied him his work.

Tesman. Oh, of course I didn't mean that literally.

Hedda. No matter—I could not bear the idea that any one should throw you into the shade.

Tesman. [*In an outburst of mingled doubt and joy.*] Hedda! Oh, is this true? But—but—I never knew you to show your love like that before. Fancy that!

Hedda. Well, I may as well tell you that—just at this time— [*Impatiently, breaking off.*] No, no; you can ask Aunt Julia. She will tell you, fast enough.

Tesman. Oh, I almost think I understand you, Hedda! [*Clasps his hands together.*] Great heavens! do you really mean it! Eh?

Hedda. Don't shout so. The servant might hear.

Tesman. [*Laughing in irrepressible glee.*] The servant! Why, how absurd you are, Hedda. It's only my old Berta! Why, I'll tell Berta myself.

Hedda. [*Clenching her hands together in desperation.*] Oh, it is killing me—it is killing me, all this!

Tesman. What is, Hedda? Eh?

Hedda. [*Coldly, controlling herself.*] All this—absurdity—George.

Tesman. Absurdity! Do you see anything absurd in my being overjoyed at the news! But after all perhaps I had better not say anything to Berta.

Hedda. Oh—why not that too?

Tesman. No, no, not yet! But I must certainly tell Aunt Julia. And then that you have begun to call me George too! Fancy that! Oh, Aunt Julia will be so happy—so happy.

Hedda. When she hears that I have burnt Eilert Lövborg's manuscript—for your sake?

Tesman. No, by-the-bye—that affair of the manuscript—of course nobody must know about that. But that you love me so much, Hedda—Aunt Julia must really share my joy in that! I wonder, now, whether this sort of thing is usual in young wives? Eh?

Hedda. I think you had better ask Aunt Julia that question too.

Tesman. I will indeed, some time or other. [*Looks uneasy and downcast again.*] And yet the manuscript—the manuscript! Good God! It is terrible to think what will become of poor Eilert now.

[MRS. ELVSTED, *dressed as in the first Act, with hat and cloak, enters by the hall door.*]

Mrs. Elvsted. [*Greets them hurriedly, and says in evident agitation.*] Oh, dear Hedda, forgive my coming again.

Hedda. What is the matter with you, Thea?

Tesman. Something about Eilert Lövborg again—eh?

Mrs. Elvsted. Yes! I am dreadfully afraid some misfortune has happened to him.

Hedda. [*Seizes her arm.*] Ah, do you think so?

Tesman. Why, good Lord—what makes you think that, Mrs. Elvsted?

Mrs. Elvsted. I heard them talking of him at my boarding house—just as I came in. Oh, the most incredible rumors are afloat about him today.

Tesman. Yes, fancy, so I heard too! And I can bear witness that he went straight home to bed last night. Fancy that!

Hedda. Well, what did they say at the boarding house?

Mrs. Elvsted. Oh, I couldn't make out anything clearly. Either they knew nothing definite, or else—They stopped talking when they saw me; and I did not dare to ask.

Tesman. [*Moving about uneasily.*] We must hope—we must hope that you misunderstood them, Mrs. Elvsted.

Mrs. Elvsted. No, no; I am sure it was of him they were talking. And I heard something about the hospital or—

Tesman. The hospital?

Hedda. No—surely that cannot be!

Mrs. Elvsted. Oh, I was in such mortal terror! I went to his lodgings and asked for him there.

Hedda. You could make up your mind to that, Thea!

Mrs. Elvsted. What else could I do? I really could bear the suspense no longer.

Tesman. But you didn't find him either—eh?

Mrs. Elvsted. No. And the people knew nothing about him. He hadn't been home since yesterday afternoon, they said.

Tesman. Yesterday! Fancy, how could they say that?

Mrs. Elvsted. Oh, I am sure something terrible must have happened to him.

Tesman. Hedda dear—how would it be if I were to go and make inquiries—?

Hedda. No, no—don't you mix yourself up in this affair.

[JUDGE BRACK, *with his hat in his hand, enters by the hall door, which* BERTA *opens, and closes behind him. He looks grave and bows in silence.*]

Tesman. Oh, is that you, my dear Judge? Eh?

Brack. Yes. It was imperative I should see you this evening.

Tesman. I can see you have heard the news about Aunt Rina.

Brack. Yes, that among other things.

Tesman. Isn't it sad—eh?

Brack. Well, my dear Tesman, that depends on how you look at it.

Tesman. [*Looks doubtfully at him.*] Has anything else happened?

Brack. Yes.

Hedda. [*In suspense.*] Anything sad, Judge Brack?

Brack. That, too, depends on how you look at it, Mrs. Tesman.

Mrs. Elvsted [*Unable to restrain her anxiety.*] Oh! it is something about Eilert Lövborg!

Brack. [*With a glance at her.*] What makes you think that, Madam? Perhaps you have already heard something—?

Mrs. Elvsted. [*In confusion.*] No, nothing at all, but—

Tesman. Oh, for heaven's sake, tell us!

Brack. [*Shrugging his shoulders.*] Well, I regret to say Eilert Lövborg has been taken to the hospital. He is lying at the point of death.

Mrs. Elvsted. [*Shrieks.*] Oh God! Oh God—

Tesman. To the hospital! And at the point of death.

Hedda. [*Involuntarily.*] So soon then—

Mrs. Elvsted. [*Wailing.*] And we parted in anger, Hedda!

Hedda. [*Whispers.*] Thea—Thea—be careful!

Mrs. Elvsted. [*Not heeding her.*] I must go to him! I must see him alive!

Brack. It is useless, Madam. No one will be admitted.

Mrs. Elvsted. Oh, at least tell me what has happened to him? What is it?

Tesman. You don't mean to say that he has himself—Eh?

Hedda. Yes, I am sure he has.

Tesman. Hedda, how can you—?

Brack. [*Keeping his eyes fixed upon her.*] Unfortunately you have guessed quite correctly, Mrs. Tesman.

Mrs. Elvsted. Oh, how horrible!

Tesman. Himself, then! Fancy that!

Hedda. Shot himself!

Brack. Rightly guessed again, Mrs. Tesman.

Mrs. Elvsted. [*With an effort at self-control.*] When did it happen, Mr. Brack?

Brack. This afternoon—between three and four.

Tesman. But, good Lord, where did he do it? Eh?

Brack. [*With some hesitation.*] Where? Well—I suppose at his lodgings.

Mrs. Elvsted. No, that cannot be; for I was there between six and seven.

Brack. Well, then, somewhere else. I don't know exactly. I only know that he was found—. He had shot himself—in the breast.

Mrs. Elvsted. Oh, how terrible! That he should die like that!

Hedda. [*To* BRACK.] Was it in the breast?

Brack. Yes—as I told you.

Hedda. Not in the temple?

Brack. In the breast, Mrs. Tesman.

Hedda. Well, well—the breast is a good place, too.

Brack. How do you mean, Mrs. Tesman?

Hedda. [*Evasively.*] Oh, nothing—nothing.

Tesman. And the wound is dangerous, you say—eh?

Brack. Absolutely mortal. The end has probably come by this time.

Mrs. Elvsted. Yes, yes, I feel it. The end! The end! Oh, Hedda—!

Tesman. But tell me, how have you learnt all this?

Brack. [*Curtly.*] Through one of the police. A man I had some business with.

Hedda. [*In a clear voice.*] At last a deed worth doing!

Tesman [*Terrified.*] Good heavens, Hedda! what are you saying?

Hedda. I say there is beauty in this.

Brack. H'm, Mrs. Tesman—

Tesman. Beauty! Fancy that!

Mrs. Elvsted. Oh, Hedda, how can you talk of beauty in such an act!

Hedda. Eilert Lövborg has himself made up his account with life. He has had the courage to do—the one right thing.

Mrs. Elvsted. No, you must never think that was how it happened! It must have been in delirium that he did it.

Tesman. In despair!

Hedda. That he did not. I am certain of that.

Mrs. Elvsted. Yes, yes! In delirium! Just as when he tore up our manuscript.

Brack. [*Starting.*] The manuscript? Has he torn that up?

Mrs. Elvsted. Yes, last night.

Tesman. [*Whispers softly.*] Oh, Hedda, we shall never get over this.

Brack. H'm, very extraordinary.

Tesman. [*Moving about the room.*] To think of Eilert going out of the world in this way! And not leaving behind him the book that would have immortalized his name—

Mrs. Elvsted. Oh, if only it could be put together again!

Tesman. Yes, if it only could! I don't know what I would not give—

Mrs. Elvsted. Perhaps it can, Mr. Tesman.

Tesman. What do you mean?

Mrs. Elvsted. [*Searches in the pocket of her dress.*] Look here. I have kept all the loose notes he used to dictate from.

Hedda. [*A step forward.*] Ah—!

Tesman. You have kept them, Mrs. Elvsted! Eh?

Mrs. Elvsted. Yes, I have them here. I put them in my pocket when I left home. Here they still are—

Tesman. Oh, do let me see them!

Mrs. Elvsted. [*Hands him a bundle of papers.*] But they are in such disorder—all mixed up.

Tesman. Fancy, if we could make something out of them, after all! Perhaps if we two put our heads together—

Mrs. Elvsted. Oh, yes, at least let us try—

Tesman. We will manage it! We must! I will dedicate my life to this task.

Hedda. You, George? Your life?

Tesman. Yes, or rather all the time I can spare. My own collections must wait in the meantime. Hedda—you understand, eh? I owe this to Eilert's memory.

Hedda. Perhaps.

Tesman. And so, my dear Mrs. Elvsted, we will give our whole minds to it. There is no use in brooding over what can't be undone—eh? We must try to control our grief as much as possible, and—

Mrs. Elvsted. Yes, yes, Mr. Tesman, I will do the best I can.

Tesman. Well then, come here. I can't rest until we have looked through the notes. Where shall we sit? Here? No, in there, in the back room. Excuse me, my dear Judge. Come with me, Mrs. Elvsted.

Mrs. Elvsted. Oh, if only it were possible!

[TESMAN *and* MRS. ELVSTED *go into the back room. She takes off her hat and cloak. They both sit at the table under the hanging lamp, and are soon deep in an eager examination of the papers.* HEDDA *crosses to the stove and sits in the armchair. Presently* BRACK *goes up to her.*]

Hedda. [*In a low voice.*] Oh, what a sense of freedom it gives one, this act of Eilert Lövborg's.

Brack. Freedom, Mrs. Hedda? Well, of course, it is a release for him—

Hedda. I mean for me. It gives me a sense of freedom to know that a deed of deliberate courage is still possible in this world—a deed of spontaneous beauty.

Brack. [*Smiling.*] H'm—my dear Mrs. Hedda—

Hedda. Oh, I know what you are going to say. For you are a kind of a specialist too, like—you know!

Brack. [*Looking hard at her.*] Eilert Lövborg was more to you than perhaps you are willing to admit to yourself. Am I wrong?

Hedda. I don't answer such questions. I only know Eilert Lövborg has had the courage to live his life after his own fashion. And then—the last great act, with its beauty! Ah! that he should have the will and the strength to turn away from the banquet of life—so early.

Brack. I am sorry, Mrs. Hedda—but I fear I must dispel an amiable illusion.

Hedda. Illusion?

Brack. Which could not have lasted long in any case.

Hedda. What do you mean?

Brack. Eilert Lövborg did not shoot himself voluntarily.

Hedda. Not voluntarily?

Brack. No. The thing did not happen exactly as I told it.

Hedda. [*In suspense.*] Have you concealed something? What is it?

Brack. For poor Mrs. Elvsted's sake I idealized the facts a little.

Hedda. What are the facts?

Brack. First, that he is already dead.

Hedda. At the hospital?

Brack. Yes—without regaining consciousness.

Hedda. What more have you concealed?

Brack. This—the event did not happen at his lodgings.

Hedda. Oh, that can make no difference.

Brack Perhaps it may. For I must tell you—Eilert Lövborg was found shot in—in Mademoiselle Diana's boudoir.

Hedda. [*Makes a motion as if to rise, but sinks back again.*] That is impossible, Judge Brack! He cannot have been there again today.

Brack. He was there this afternoon. He went there, he said, to demand the return of something which they had taken from him. Talked wildly about a lost child—

Hedda. Ah—so that was why—

Brack. I thought probably he meant his manuscript; but now I hear he destroyed that himself. So I suppose it must have been his pocketbook.

Hedda. Yes, no doubt. And there—there he was found?

Brack. Yes, there. With a pistol in his breast-pocket, discharged. The ball had lodged in a vital part.

Hedda. In the breast—yes.

Brack. No—in the bowels.

Hedda. [*Looks up at him with an expression of loathing.*] That too! Oh what curse is it that makes everything I touch turn ludicrous and mean?

Brack. There is one point more, Mrs. Hedda—another disagreeable feature in the affair.

Hedda. And what is that?

Brack. The pistol he carried—

Hedda. [*Breathless.*] Well? What of it?

Brack. He must have stolen it.

Hedda. [*Leaps up.*] Stolen it! That is not true! He did not steal it!

Brack. No other explanation is possible. He must have stolen it—Hush!

[TESMAN *and* MRS. ELVSTED *have risen from the table in the back room, and come into the drawing room.*]

Tesman. [*With the papers in both his hands.*] Hedda dear, it is almost impossible to see under that lamp. Think of that!

Hedda. Yes, I am thinking.

Tesman. Would you mind our sitting at your writing table—eh?

Hedda. If you like. [*Quickly.*] No, wait! Let me clear it first!

Tesman. Oh, you needn't trouble, Hedda. There is plenty of room.

Hedda. No, no; let me clear it, I say! I will take these things in and put them on the piano. There! [*She has drawn out an object, covered with sheet music, from under the bookcase, places several other pieces of music upon it, and carries the whole into the inner room, to the left.* TESMAN *lays the scraps of paper on the writing table, and moves the lamp there from the corner table.* HEDDA *returns.*]

Hedda. [*Behind* MRS. ELVSTED'S *chair, gently ruffling her hair.*] Well, my sweet Thea, how goes it with Eilert Lövborg's monument?

Mrs. Elvsted. [*Looks dispiritedly up at her.*] Oh, it will be terribly hard to put in order.

Tesman. We must manage it. I am determined. And arranging other people's papers is just the work for me.

[HEDDA *goes over to the stove, and seats herself on one of the footstools.* BRACK *stands over her, leaning on the armchair.*]

Hedda. [*Whispers.*] What did you say about the pistol?

Brack. [*Softly.*] That he must have stolen it.

Hedda. Why stolen it?

Brack. Because every other explanation ought to be impossible, Mrs. Hedda.

Hedda. Indeed?

Brack. [*Glances at her.*] Of course Eilert Lövborg was here this morning. Was he not?

Hedda. Yes.

Brack. Were you alone with him?

Hedda. Part of the time.

Brack. Did you not leave the room whilst he was here?

Hedda. No.

Brack. Try to recollect. Were you not out of the room a moment?

Hedda. Yes, perhaps just a moment—out in the hall.

Brack. And where was your pistol case during that time?

Hedda. I had it locked up in—

Brack. Well, Mrs. Hedda?

Hedda. The case stood there on the writing table.

Brack. Have you looked since, to see whether both the pistols are there?

Hedda. No.

Brack. Well, you need not. I saw the pistol found in Lövborg's pocket, and I knew it at once as the one I had seen yesterday—and before, too.

Hedda. Have you it with you?

Brack. No; the police have it.

Hedda. What will the police do with it?

Brack. Search till they find the owner.

Hedda. Do you think they will succeed?

Brack. [*Bends over her and whispers.*] No, Hedda Gabler—not so long as I say nothing.

Hedda. [*Looks frightened at him.*] And if you do not say nothing—what then?

Brack. [*Shrugs his shoulders.*] There is always the possibility that the pistol was stolen.

Hedda. [*Firmly.*] Death rather than that.

Brack. [*Smiling.*] People say such things—but they don't do them.

Hedda. [*Without replying.*] And supposing the pistol was stolen, and the owner is discovered? What then?

Brack. Well, Hedda—then comes the scandal.

Hedda. The scandal!

Brack. Yes, the scandal—of which you are mortally afraid. You will, of course, be brought before the court—both you and Mademoiselle Diana. She will have to explain how the thing happened—whether it was an accidental shot or murder. Did the pistol go off as he was trying to take it out of his pocket, to threaten her with? Or did she tear the pistol out of his hand, shoot him, and push it back into his pocket? That would be quite like her; for she is an able-bodied young person, this same Mademoiselle Diana.

Hedda. But *I* have nothing to do with all this repulsive business.

Brack. No. But you will have to answer the question: Why did you give Eilert Lövborg the pistol? And what conclusions will people draw from the fact that you did give it to him?

Hedda. [*Lets her head sink.*] That is true. I did not think of that.

Brack. Well, fortunately, there is no danger, so long as I say nothing.

Hedda. [*Looks up at him.*] So I am in your power, Judge Brack. You have me at your beck and call, from this time forward.

Brack. [*Whispers softly.*] Dearest Hedda—believe me—I shall not abuse my advantage.

Hedda. I am in your power none the less. Subject to your will and your demands. A slave, a slave then! [*Rises impetuously.*] No, I cannot endure the thought of that! Never!

Brack. [*Looks half-mockingly at her.*] People generally get used to the inevitable.

Hedda. [*Returns his look.*] Yes, perhaps. [*She crosses to the writing table. Suppressing an involuntary smile, she imitates* TESMAN'S *intonations.*] Well? Are you getting on, George? Eh?

Tesman. Heaven knows, dear. In any case it will be the work of months.

Hedda. [*As before.*] Fancy that! [*Passes her hands softly through* MRS. ELVSTED'S *hair.*] Doesn't it seem strange to you, Thea? Here are you sitting with Tesman—just as you used to sit with Eilert Lövborg?

Mrs. Elvsted. Ah, if I could only inspire your husband in the same way.

Hedda. Oh, that will come too—in time.

Tesman. Yes, do you know, Hedda—I really think I begin to feel something of the sort. But won't you go and sit with Brack again?

Hedda. Is there nothing I can do to help you two?

Tesman. No, nothing in the world. [*Turning his head.*] I trust to you to keep Hedda company, my dear Brack.

Brack. [*With a glance at* HEDDA.] With the very greatest of pleasure.

Hedda. Thanks. But I am tired this evening. I will go in and lie down a little on the sofa.

Tesman. Yes, do dear—eh?

[HEDDA *goes into the back room and draws the curtains. A short pause. Suddenly she is heard playing a wild dance on the piano.*]

Mrs. Elvsted. [*Starts from her chair.*] Oh—what is that?

Tesman. [*Runs to the doorway.*] Why, my dearest Hedda—don't play dance music tonight! Just think of Aunt Rina! And of Eilert too!

Hedda. [*Puts her head out between the curtains.*] And of Aunt Julia. And of all the rest of them. After this, I will be quiet. [*Closes the curtains again.*]

Tesman. [*At the writing table.*] It's not good for her to see us at this distressing work. I'll tell you what, Mrs. Elvsted, you shall take the empty room at Aunt Julia's and then I will come over in the evenings and we can sit and work there—eh?

Hedda. [*In the inner room.*] I hear what you are saying, Tesman. But how am *I* to get through the evenings out here?

Tesman. [*Turning over the papers.*] Oh, I daresay Judge Brack will be so kind as to look in now and then, even though I am out.

Brack. [*In the armchair, calls out gaily.*] Every blessed evening, with all the pleasure in life, Mrs. Tesman! We shall get on capitally together, we two!

Hedda. [*Speaking loud and clear.*] Yes, don't you flatter yourself we will, Judge Brack? Now that you are the one cock in the basket—

[*A shot is heard within.* TESMAN, MRS. ELVSTED, *and* BRACK *leap to their feet.*]

Tesman. Oh, now she is playing with those pistols again.

[*He throws back the curtains and runs in, followed by* MRS. ELVSTED. HEDDA *lies stretched on the sofa, lifeless. Confusion and cries.* BERTA *enters in alarm from the right.*]

Tesman. [*Shrieks to* BRACK.] Shot herself! Shot herself in the temple! Fancy that!

Brack. [*Half-fainting in the armchair.*] Good God!—people don't do such things.

Further Assignment: Write an analysis of character and conflict on either of the following stories in Appendix II:

1. J. F. Powers' story "The Devil Was The Joker." Focus on the conflict in values—for example, conservative Catholicism and liberal Catholicism—that exists between Mac and Myles.
2. Lionel Trilling's story "Of This Time, Of That Place." Focus on Tertan and Blackburn. Show how they reflect externally the internal conflict of the narrator.

Suggested Assignment Outside the Text: Write a similar analysis of any of the following:

1. James Joyce's story "A Little Cloud." Focus on Little Chandler and Gallagher.
2. James Joyce's story "Two Gallants." Focus on Corley and Lenehan.
3. Scott Fitzgerald's novel *The Great Gatsby*. Focus on Nick and Gatsby.
4. Mark Twain's novel *Huckleberry Finn*. Focus on Tom and Huck.
5. Robert Penn Warren's novel *All the King's Men*. Focus on Willy Stark and Adam Stanton. Show how they reflect externally the internal conflict of the narrator.
6. Kingsley Amis' novel *Lucky Jim*. Focus on Jim Dixon and Bertrand Welch.
7. Flannery O'Connor's novel *The Violent Bear It Away*. Focus on Rayber and Tarwater.
8. Tennessee Williams' play *Streetcar Named Desire*. Focus on Blanche and Stanley.
9. Edward Albee's play *The Zoo Story*. Focus on Peter and Jerry.

ASSIGNMENT 7: ANALYSIS OF SYMBOL* AND PURPOSE*

What is the purpose of the play, story or novel? How do the symbols in the play, story, or novel help to develop that purpose? These are the major questions the writer analyzing the relationship between symbol and purpose must answer.

SAMPLE ANALYSIS OF PURPOSE AND SYMBOL IN IBSEN'S HEDDA GABLER

One way to arrive at a statement of the purpose of *Hedda Gabler* is to ask these questions: What ultimately is wrong with Hedda Gabler? What causes her destruction? The answer, in large part, is that Hedda expects great things from life but is unwilling (perhaps unable) to make the sacrifices and to endure the suffering that such expectations necessitate. She wants freedom without responsibility, adventure without risk, and such expectations create in her a psychic ambivalence that ultimately destroys her. Therefore, we may say that the purpose of *Hedda Gabler* is to dramatize the effects of this psychic ambivalence. (Such ambivalence is described in detail in Karl Menninger's classic study of suicide, *Man Against Himself*, a book helpful in understanding *Hedda*.) Various symbols in the play function to enable Ibsen to achieve this purpose. For example, we immediately see Hedda's ambivalent nature in her attitude toward flowers and sunlight, symbols of life and femininity. Hedda dislikes both. Rather than flowers, Hedda is attracted to her father's pistols, symbols of death and masculinity.

Yet Hedda maintains throughout the play that she wants the full life, the life of feminine fulfillment that she envies Mrs. Elvsted.

What these symbols—the flowers and pistols—tell us indirectly is parallel to what details like Hedda's fear of pregnancy and scandal tell us more directly: that Hedda wants the impossible, the best of both worlds, the privileges of womanhood and manhood, and the reponsibilities of neither. And, of course, trapped in such ambivalence, Hedda's ultimate choice of the pistols as her way out is dramatically inevitable.

That the pistols are *inherited* by Hedda from her father and that Hedda keeps a portrait of her father prominently displayed in the Tesman house, are details suggesting a further dimension of Hedda's ambivalence. Apparently, the one time in her life when Hedda was happy was as a child living with her father. A domineering figure (who continues to dominate her life, as such details as the portrait and her late marriage suggest), a figure of romance and adventure as well as of security, the General provided an ideal world for Hedda (though, even as a child Hedda wears black suggesting her tragic future.) Thus Hedda's impossible goal is to replace the father with a husband, a husband who, like Lövborg would offer romance and the promise of an exciting future and, at the same time, the security that Tesman offers. Wanting the future yet unwilling to surrender the past, wanting romance yet unwilling to surrender security, wanting, in short, both a father and a husband in the same person, Hedda, of course, can have neither; and her frustration ultimately leads to her fate—self-destruction by the weapon which is her literal and symbolic inheritance.

COMMENTS ON SAMPLE ANALYSIS OF SYMBOL AND PURPOSE

An examination of the sample analysis of symbol and purpose in *Hedda Gabler* reveals that the writer of the analysis has used a method we studied in the section on the analysis of poetry: demonstrating how images and symbols contribute to the overall purpose of a literary work of art. Having raised and answered the question of what causes the ultimate destruction of Hedda, the writer is able to state the purpose of the play. Then, using a pattern of organization similar to those used by the writers of the sample analyses on Frost's "Design" and Rodgers' "White Christmas," the writer proceeds to show how two (of several he could have chosen) key symbols in the play—the pistols and flowers—work to fulfill that purpose.

The key word in the sample analysis is *ambivalent.* Ambivalence is Hedda's main problem, and, as the writer of the sample analysis shows us, her attitude toward the pistols and flowers symbolically tells us this early in the drama. Notice that the writer by focusing closely on the symbol of the pistols introduces a symbolic pattern of associated images, for example, General Gabler's portrait and Hedda's black riding habit. This pattern suggests that heredity as well as free will is a cause of Hedda's destruction. Notice also how the writer's parallel sentences rhetorically develop the idea of ambivalance.

Although the writer does a good job of analysis, there are major questions about the symbol of the pistols that he fails to answer: Why are there two pistols? What does Lövborg's being destroyed by one and Hedda's being destroyed by the other symbolize? What is the significance of Hedda's physical movements toward and away from the pistols at various times in the play?

The writer of the sample analysis obviously realizes two major points about successful plays: (1) successful plays, because they must always show, never tell, must be organized so that every detail—every costume, every piece of furniture, every speech, gesture, and movement—functions to fulfill the play's overall purpose; and (2) that understanding plays, especially tragedies like *Hedda Gabler,* is largely a matter of thoroughly understanding the protagonists of such plays, the tragic heroes and heroines. What ultimately causes the destruction of the hero or heroine? This is the question we must always ask if we are to understand tragedy.

Assignment: Write an analysis of symbol and purpose on James Joyce's "An Encounter." Show how Joyce uses the color green to fulfill his purpose. Your analysis should attempt to answer such questions as the following:

1. What is it about the color green that helps to fulfill Joyce's purpose of dramatizing that appearances are not reality?
2. What does the narrator's looking for green eyes in the sailors and finding them in the pervert have to do with the purpose of the story?
3. Why is green essentially an ambiguous color? (Check the unabridged dictionary for an answer to this.)
4. Is green used in conjunction with any other color imagery to help to fulfill the purpose of the story?

Further Assignment: Write an analysis of symbol and purpose on any of the following works of literature:

1. Jean Stafford's story, "A Country Love Story." Focus on such symbols as:
   a. The antique sleigh
   b. The house
   c. The seasons of the year
2. Tennessee Williams' play *Streetcar Named Desire.* Focus on such symbols as the moth and the electric light.

3. Ibsen's play *The Wild Duck*. Focus on such symbols as:
   a. The net
   b. The lighting
4. Arthur Miller's play *Death of a Salesman*. Examine the symbolic significance of the set described in the text of the play. Focus on the significance of such symbols as:
   a. The house surrounded by a "vault" of apartment houses
   b. The athletic trophy
   c. The failed garden
5. Ernest Hemingway's story "Soldier's Home." Focus on the significance of such symbols as the game of pool.
6. In *Hedda Gabler* focus on the symbolic significance of:
   a. Lövborg's manuscript
   b. Tesman's manuscript

GLOSSARIES

GENERAL GLOSSARY

Action: What happens literally and symbolically in a work of fiction or drama. Symbolic action is physical action—for instance, gestures, movements, speeches—suggesting deeper, psychological, levels of meaning. In Joyce's "An Encounter," for example, Mahony's running across the field to bring "aid" to the narrator symbolically suggests the dependence of the introverted part of human nature on the extroverted part, of the part dominated by the super ego on the part dominated by the id, of conscience on instinct.

Antagonist: The character or force directly opposed to the interests of the protagonist, the main character, in a work of fiction or drama.

Apollian-Dionysian: Taken from Nietzsche's *Birth of Tragedy,* these terms suggest the conflict in man and in art between reason and instinct, conscious and unconscious, civilization and primitivism. Roughly equivalent are such terms as classicism and romanticism, super ego and id, Hellenism and Hebraism.

Conflict: The literal and symbolic struggle in a work of fiction or drama between the protagonist, and the values he may represent, and the antagonist, and the values he may represent. Conflict can be largely external, that is, on a public level, as in the open argument between Mac and Myles in Powers' "The Devil Was The Joker"; or internal, that is, largely within the mind of the protagonist, as in Joyce's "An Encounter." Often external conflict is a reflection of internal conflict. For example, the external conflict of Ibsen's *Hedda Gabler* reflects Hedda's internal conflict just as the external conflict in Trilling's "Of This Time, Of That Place" reflects Howe's internal conflict. Defining conflict, identifying the major conflicting characters and forces and their respective values is perhaps the most important task of the explicator of fiction and drama.

Complication: That part of a work of fiction or drama that develops the conflict implicit in the opening situation of a work of fiction or drama.

Connotation-denotation: The denotative meaning of a word is its literal, its exact, dictionary definition. The connotative meaning of a word, however, includes all the associations or suggestions that word brings to mind.

Denouement: The final stage in the resolution of the conflict in a work of fiction or drama.

Dominant image: The main sense impression, for example, the main picture or sound, in a work of literature.

Dramatic: In poetry *dramatic* suggests the presence of at least two characters within the poem, that is, of a person speaking and a person spoken to. Matthew Arnold's "Dover Beach" is an example of such a poem. In fiction and drama, *dramatic,* besides suggesting strong conflict, suggests that the reader or auditor is shown much and told little; that is, that the reader or auditor of a dramatic work must *infer* meanings from symbolic actions.

Exposition: That part of a work of fiction or drama that provides necessary background information.

Form: The principle of organization that enables all the parts of a work of literature—for example, ideas, images, setting, tone, diction—to cohere, to achieve the work's total effect.

Formalistic criticism: Literary criticism which attempts to demonstrate how the parts of a work of literature function to advance the purpose of that work.

Image: Any sense impression in a work of literature. Image patterns are arrangements of sense impressions to suggest ideas and to advance the purpose of a work of literature. In Frost's "Design," for example, the juxtaposition of images of innocence and evil suggests the deceptive, evil design that the poem implies is the design of the world.

Irony: Doing or saying one thing and meaning another. Seemingly inappropriate speech or action which, when examined carefully, is really quite appropriate in the full context of a work of literature.

Meaningful ambiguity: When the two or more different meanings of a word or other verbal construction in a work of literature combine to form the author's single meaning. Puns are good examples of words that are used with meaningful ambiguity. In Frost's "Design," for instance, the word "appall" means both to make fearful and to make white; and both meanings, though apparently far apart, fit nicely into the overall meaning of the poem.

Meaningful repetition: Repetition of a word, phrase, or sentence in order to gain emphasis, clarity, and coherence.

Paradox: An apparent contradiction which nevertheless is true. For example, the Christian paradox that man must die if he is to live forever.

Point of view: The point of view character in a story or novel is the character through whose eyes we view the action; he is the *voice,* the intelligence, of the story or novel. Point of view is usually: (1) omniscient, that is, the narrator knows all and goes from the mind of one character to the next; (2) central intelligence or third person, that is, the narrator is a character in the story through whose eyes we see and interpret the action; and (3) first person, the *I* narrator.

Protagonist: The protagonist is the main character in a work of fiction or drama. Usually, but not always, the protagonist is the character with whom we are supposed to sympathize.

Pun: Puns are words having the same sound but different meanings. For example, in "Design" Frost puns on the words "morning right" by implying that they might well read "mourning rite."

Purpose: The intention of a work of literature, what the writer is trying to do in a work of literature. For example, after reading Ibsen's *Hedda Gabler,* we may say that the purpose of that play is to dramatize the tragic effects of wanting freedom without responsibility. Purpose, of course, can be stated in many ways, but it should always be stated as a complete sentence and should be stated only *after* the work has been carefully read. Stating the purpose of a work of literature is not an exercise in biographical scholarship; that is, we need no information about the author's life to state the purpose of any of his works. We can state the purpose of unsigned works, after reading them, with as much assurance as we can signed works.

Resolution: That part of a work of fiction or drama in which the major issue raised by the conflict and developed through the complication is settled.

Structure: Part of the overall form of a work of literature, structure usually refers to the bigger elements in a work of literature: for example, episodes, scenes, and major psychological linking devices (such as those mentioned in the discussion of Yeats' "Lapis Lazuli.") While structure refers to the arrangement of a work's bigger elements, style refers to the arrangement of words in a work of literature.

Super ego-id: In Freudian terms the super ego is the civilizing agent in man, an agent equivalent to the Christian conscience. Man's super-ego tells him what he *ought* to do. The product of church and school and home, the product of tradition and of many and various moral authorities, the super ego, according to Freud, is the "morality principle." In contrast is the id, the unconscious source of man's passions, desires, instinctual energies and aggressions. Causing man to wish to gratify his instincts, to do what he wants instead of what he ought, the id is the natural enemy of the super ego and is the "pleasure principle." Trying to balance the constantly conflicting claims of the super ego and the id, trying to become a mature human rather than the angel the super ego would have him or the ape the id would have him, is, according to Freud, the central struggle of man in civilization.

Symbol: A symbol is an image that suggests one or more ideas. As literary works develop, images in those works often become symbols. For example, in Arnold's "Dover Beach" Dover Beach to begin with is merely an image, that is, the picture of a slate beach on the English Channel. As the poem develops, however, Dover Beach becomes a symbol for a world devoid of meaning, for, possibly, the Nietzschean, post Darwinian world of the nineteenth century.

Tone: The attitude a writer takes toward his audience and toward his material. In "The Devil Was the Joker" it is clear that J. F. Powers' attitude toward both Mac and Myles is ironical; therefore, we understand that neither Mac nor Myles is to be viewed with total sympathy, that neither is a clear cut hero, that both have ludicrous human faults.

A GLOSSARY
OF PROSODY

Alliteration: The repetition of a consonant sound usually at the beginning of a word.

    Example: Though worlds of wanwood leafmeal lie
             Gerard Manley Hopkins, "Spring and Fall: To a Young Child"

Assonance: The repetition of the same vowel sound. Note, however, that the same vowels will not always produce the same sounds.

    Example: Over Goldengrove unleaving
             Gerard Manley Hopkins, "Spring and Fall: To a Young Child"

End-stopped-lines and run-on-lines: Lines of poetry are *end-stopped* when the sense of the line terminates at the end of the line (or in a couplet, at the end of the couplet). *Run-on* or *enjambed* lines, on the other hand, are lines in which the sense continues into the following line. A fairly safe rule, although not a completely foolproof one, to determine whether a line or couplet is end-stopped is to look for terminal punctuation (period, semi-colon, question mark or exclamation point) at the end of the line or couplet. If the line ends in terminal punctuation, it is usually end-stopped; if not, it is usually run-on.

    Example: *End-stopped couplet:*
             Nature to all things fixed the limits fit,
             And wisely curbed proud man's pretending wit.
                       Alexander Pope, "Essay on Criticism"

        Run-on or *enjambed couplet:*
             The Mighty Mother, and her Son, who brings
             The Smithfield Muses to the ear of Kings,
             I sing.
                       Alexander Pope, "The Dunciad"

Meter: The rhythm of a line of poetry based on the pattern of stressed and unstressed syllables. The *meter* is determined by scanning the line, that is, first,
describing the basic *foot* of a line; second, counting the number of feet in a line.
A *foot* consists of a combination of two or more stressed or unstressed syllables. The basic feet used in English poetry are:

Iamb — /	ob scure (— /)
Trochee / —	in dex (/ —)
Anapest — — /	com man deer (— — /)
Dactyl / — —	grad u al (/ — —)
Spondee / /	mad cap (/ /)
Pyrrhic — —	Since no word is, in itself, without accent, this foot can only be demonstrated in the context of a line of poetry. See the example below.

The following lines illustrate the basic feet:

Iamb And now upon his western wing he leaned
George Meredith, "Lucifer in Starlight"

Trochee Laughter soft as tears and tears that turned to laughter
A. S. Swinburne, "Stage Love"

Anapest 'In my youth,' Father William replied to his son
Lewis Carroll, "Father William"

Dactyl Just for a handful of silver he left us
Robert Browning, "The Lost Leader"

Pyrrhic and Spondee At its own stable door
Emily Dickinson, "I like to See It Lap the Miles"

The number of feet employed in a line is described as follows:

monometer: one foot
dimeter: two feet
trimeter: three feet
tetrameter: four feet
pentameter: five feet
hexameter: six feet
heptameter: seven feet

The iambic and trochaic lines above, for example, would be described as
iambic pentameter, and *trochaic hexameter.*

Onomatopoeia: The use of words which, approximately, imitate the sounds they represent. For example, <u>hiss,</u> <u>bang,</u> <u>boom,</u> and so on. Sometimes alliteration and assonance can combine to produce the effect of onomatopoeia.

Example: But when <u>loud</u> <u>surges</u> <u>lash</u> the <u>sounding</u> <u>shore,</u>
The <u>hoarse,</u> <u>rough</u> <u>verse</u> should <u>like</u> the <u>torrent</u> <u>roar.</u>
Alexander Pope, "Essay on Criticism"

Prosody: The art of versification which includes stanza form, meter, rhyme, and other related sound effects, such as assonance, alliteration and onomatopoeia.

Rhyme: The correspondence in the end sounds of words. *Exact* or *full rhyme* occurs when two words correspond completely in their terminal sound.

Example: This thou perceiv'st which makes thy love more strong,
To love that well which thou must leave ere long.
Shakespeare, Sonnet LXXIII
Slant rhyme or *half rhyme* occurs when there is an incomplete correspondence in the final sound of the rhyming words.

Example: up/step, peer/pare, star/door.

Sometimes a *half rhyme* is used for comic effect by forcing the reader to pronounce it as a *full rhyme.*

Example: That Latin was no more difficile,
Than to a blackbird 'tis to whistle.
Samuel Butler, "Hudibras"

Stanza: A group of lines forming one of the divisions of a poem. The number and length of such lines are usually determined according to a traditional pattern.

Example: Two lines: *couplet*
Great wits are sure to madness near ally'd;
And thin partitions do their bounds divide.
John Dryden, "Absalom & Achitophel"

Three lines: *tercet*
Whenas in silks my Julia goes
Then, then (methinks) how sweetly flows
That liquefaction of her clothes.
Robert Herrick, "Upon Julia's Clothes"

Four lines: *quatrain*
I looked upon the rotting sea,
And drew my eyes away;
I looked upon the rotting deck,
And there the dead men lay.
Samuel Taylor Coleridge, "Rime of the Ancient Mariner"

Quintain (five-line stanza), *sestet* (six-line stanza), *rime royal* (one kind of seven-line stanza), *ottava rima* (one kind of eight-line stanza), and so forth. One of the most frequently used stanza forms is the *sonnet,* a lyric poem of fourteen lines written in iambic pentameter. For examples of the *sonnet,* see Robert Frost's "Design" and George Meredith's "Lucifer in Starlight" in the text.

APPENDIXES

APPENDIX I

1. Demonstrate how recurring symbols help to develop recurring themes in the poems of any one of the following: Robert Frost, Emily Dickinson, or Richard Wilbur.
2. Demonstrate James Joyce's symbolic use of setting in his collection of short stories, *Dubliners*.
3. Demonstrate that Puritanism is a dominant attitude in the poetry of Robert Frost.
4. Read ten or twelve of Ibsen's plays and do a paper on one of the following topics:
   a. The struggle between Apollonian and Dionysian values in Ibsen
   b. Ibsen, the logical positivist
   c. a comparison between the values of Ibsen and those of Kierkegaard, the Danish philosopher.
5. Demonstrate how the super ego-id, the introvert-extrovert conflict, of "An Encounter" is dramatized in other stories in *Dubliners*.
6. Show how the various explicators of Gerard Manley Hopkins' "The Windover: To Christ Our Lord" are divided in their interpretations of the key word, "Buckle." Agree with or disagree with one or the other of the critical camps, and support your position with textual evidence from your own reading.
7. Demonstrate the transition from classicism to romanticism in the poems of Robert Lowell.

137

SAMPLE CRITICAL TERM PAPER

A CATHOLIC COMEDY

Rereading J. F. Powers in the light of the Vatican Council and after the various and many liberal-conservative fights in this country and abroad—for example, the classic battle between Cardinal McIntyre and Father DuBay—I have often been struck by the truth that life indeed does imitate art. For long before the life of the Vatican Council made the liberal-conservative Roman Catholic battles fashionable—twenty years before, to be exact—Powers was dramatizing these battles in his satirical stories, using these battles, in fact, as the basis of his art, as the rhetoric of his fiction. And quite frequently issues argued comically in Powers are the same issues argued solemnly twenty years later at the Council.

Although Powers has not produced a large body of literature, he has long been regarded as one of the world's great satirical talents. Frank O'Connor has called Powers "one of the world's greatest living storytellers," and O'Connor's opinion has been echoed many times by such major literary figures as Evelyn Waugh, V. S. Pritchett, Alfred Kazin, Sean O'Faolain and others.

Part of Powers' "greatness" is technical. A literary perfectionist, Powers works with a story until it possesses an almost poetic ironic tightness. But more than great natural talent and craftsmanship what accounts for Powers' achievement is that he alone of today's major working satirists has discovered (perhaps rediscovered would be more accurate) and developed a great *subject* for satire: the comedy of Roman Catholicism, especially the comedy of American Catholicism, but essentially the comedy of Catholicism through the ages (the comedy prominently displayed but unreported at the Council). It is a critical cliché that America is a poor country for classical satire because such satire depends on stable institutions, and America's institutions are constantly changing (Mary McCarthy's work has suffered because of this); however, Powers has found in Roman Catholicism, American Roman Catholicism, a relatively stable (up to now at least) institution, a nonmoving target.

Like all comedy, the comedy of Catholicism which Powers dramatizes is based on incongruity: pretending to be one thing the Church turns out to be another. Pretending, for example, to be a positive, unifying instrument of Christ's love, the Church turns out frequently to be a negative, divisive instrument of fear and hatred; pretending to universality she has regularly served the interests of nationalism; pretending to absolute certainty, to "unchanging positions" she has regularly turned out to be wrong. As Julian

Pleasants of Notre Dame's science faculty puts it: "And so, well armed with *clear* knowledge of the natural limits beyond which a thing cannot go, the Church's spokesmen have, at various times, been able to defend slavery, to disparage the intellectual abilities of woman, underestimate the capabilities of science, oppose the rise of democracy, and tolerate segregation. I have every confidence that the Church can back out of her birth control position as successfully as she has been able to back out of the above positions. . . ."

Though it appears somewhat digressive, Mr. Pleasants' remark about the Church "backing out" of its birth control position is a good illustration of the almost perfect incongruity that is the basis for the comedy of Catholicism and for the satirical art of J. F. Powers. What, for instance, could be more incongruous, what could provide a more perfect subject for satire, than the Church that pretends "indivisibility" divided and arguing over an "inarguable," that is, dogmatic matter? (This is essentially the comedy of the Council, a comedy one suspects Pope John, more than anyone else, understood and richly enjoyed.) On the one hand we have in the indivisible Church, the liberals who are for the pill and who appear, as Mr. Pleasants points out, to be "backing out;" and, on the other hand, we have the conservatives who are against the pill and who appear to be supporting (in an institution that pretends to be the world's bastion of Truth) the rationally insupportable. And both to the satirist, of course, appear comical.

Thus what Mr. Powers does in his best and most representative work, in his satirical stories and in his novel about American Catholics—especially American, diocesan, midwestern priests—is to dramatize in contemporary form, the age old substance, the age old incongruity, that is the comedy of Catholicism. And it is this rich tradition of comedy (and of tragedy too, since all serious comedy borders on tragedy), coupled with Powers' technical skill that helps to account for Powers' greatness—for his universality, his classical irony, his living, memorable characters.

What Powers has found in American Catholicism is the perfect juxtaposition of the sacred and the profane, the exalted and the vulgar, the material and the spiritual, which provides the classical satirical irony of his fiction. At the heart of a Powers' satire, for example, is a contemporary figure of incongruity who is also a traditional figure of incongruity (a figure satirized by Dante and Chaucer and Erasmus)—the servant of two masters, the Man of God serving Mammon. In Powers' work such a figure is typically a diocesan "builder-priest," a midwestern businessman cleric, a money raiser whose vocation ironically is to attract money changers into the temple rather than to drive them out. A Chamber of Commerce type, he is luxury loving, vain, vulgar, usually politically conservative, ambitious (in the most vulgar way: if an assistant, he connives to be a pastor, if a pastor, a bishop, and so on) and either anti-intellectual or nonintellectual. He usually loves golf and automobiles and "good dinners;" and he gets a lot "out of *Life* and *Reader's Digest. . . .*"

Focusing on this classically incongruous figure, Powers creates his satires with extraordinary economy. Focusing, for example, on Monsignor Sweeney—a Man of God serving Mammon—in the story "The Forks," Powers, in fifteen pages says as much as lesser writers say in entire novels. Timely as the quarrel between liberals and conservatives at the Council; yet timeless as the eternal quarrel between God and Mammon, youth and age, the practical and the ideal, "The Forks," though it was written twenty years before Pope John and the open warfare between Church liberals and conservatives, is a comic dramatization of that warfare. The story, in fact, sounds like a fictive account of that prototypical American liberal-conservative fight in the Church—the now classic Cardinal McIntyre-Father DuBay battle in Los Angeles, a battle that like the Councils occurred over twenty years after "The Forks" was first published. Simply plotted, the story pits young, idealistic, liberal Father Eudex, a "social action priest," a "*Commonweal* Catholic," against aging, materialistic, reactionary Monsignor Sweeney, a "builder priest," a *"The Tidings"* or a *"Brooklyn Tablet"* Catholic. As did Father DuBay, Father Eudex wants to apply the Church's teachings to practical matters in an immediate and practical way: he is, as Father DuBay was, strongly opposed to segregation, and he preaches the doctrines of the fair wage and is prolabor in an antilabor parish—Monsignor Sweeney's parish. Monsignor, however, views all this "talk" about race and labor as inspired by "atheistic Communism." Gently reminded by Eudex that the Holy Father himself declares in the encyclicals that the Church must take strong stands on these matters, the Monsignor declares hotly: "The Holy Father's in Rome." For Monsignor (and apparently for prelates like Cardinal McIntyre) the Church's mission, to quote Monsignor Sweeney, is not to "get involved in unions, race riots, strikes . . . all that stuff," but rather to wage war on the truly big sins: "birth control, salacious books, and indecent movies."

Incongruous to begin with, the Monsignor becomes the essence of incongruity as Powers' story develops. Representing an institution that claims to be the most universal on earth, Monsignor is provincial and nationalistic. He sees no incongruity in answering Eudex's question about the encyclicals with the statement: "The Holy Father's in Rome." Nor does he see the incongruity of following that up with: "Mr. Memmers lives in this parish. I'm *his* priest. (Mr. Memmers is an official of the First National.) ". . . it's damn little cheer I can give a man like Memmers. Catholics, priests, and laity alike—yes, and princes of the Church, all talking atheistic Communism!"

Dedicated to imitating Christ, dedicated to spirituality and humility, Monsignor ironically is materalistic and vain; he is not Christ's priest, but Memmers' (that is, Mammon's). He is devoted to the things of Memmers and Mammon: Monsignor is devoted to his automobile, a vehicle he affectionately calls "her," and to "whom" he applies "amorous chucks," and "feeds only the best of gas and oil and grease." (Monsignor, the story tells us, "knew automobiles;" and one thinks of the bemused Los Angeles priest who said recently of Cardinal McIntyre: "Social action, no—but concrete and cost estimates, those he understands.") Monsignor is also devoted to the "Rival Company" which underpays its workers and sends "offerings" to the parish priests in hopes that the priests will forget the encyclicals and preach antistrike sermons. (Monsignor happily endorses his check; Father Eudex labels his "hush money," and flushes it down the toilet—which action Powers with great comic invention converts into a contemporary version of the parable of the talents.) And Monsignor is devoted to the elegancies of the table and dress. To him, it's bad enough that Eudex reads the *Catholic Worker,* is willing to drive an aged Ford and to be seen doing manual labor with the parish janitor; but worse, that Eudex is indifferent to "the forks" (that is, that Eudex absentmindedly uses his salad fork to eat vegetables), can't seem to remember that green olives do *not* belong in "tutti-frutti salad," and habitually walks down the hall outside his bedroom clad only in "pajama bottoms." This latter crime so disturbs Monsignor that he gives Eudex a severe lecture on the "history and purpose of the dressing gown," on the "wisdom of barbering the armpits—it's being done all over now . . ." and on the desirability of using "Steeple," the clergyman's cologne."

Given such a perfect vehicle for satire as Monsignor, a lesser satirist—a Sinclair Lewis, for instance—would create propaganda not art; he would write liberal tracts against the Church conservatives. But Powers is always the artist, never the propagandist. Powers, for example, often makes his "liberals" unattractive and sometimes downright obnoxious. (Considering the rise of the liberal Establishment in the Church since the Council, it is interesting to speculate what Powers will do with his liberals in future stories. Considering what he's done with his radical liberals in the past, however, it is safe to assume that the Dutch theologians with their unpronounceable names and unintelligible doctrine and the "love" priests with their Hootenanny Masses are in for a bad time.) Even Father Eudex in "The Forks"—the nearest thing to a "good liberal" in Powers' works—has strong weaknesses: he is self-pitying, vain about his humility, and perverse in his desire to "rub salt in Monsignor's wounds." Other of Powers' more famous liberals: Fathers Quinlan and Keefe in "Prince of Darkness" and other stories; Myles, the ex-seminarian in "The Devil Was the Joker"; and the wonderful Dickie Thwaites in Powers' novel, *Morte d'Urban,* possess the characteristic liberal weaknesses; they are self-pitying, self-righteous, full of the "thank God I'm not as evil as the publican" spirit, humorless (as in the case of Myles and Dickie), and full of a brand of smugness characteristic of the avant-garde, but especially and most obnoxiously characteristic of the avant-garde of "Catholic intellectuals" who turned up in the late 1940s and who have been around ever since. It's the kind of smugness one finds, for example, at its earliest, in that monument of Roman Catholic smugness— Thomas Merton's *Seven Storey Mountain;* the kind of smugness that expresses itself in cultivated eccentricity, in homemade sandals and return to the soil movements; the kind of smugness that contemns the rational and reveres the mystical and the obscure. It is the kind of smugness that can be found in Catholic writers as apparently diverse as Chesterton, Leon Bloy, Mauriac, Green, Claudel and Waugh, the kind of smugness and irrationality that Andre Gide held out against in France during and after World War II. It's the kind of smugness that causes Dickie Thwaites to have nothing but contempt for a world (today's, of course) that isn't thrilled about his plan to "bring out" in "popular editions" such works as "Denzinger's Enchiridion and the lost books of Tertullian." (Dickie, forty-six, called fondly by his mother, " 'the boy', in and out of more religious orders than you can count," is proprietor of a "liturgical church goods store" featuring the "sacred art of Varian and Foo, plus chalices done in the manner of Henry More." The store is named by Dickie "The Eight Seasons" and to the inevitable bourgeois question: "What eight seasons?" Dickie, with withering contempt, answers: "Why the eight seasons of the Church, of course!")

More important, however, Powers is always the artist, never the propagandist, because he never sensationalizes. Of the major contemporary satirists—of, for instance, Kingsley Amis, Mary McCarthy, John Barth, Anthony Powell—Powers least of all depends on the outrageous, the bizarre, the eccentric, to get his comic effects. Concentrating on the "average" priest in the "ordinary" situation, Powers' art is always credible (in the way Moliere is credible and in the quiet, deceptively simple way Thurber is credible when he turns his hand to serious satire). In the Aristotelian sense, in fact, Powers' art improves on life by making life seem more credible than it actually is. Earlier, for example, when I said that "The Forks" sounded like a fictive account of the classic, real-life, modern liberal-conservative battle between Cardinal McIntyre and Father DuBay, I was, in a sense, inaccurate. For "The Forks" is credible, while the McIntyre-DuBay affair fictionalized would really be too bizarre to seem credible. Powers, through a character like Monsignor Sweeney may satirize Church conservatives—American builder-priests; but Powers would never create a "builder" so grotesquely conservative as Cardinal McIntyre or even the late Cardinal Spellman. Not that these men (like their liberal counterparts, the Father DuBays, for instance) aren't naturals for satire; they are. One has only to think of a few of their actions—Cardinal McIntyre's suppressions of such "dangerous" magazines as *America* and *The Commonweal* in the Los Angeles diocese and Cardinal Spellman's blessing of American troops for fighting "Christ's war in Viet Nam," for instance—to see that; but the kind of comedy inherent in such actions is too bizarre for Powers, the classical satirist, to dramatize. Powers is simply too decent, too quiet, too consistently Horatian, to use a Church figure like Cardinal McIntyre as a satirical vehicle. One can imagine a Sinclair Lewis using the Cardinal as a model for a celibate Elmer Gantry or a Kurt Vonnegut using the Cardinal's real behavior as a source for surrealistic humor; but not Powers.

In fact, with the exception of one bishop—Bishop Dullinger of *Morte d'Urban* whose favorite song is "Trees" and who dislikes liturgical changes—Powers' comic conservatives, his Men of God Serving Mammon, are almost never higher than Monsignors. Typically in Powers (if not in reality) high ranking clerics are rather decent, even Christ-like compared to the "builders," the Mammon servers at the bottom. The men at the top, in fact, regularly thwart the Mammon servers down the line. In "The Forks," for instance, Monsignor Sweeney's ambition to be a bishop is thwarted by the present bishop, a bishop whom Monsignor calls "that crazy man," because, of course, the bishop stands for everything Monsignor doesn't. One of the many fine lines in "The Forks"—a line that capsulizes the essential comedy of the Catholic conservatives, of the unbending absolutists—is Monsignor's reference to a decision made by the "crazy" bishop: "If that fellow's right," says Monsignor, pausing a long time to let his unimaginable conclusion sink in, "then (another long pause) I'm wrong!" And in the story "Prince of Darkness" it is the saintly (if somewhat shadowy) Archbishop who checks the ambition of Father Burner, who wants to be a pastor, "to have a Church of his own," to become, in his words, "the biggest builder of them all." Just before refusing Burner's request for a Church, the Archbishop tells Burner that the trouble with many priests is that they toady to the rich. "We," says the Archbishop (and by "we" it's clear he means Father Burner and his ilk) "give them (the rich) consolation and make of the eye of the needle a gate." In the same story, the Vicar General, next in line to succeed the Archbishop, is portrayed also as a saintly man. And even the most famous of all Powers' "builders," of all his Men of God Serving Mammon, Father Urban of *Morte d'Urban,* becomes "spiritualized," that is, ceases to serve Mammon, when he becomes Provincial of his order.

Powers sparing the hierarchy gives his satire a degree of fairness, of charity, lacking in many satirists; but, more important, Powers (consciously or unconsciously) spares the hierarchy to gain an artistic effect I've already mentioned: he realizes apparently that when one satirizes a really high ranking official, a Cardinal, for example, one almost always risks producing not a character, but a caricature, someone historically credible but artistically unbelievable (a Cardinal McIntyre); or, worse, of producing a mere propaganda vehicle.

Thus, that Powers consistently produces credible, living, memorable characters, never caricatures or propaganda vehicles, can be attributed to his concentration on the "average character," the "average priest" in the "ordinary" situation. More than any other important writer Powers knows to the smallest detail what goes on in American Catholic parishes and rectories; and, a great part of his achievement is simply that he takes us into the typical Catholic parish, into the typical diocesan rectory, and lets us see and hear what's really happening in these places. And what's happening, of course, in place after place, character after character, event after event, is the perfect low key drama that is the comedy of Catholicism.

In the kitchen of a typical midwestern rectory on a hot Sunday afternoon in the late 1940s, Sister Paula (Sister "Cigar Box" to the parish school children) counts money from the Sunday collection envelopes. In the room next to her, Father O'Hannon (known to the nuns as Father O'Mammon) sits drinking beer and listening to the Chicago Cubs' game over the radio. Sister wants to listen to the symphony but says nothing, choosing instead to "mumble over the money." The other parish priests are "out on the golf course." In a Minnesota parish, Monsignor Renton, who drives an Imperial and loves cigars—"Dunhill Monte Cristo Colorada Maduro Number 1's"—and Father Phil Smith plan their annual vacation (a vacation that annually begins with a champagne going away party in early January) to Miami and the Bahamas for a few months to "play a little golf." On the grounds of the Clementine Order, Father Urban (who secretly dreams of having a TV show that will rival Oral Roberts' or Billy Graham's) and businessman, Billy Cosgrove, drink from Our Lady's fountain: "You ought to bottle it," Billy solemnly suggests. At breakfast over a plate of pancakes with "butter bubbling at the pores," Father Burner, who "during grace," somehow manages to "stop chewing and reaching for things," (and who dreams of becoming a great clerical golfer—"Boomer Burner, Par Shattering Padre," he envisions the headlines reading), denounces Gerard Manley Hopkins' poetry. "Hopkins is okay if you like jabberwockey and jebbies"; but in Father Burner's eyes Hopkins is far inferior to "Francis Thompson, the only limey worth his salt." In the confessional later on that day, Father Burner reprimands a birth control practitioner: "Don't you know it's a crime against nature?" he demands of the miserable penitent. "Don't you know France fell because of birth control?" Elsewhere in the parish, Father Quinlan, "liberal" enemy of the conservative Burner, invents a prayer that future generations will offer to Burner: "St. Ernest Burner, Help of golfers, Pray for us." In another midwestern parish, two young priests matter-of-factly discuss why their pastor, old Father Malt, lost his job as County Exorcist: "As an exorcist," one priest explains, "Malt was pretty trigger happy . . ." to which the other priest solemnly replies, "yes, but you have to admit he did stick pretty much to livestock." (The situation and the rare conceit of a "trigger happy exorcist" are worthy of Thurber at his best.) At the Clementine golf course (a promotion of Father Urban's to attract the "*right* kind of retreatants" to the Clementine retreat house) the golf course architect explains to Father Urban, "A golf course is like a fancy woman . . . you take care of her, she'll take care of you." "I'll remember that," Father Urban promises. In other parishes, priests are filling the church pamphlet racks with pamphlets like "Help, Murder!," a tract against euthanasia; buying wholesale orders of "automatic Bingo cards with built-in simulated corn counters"; discussing ways to "terminate perpetual novenas"; and trying to raise money by creating (this during World War II in the story, but also in reality today in connection with Viet Nam) Victory Alters with "vigil lights in the shape of a V at a dollar a throw." And in still other parishes, priests are hearing the confessions of rich old women like Mrs. Thwaites (Dickie's mother) who worries a lot about the "place of her soul in the next world," who watches two TV sets simultaneously, who has a bomb shelter in case of atomic attack, and who cheats (at dominoes) her simpleminded maid out of her (the maid's) meager weekly wages; or having dinner with other old women who explain that they always "flush the toilet before making coffee, because it brings fresh water into the house"; or merely planning (unsuccessfully) moral ways of divesting themselves of horrible housekeepers who have been with the priests for years.

If Powers gave us nothing more than these "ordinary" characters and situations made extraordinary by his brilliant eye and ear for detail and his unparalleled talent for perceiving and dramatizing the irony that lies behind these characters and situations, he would have established himself as a unique and important writer. He would have given us what critics like Lionel Trilling and Marius Bewley and Richard Chase tell us few first rate American writers have given us: an original and rich picture of, to quote Trilling, "the manners and morals . . . the social texture," of American middle class life. But Powers has given us much more than brilliantly ironic sociological reportage. Because he has seen in the topical the timeless, in the parochial the universal, in the ordinary the extraordinary, because he has rediscovered what is probably the greatest comic tradition in the Western World—the comedy of Catholicism—he has given us a classical art, a classical body of satirical comedy, a comedy growing immediately from the perfect incongruity that Powers sees at the heart of American Catholicism, but a comedy with much deeper roots: a comedy that grows ultimately from the incongruity in the heart of man, a comedy, not merely of Catholics, but a truly catholic comedy.

APPENDIX II

OF THIS TIME, OF THAT PLACE

Lionel Trilling

It was a fine September day. By noon it would be summer again, but now it was true autumn with a touch of chill in the air. As Joseph Howe stood on the porch of the house in which he lodged, ready to leave for his first class of the year, he thought with pleasure of the long indoor days that were coming. It was a moment when he could feel glad of his profession.

On the lawn the peach tree was still in fruit and young Hilda Aiken was taking a picture of it. She held the camera tight against her chest. She wanted the sun behind her, but she did not want her own long morning shadow in the foreground. She raised the camera, but that did not help, and she lowered it, but that made things worse. She twisted her body to the left, then to the right. In the end she had to step out of the direct line of the sun. At last she snapped the shutter and wound the film with intense care.

Howe, watching her from the porch, waited for her to finish and called good morning. She turned, startled, and almost sullenly lowered her glance. In the year Howe had lived at the Aikens', Hilda had accepted him as one of her family, but since his absence of the summer she had grown shy. Then suddenly she lifted her head and smiled at him, and the humorous smile confirmed his pleasure in the day. She picked up her bookbag and set off for school.

The handsome houses on the streets to the college were not yet fully awake, but they looked very friendly. Howe went by the Bradby house where he would be a guest this evening at the first dinner party of the year. When he had gone the length of the picket fence, the whitest in town, he turned back. Along the path there was a fine row of asters and he went through the gate and picked one for his buttonhole. The Bradbys would be pleased if they happened to see him invading their lawn and the knowledge of this made him even more comfortable.

He reached the campus as the hour was striking. The students were hurrying to their classes. He himself was in no hurry. He stopped at his dim cubicle of an office and lit a cigarette. The prospect of facing his class had suddenly presented itself to him and his hands were cold; the lawful seizure of power he was about to make seemed momentous. Waiting did not help. He put out his cigarette, picked up a pad of theme paper, and went to his classroom.

As he entered, the rattle of voices ceased, and the twenty-odd freshmen settled themselves and looked at him appraisingly. Their faces seemed gross, his heart sank at their massed impassivity, but he spoke briskly.

"My name is Howe," he said, and turned and wrote it on the blackboard. The carelessness of the scrawl confirmed his authority. He went on, "My office is 412 Slemp Hall, and my office-hours are Monday, Wednesday and Friday from eleven-thirty to twelve-thirty."

He wrote, "M., W., F., 11:30–12:30." He said, "I'll be very glad to see any of you at that time. Or if you can't come then, you can arrange with me for some other time."

He turned again to the blackboard and spoke over his shoulder. "The text for the course is Jarman's *Modern Plays,* revised edition. The Co-op has it in stock." He wrote the name, underlined "revised edition" and waited for it to be taken down in the new notebooks.

When the bent heads were raised again he began his speech of prospectus. "It is hard to explain—" he said, and paused as they composed themselves. "It is hard to explain what a course like this is intended to do. We are going to try to learn something about modern literature and something about prose composition."

As he spoke, his hands warmed and he was able to look directly at the class. Last year on the first day the faces had seemed just as cloddish, but as the term wore on they became gradually alive and quite likable. It did not seem possible that the same thing could happen again.

"I shall not lecture in this course," he continued. "Our work will be carried on by discussion and we will try to learn by an exchange of opinion. But you will soon learn to recognize that my opinion is worth more than anyone else's here."

He remained grave as he said it, but two boys understood and laughed. The rest took permission from them and laughed too. All Howe's private ironies protested the vulgarity of the joke, but the laughter made him feel benign and powerful.

When the little speech was finished, Howe picked up the pad of paper he had brought. He announced that they would write an extemporaneous theme. Its subject was traditional, "Who I am and why I came to Dwight College." By now the class was more at ease and it gave a ritualistic groan of protest. Then there was a stir as fountain pens were brought out and the writing-arms of the chairs were cleared, and the paper was passed about. At last, all the heads bent to work, and the room became still.

Howe sat idly at his desk. The sun shone through the tall clumsy windows. The cool of the morning was already passing. There was a scent of autumn and of varnish and the stillness of the room was deep and oddly touching. Now and then a student's head was raised and scratched in the old, elaborate students' pantomime that calls the teacher to witness honest intellectual effort.

Suddenly a tall boy stood within the frame of the open door. "Is this," he said, and thrust a large nose into a college catalogue, "is this the meeting place of English 1A? The section instructed by Dr. Joseph Howe?"

He stood on the very sill of the door, as if refusing to enter until he was perfectly sure of all his rights. The class looked up from work, found him absurd and gave a low mocking cheer.

The teacher and the new student, with equal pointedness, ignored the disturbance. Howe nodded to the boy, who pushed his head forward and then jerked it back in a wide elaborate arc to clear his brow of a heavy lock of hair. He advanced into the room and halted before Howe, almost at attention. In a loud, clear voice he announced, "I am Tertan, Ferdinand R., reporting at the direction of Head of Department Vincent."

The heraldic formality of this statement brought forth another cheer. Howe looked at the class with a sternness he could not really feel, for there was indeed something ridiculous about this boy. Under his displeased regard the rows of heads dropped to work again. Then he touched Tertan's elbow, led him up to the desk and stood so as to shield their conversation from the class.

"We are writing an extemporaneous theme," he said. "The subject is, 'Who I am and why I came to Dwight College.'"

He stripped a few sheets from the pad and offered them to the boy. Tertan hesitated and then took the paper, but he held it only tentatively. As if with the effort of making something clear, he gulped, and a slow smile fixed itself on his face. It was at once knowing and shy.

"Professor," he said, "to be perfectly fair to my classmates"—he made a large gesture over the room—"and to you"—he inclined his head to Howe—"this would not be for me an extemporaneous subject."

Howe tried to understand. "You mean you've already thought about it—you've heard we always give the same subject? That doesn't matter."

Again the boy ducked his head and gulped. It was the gesture of one who wishes to make a difficult explanation with perfect candor. "Sir," he said, and made the distinction with great care, "the topic I did not expect, but I have given much ratiocination to the subject."

Howe smiled and said, "I don't think that's an unfair advantage. Just go ahead and write."

Tertan narrowed his eyes and glanced sidewise at Howe. His strange mouth smiled. Then in quizzical acceptance, he ducked his head, threw back the heavy, dank lock, dropped into a seat with a great loose noise and began to write rapidly.

The room fell silent again and Howe resumed his idleness. When the bell rang, the students who had groaned when the task had been set now groaned again because they had not finished. Howe took up the papers, and held the class while he made the first assignment. When he dismissed it, Tertan bore down on him, his slack mouth held ready for speech.

"Some professors," he said, "are pedants. They are Dryasdusts. However, some professors are free souls and creative spirits. Kant, Hegel and Nietzsche were all professors." With this pronouncement he paused. "It is my opinion," he continued, "that you occupy the second category."

Howe looked at the boy in surprise and said with good-natured irony, "With Kant, Hegel and Nietzsche?"

Not only Tertan's hand and head but his whole awkward body waved away the stupidity. "It is the kind and not the quantity of the kind," he said sternly.

Rebuked, Howe said as simply and seriously as he could, "It would be nice to think so." He added, "Of course I am not a professor."

This was clearly a disappointment but Tertan met it. "In the French sense," he said with composure. "Generically, a teacher."

Suddenly he bowed. It was such a bow, Howe fancied, as a stage-director might teach an actor playing a medieval student who takes leave of Abelard—stiff, solemn, with elbows close to the body and feet together. Then, quite as suddenly, he turned and left.

A queer fish, and as soon as Howe reached his office, he sifted through the batch of themes and drew out Tertan's. The boy had filled many sheets with his unformed headlong scrawl. "Who am I?" he had begun. "Here, in a mundane, not to say commercialized academe, is asked the question which from time long immemorably out of mind has accreted doubts and thoughts in the psyche of man to pester him as a nuisance. Whether in St.

Augustine (or Austin as sometimes called) or Miss Bashkirtsieff or Frederic Amiel or Empedocles, or in less lights of the intellect than these, this posed question has been ineluctable."

Howe took out his pencil. He circled "academe" and wrote "vocab." in the margin. He underlined "time long immemorably out of mind" and wrote "Diction!" But this seemed inadequate for what was wrong. He put down his pencil and read ahead to discover the principle of error in the theme. "Today as ever, in spite of gloomy prophets of the dismal science (economics) the question is uninvalidated. Out of the starry depths of heaven hurtles this spear of query demanding to be caught on the shield of the mind ere it pierces the skull and the limbs be unstrung."

Baffled but quite caught, Howe read on. "Materialism, by which is meant the philosophic concept and not the moral idea, provides no aegis against the question which lies beyond the tangible (metaphysics). Existence without alloy is the question presented. Environment and heredity relegated aside, the rags and old clothes of practical life discarded, the name and the instrumentality of livelihood do not, as the prophets of the dismal science insist on in this connection, give solution to the interrogation which not from the professor merely but veritably from the cosmos is given. I think, therefore I am (cogito etc.) but who am I? Tertan I am, but what is Tertan? Of this time, of that place, of some parentage, what does it matter?"

Existence without alloy: the phrase established itself. Howe put aside Tertan's paper and at random picked up another. "I am Arthur J. Casebeer, Jr.," he read. "My father is Arthur J. Casebeer and my grandfather was Arthur J. Casebeer before him. My mother is Nina Wimble Casebeer. Both of them are college graduates and my father is in insurance. I was born in St. Louis eighteen years ago and we still make our residence there."

Arthur J. Casebeer, who knew who he was, was less interesting than Tertan, but more coherent. Howe picked up Tertan's paper again. It was clear that none of the routine marginal comments, no "sent. str." or "punct." or "vocab." could cope with this torrential rhetoric. He read ahead, contenting himself with underscoring the errors against the time when he should have the necessary "conference" with Tertan.

It was a busy and official day of cards and sheets, arrangements and small decisions, and it gave Howe pleasure. Even when it was time to attend the first of the weekly Convocations he felt the charm of the beginning of things when intention is still innocent and uncorrupted by effort. He sat among the young instructors on the platform, and joined in their humorous complaints at having to assist at the ceremony, but actually he got a clear satisfaction from the ritual of prayer, and prosy speech, and even from wearing his academic gown. And when the Convocation was over the pleasure continued as he crossed the campus, exchanging greetings with men he had not seen since the spring. They were people who did not yet, and perhaps never would, mean much to him, but in a year they had grown amiably to be part of his life. They were his fellow-townsmen.

The day had cooled again at sunset, and there was a bright chill in the September twilight. Howe carried his voluminous gown over his arm, he swung his doctoral hood by its purple neckpiece, and on his head he wore his mortarboard with its heavy gold tassel bobbing just over his eye. These were the weighty and absurd symbols of his new profession and they pleased him. At twenty-six Joseph Howe had discovered that he was neither so well off nor so bohemian as he had once thought. A small income, adequate when supplemented by a sizable cash legacy, was genteel poverty when the cash was all spent. And the literary life—the room at the Lafayette, or the small apartment without a lease, the long summers on the Cape, the long afternoons and the social evenings—began to weary him. His writing filled his mornings, and should perhaps have filled his life, yet it did not. To the amusement of his friends, and with a certain sense that he was betraying his own freedom, he had used the last of his legacy for a year at Harvard. The small but respectable reputation of his two volumes of verse had proved useful—he continued at Harvard on a fellowship and when he emerged as Doctor Howe he received an excellent appointment, with prospects, at Dwight.

He had his moments of fear when all that had ever been said of the dangers of the academic life had occurred to him. But after a year in which he had tested every possibility of corruption and seduction he was ready to rest easy. His third volume of verse, most of it written in his first years of teaching, was not only ampler but, he thought, better that its predecessors.

There was a clear hour before the Bradby dinner party, and Howe looked forward to it. But he was not to enjoy it, for lying with his mail on the hall table was a copy of this quarter's issue of *Life and Letters,* to which his landlord subscribed. Its severe cover announced that its editor, Frederic Woolley, had this month contributed an essay called 'Two Poets,' and Howe, picking it up, curious to see who the two poets might be, felt his own name start out at him with cabalistic power—Joseph Howe. As he continued to turn the pages his hand trembled.

Standing in the dark hall, holding the neat little magazine, Howe knew that his literary contempt for Frederic Woolley meant nothing, for he suddenly understood how he respected Woolley in the way of the world. He knew this by the trembling of his hand. And of the little world as well as the great, for although the literary groups of New York might dismiss Woolley, his name carried high authority in the academic world. At Dwight it was even a revered name, for it had been here at the college that Frederic

Woolley had made the distinguished scholarly career from which he had gone on to literary journalism. In middle life he had been induced to take the editorship of *Life and Letters,* a literary monthly not widely read but heavily endowed, and in its pages he had carried on the defense of what he sometimes called the older values. He was not without wit, he had great knowledge and considerable taste, and even in the full movement of the "new" literature he had won a certain respect for his refusal to accept it. In France, even in England, he would have been connected with a more robust tradition of conservatism, but America gave him an audience not much better than genteel. It was known in the college that to the subsidy of *Life and Letters* the Bradbys contributed a great part.

As Howe read, he saw that he was involved in nothing less than an event. When the Fifth Series of *Studies in Order and Value* came to be collected, this latest of Frederic Woolley's essays would not be merely another step in the old direction. Clearly and unmistakably, it was a turning point. All his literary life Woolley had been concerned with the relation of literature to morality, religion, and the private and delicate pieties, and he had been unalterably opposed to all that he had called "inhuman humanitarianism." But here, suddenly, dramatically late, he had made an about-face, turning to the public life and to the humanitarian politics he had so long despised. This was the kind of incident the histories of literature make much of. Frederic Woolley was opening for himself a new career and winning a kind of new youth. He contrasted the two poets, Thomas Wormser, who was admirable, Joseph Howe, who was almost dangerous. He spoke of the "precious subjectivism" of Howe's verse. "In times like ours," he wrote, "with millions facing penury and want, one feels that the qualities of the *tour d'ivoire* are well-nigh inhuman, nearly insulting. The *tour d'ivoire* becomes the *tour d'ivresse,* and it is not self-intoxicated poets that our people need." The essay said more: "The problem is one of meaning. I am not ignorant that the creed of the esoteric poets declares that a poem does not and should not *mean* anything, that it *is* something. But poetry is what the poet makes it, and if he is a true poet he makes what his society needs. And what is needed now is the tradition in which Mr. Wormser writes, the true tradition of poetry. The Howes do no harm, but they do no good when positive good is demanded of all responsible men. Or do the Howes indeed do no harm? Perhaps Plato would have said they do, that in some ways theirs is the Phrygian music that turns men's minds from the struggle. Certainly it is true that Thomas Wormser writes in the lucid Dorian mode which sends men into battle with evil."

It was easy to understand why Woolley had chosen to praise Thomas Wormser. The long, lilting lines of *Corn Under Willows* hymned, as Woolley put it, the struggle for wheat in the Iowa fields, and expressed the real lives of real people. But why out of the dozen more notable examples he had chosen Howe's little volume as the example of "precious subjectivism" was hard to guess. In a way it was funny, this multiplication of himself into "the Howes." And yet this becoming the multiform political symbol by whose creation Frederic Woolley gave the sign of a sudden new life, this use of him as a sacrifice whose blood was necessary for the rites of rejuvenation, made him feel oddly unclean.

Nor could Howe get rid of a certain practical resentment. As a poet he had a special and respectable place in the college life. But it might be another thing to be marked as the poet of a wilful and selfish obscurity.

As he walked to the Bradbys', Howe was a little tense and defensive. It seemed to him that all the world knew of the "attack" and agreed with it. And, indeed, the Bradbys had read the essay but Professor Bradby, a kind and pretentious man, said, "I see my old friend knocked you about a bit, my boy." and his wife Eugenia looked at Howe with her childlike blue eyes and said, "I shall *scold* Frederic for the untrue things he wrote about you. You aren't the least obscure." They beamed at him. In their genial snobbery they seemed to feel that he had distinguished himself. He was the leader of Howeism. He enjoyed the dinner party as much as he had thought he would.

And in the following days, as he was more preoccupied with his duties, the incident was forgotten. His classes had ceased to be mere groups. Student after student detached himself from the mass and required or claimed a place in Howe's awareness. Of them all it was Tertan who first and most violently signaled his separate existence. A week after classes had begun Howe saw his silhouette on the frosted glass of his office door. It was motionless for a long time, perhaps stopped by the problem of whether or not to knock before entering. Howe called, "Come in!" and Tertan entered with his shambling stride.

He stood beside the desk, silent and at attention. When Howe asked him to sit down, he responded with a gesture of head and hand, as if to say that such amenities were beside the point. Nevertheless, he did take the chair. He put his ragged, crammed briefcase between his legs. His face, which Howe now observed fully for the first time, was confusing, for it was made up of florid curves, the nose arched in the bone and voluted in the nostril, the mouth loose and soft and rather moist. Yet the face was so thin and narrow as to seem the very type of asceticism. Lashes of unusual length veiled the eyes and, indeed, it seemed as if there were a veil over the whole countenance. Before the words actually came, the face screwed itself into an attitude of preparation for them.

"You can confer with me now?" Tertan said.

"Yes, I'd be glad to. There are several things in your two themes I want to talk to you about." Howe reached for the packet of themes on his desk and sought for Tertan's. But the boy was waving them away.

"These are done perforce," he said. "Under the pressure of your requirement. They are not significant; mere duties." Again his great hand flapped vaguely to dismiss his themes. He leaned forward and gazed at his teacher.

"You are," he said, "a man of letters? You are a poet?" It was more declaration than question.

"I should like to think so," Howe said.

At first Tertan accepted the answer with a show of appreciation, as though the understatement made a secret between himself and Howe. Then he chose to misunderstand. With his shrewd and disconcerting control of expression, he presented to Howe a puzzled grimace. "What does that mean?" he said.

Howe retracted the irony. "Yes. I am a poet." It sounded strange to say.

"That," Tertan said, "is a wonder." He corrected himself with his ducking head. "I mean that is wonderful."

Suddenly, he dived at the miserable briefcase between his legs, put it on his knees, and began to fumble with the catch, all intent on the difficulty it presented. Howe noted that his suit was worn thin, his shirt almost unclean. He became aware, even, of a vague and musty odor of garments worn too long in unaired rooms. Tertan conquered the lock and began to concentrate upon a search into the interior. At last he held in his hand what he was after, a torn and crumpled copy of *Life and Letters*.

"I learned it from here," he said, holding it out.

Howe looked at him sharply, his hackles a little up. But the boy's face was not only perfectly innocent, it even shone with a conscious admiration. Apparently nothing of the import of the essay had touched him except the wonderful fact that his teacher was a "man of letters." Yet this seemed too stupid, and Howe, to test it, said, "The man who wrote that doesn't think it's wonderful."

Tertan made a moist hissing sound as he cleared his mouth of saliva. His head, oddly loose on his neck, wove a pattern of contempt in the air. "A critic," he said, "who admits *prima facie* that he does not understand." Then he said grandly, "It is the inevitable fate."

It was absurd, yet Howe was not only aware of the absurdity but of a tension suddenly and wonderfully relaxed. Now that the "attack" was on the table between himself and this strange boy, and subject to the boy's funny and absolutely certain contempt, the hidden force of his feeling was revealed to him in the very moment that it vanished. All unsuspected, there had been a film over the world, a transparent but discoloring haze of danger. But he had no time to stop over the brightened aspect of things. Tertan was going on. "I also am a man of letters. Putative."

"You have written a good deal?" Howe meant to be no more than polite, and he was surprised at the tenderness he heard in his words.

Solemnly the boy nodded, threw back the dank lock, and sucked in a deep, anticipatory breath. "First, a work of homiletics, which is a defense of the principles of religious optimism against the pessimism of Schopenhauer and the humanism of Nietzsche."

"Humanism? Why do you call it humanism?"

"It is my nomenclature for making a deity of man," Tertan replied negligently. "Then three fictional works, novels. And numerous essays in science, combating materialism. Is it your duty to read these if I bring them to you?"

Howe answered simply, "No, it isn't exactly my duty, but I shall be happy to read them." ·

Tertan stood up and remained silent. He rested his bag on the chair. With a certain compunction—for it did not seem entirely proper that, of two men of letters, one should have the right to blue-pencil the other, to grade him or to question the quality of his "sentence structure"—Howe reached for Tertan's papers. But before he could take them up, the boy suddenly made his bow-to-Abelard, the stiff inclination of the body with hands seeming to emerge from the scholar's gown. Then he was gone.

But after his departure something was still left of him. The timbre of his curious sentences, the downright finality of so quaint a phrase as "It is the inevitable fate" still rang in the air. Howe gave the warmth of his feeling to the new visitor who stood at the door announcing himself with a genteel clearing of the throat.

"Doctor Howe, I believe?" the student said. A large hand advanced into the room and grasped Howe's hand. "Blackburn, sir, Theodore Blackburn, vice-president of the Student Council. A great pleasure, sir."

Out of a pair of ruddy cheeks a pair of small eyes twinkled good-naturedly. The large face, the large body were not so much fat as beefy and suggested something "typical"—monk, politician, or innkeeper.

Blackburn took the seat beside Howe's desk. "I may have seemed to introduce myself in my public capacity, sir," he said. "But it is really as an individual that I came to see you. That is to say, as one of your students to be."

He spoke with an English intonation and he went on, "I was once an English major, sir."

For a moment Howe was startled, for the roastbeef look of the boy and the manner of his speech gave a second's credibility to one sense of his statement. Then the collegiate meaning of the phrase asserted itself, but some perversity made Howe say what was not really in good taste even with so forward a student, "Indeed? What regiment?"

Blackburn stared and then gave a little pouf-pouf of laughter. He waved the misapprehension away. "*Very* good, sir. It certainly is an ambiguous term." He chuckled in appreciation of Howe's joke, then cleared his throat to put it aside. "I look forward to taking your course in the romantic poets, sir," he said earnestly. "To me the romantic poets are the very crown of English literature."

Howe made a dry sound, and the boy, catching some meaning in it, said, "Little as I know them, of course. But even Shakespeare who is so dear to us of the Anglo-Saxon tradition is in a sense but the preparation for Shelley, Keats and Byron. And Wadsworth."

Almost sorry for him, Howe dropped his eyes. With some embarrassment, for the boy was not actually his student, he said softly, "Wordsworth."

"Sir?"

"Wordsworth, not Wadsworth. You said Wadsworth."

"Did I, sir?" Gravely he shook his head to rebuke himself for the error. "Wordsworth, of course—slip of the tongue." Then, quite in command again, he went on. "I have a favor to ask of you, Doctor Howe. You see, I began my college course as an English major,"—he smiled—"as I said."

"Yes?"

"But after my first year I shifted. I shifted to the social sciences. Sociology and government—I find them stimulating and very *real*." He paused, out of respect for reality. "But now I find that perhaps I have neglected the other side."

"The other side?" Howe said.

"Imagination, fancy, culture. A well-rounded man." He trailed off as if there were perfect understanding between them. "And so, sir, I have decided to end my senior year with your course in the romantic poets."

His voice was filled with an indulgence which Howe ignored as he said flatly and gravely, "But that course isn't given until the spring term."

"Yes, sir, and that is where the favor comes in. Would you let me take your romantic prose course? I can't take it for credit, sir, my program is full, but just for background it seems to me that I ought to take it. I do hope," he concluded in a manly way, "that you will consent."

"Well, it's no great favor, Mr. Blackburn. You can come if you wish, though there's not much point in it if you don't do the reading."

The bell rang for the hour and Howe got up.

"May I begin with this class, sir?" Blackburn's smile was candid and boyish.

Howe nodded carelessly and together, silently, they walked to the classroom down the hall. When they reached the door Howe stood back to let his student enter, but Blackburn moved adroitly behind him and grasped him by the arm to urge him over the threshold. They entered together with Blackburn's hand firmly on Howe's biceps, the student inducting the teacher into his own room. Howe felt a surge of temper rise in him and almost violently he disengaged his arm and walked to the desk, while Blackburn found a seat in the front row and smiled at him.

II

The question was, At whose door must the tragedy be laid?

All night the snow had fallen heavily and only now was abating in sparse little flurries. The windows were valanced high with white. It was very quiet; something of the quiet of the world had reached the class, and Howe found that everyone was glad to talk or listen. In the room there was a comfortable sense of pleasure in being human.

Casebeer believed that the blame for the tragedy rested with heredity. Picking up the book he read, "The sins of the fathers are visited on their children." This opinion was received with general favor. Nevertheless, Johnson ventured to say that the fault was all Pastor Manders' because the Pastor had made Mrs. Alving go back to her husband and was always hiding the truth. To this Hibbard objected with logic enough, "Well then, it was really all her husband's fault. He *did* all the bad things." De Witt, his face bright with an impatient idea, said that the fault was all society's. "By society I don't mean upper-crust society," he said. He looked around a little defiantly, taking in any members of the class who might be members of upper-crust society. "Not in that sense. I mean the social unit."

Howe nodded and said, "Yes, of course."

"If the society of the time had progressed far enough in science," De Witt went on, "then there would be no problem for Mr. Ibsen to write about. Captain Alving plays around a little, gives way to perfectly natural biological urges, and he gets a social disease, a venereal disease. If the disease is cured, no problem. Invent salvarsan and the disease is cured. The problem of heredity disappears and li'l Oswald just doesn't get paresis. No paresis, no problem—no problem, no play."

This was carrying the ark into battle, and the class looked at De Witt with respectful curiosity. It was his usual way and on the whole they were sympathetic with his struggle to prove to Howe that science was better than literature. Still, there was something in his reckless manner that alienated them a little.

"Or take birth-control, for instance," De Witt went on. "If Mrs. Alving had some knowledge of contraception, she wouldn't have had to have li'l Oswald at all. No li'l Oswald, no play."

The class was suddenly quieter. In the back row Stettenhover swung his great football shoulders in a righteous sulking gesture, first to the right, then to the left. He puckered his mouth ostentatiously. Intellect was always ending up by talking dirty.

Tertan's hand went up, and Howe said, "Mr. Tertan." The boy shambled to his feet and began his long characteristic gulp. Howe made a motion with his fingers, as small as possible, and Tertan ducked his head and smiled in apology. He sat down. The class laughed. With more than half the term gone, Tertan had not been able to remember that one did not rise to speak. He seemed unable to carry on the life of the intellect without this mark of respect for it. To Howe the boy's habit of rising seemed to accord with the formal shabbiness of his dress. He never wore the casual sweaters and jackets of his classmates. Into the free and comfortable air of the college classroom he brought the stuffy sordid strictness of some crowded, metropolitan high school.

"Speaking from one sense," Tertan began slowly, "there is no blame ascribable. From the sense of determinism, who can say where the blame lies? The preordained is the preordained and it cannot be said without rebellion against the universe, a palpable absurdity."

In the back row Stettenhover slumped suddenly in his seat, his heels held out before him, making a loud, dry, disgusted sound. His body sank until his neck rested on the back of his chair. He folded his hands across his belly and looked significantly out of the window, exasperated not only with Tertan, but with Howe, with the class, with the whole system designed to encourage this kind of thing. There was a certain insolence in the movement and Howe flushed. As Tertan continued to speak, Howe stalked casually toward the window and placed himself in the line of Stettenhover's vision. He stared at the great fellow, who pretended not to see him. There was so much power in the big body, so much contempt in the Greek-athlete face under the crisp Greek-athlete curls, that Howe felt almost physical fear. But at last Stettenhover admitted him to focus and under his disapproving gaze sat up with slow indifference. His eyebrows raised high in resignation, he began to examine his hands. Howe relaxed and turned his attention back to Tertan.

"Flux of existence," Tertan was saying, "produces all things, so that judgment wavers. Beyond the phenomena, what? But phenomena are adumbrated and to them we are limited."

Howe saw it for a moment as perhaps it existed in the boy's mind—the world of shadows which are cast by a great light upon a hidden reality as in the old myth of the Cave. But the little brush with Stettenhover had tired him, and he said irritably, "But come to the point, Mr. Tertan."

He said it so sharply that some of the class looked at him curiously. For three months he had gently carried Tertan through his verbosities, to the vaguely respectful surprise of the other students, who seemed to conceive that there existed between this strange classmate and their teacher some special understanding from which they were content to be excluded. Tertan looked at him mildly, and at once came brilliantly to the point. "This is the summation of the play," he said and took up his book and read," 'Your poor father never found any outlet for the over-mastering joy of life that was in him. And I brought no holiday into his home, either. Everything seemed to turn upon duty and I am afraid I made your poor father's home unbearable to him, Oswald.' Spoken by Mrs. Alving."

Yes that was surely the "summation" of the play and Tertan had hit it, as he hit, deviously and eventually, the literary point of almost everything. But now, as always, he was wrapping it away from sight. "For most mortals," he said, "there are only joys of biological urgings, gross and crass, such as the sensuous Captain Alving. For certain few there are the transmutations beyond these to a contemplation of the utter whole."

Oh, the boy was mad. And suddenly the word, used in hyperbole, intended almost for the expression of exasperated admiration, became literal. Now that the word was used, it became simply apparent to Howe that Tertan was mad.

It was a monstrous word and stood like a bestial thing in the room. Yet it so completely comprehended everything that had puzzled Howe, it so arranged and explained what for three months had been perplexing him that almost at once its horror became domesticated. With this word Howe was able to understand why he had never been able to communicate to Tertan the value of a single criticism or correction of his wild, verbose themes. Their conferences had been frequent and long but had done nothing to reduce to order the splendid confusion of the boy's ideas. Yet, impossible though its expression was, Tertan's incandescent mind could always strike for a moment into some dark corner of thought.

And now it was suddenly apparent that it was not a faulty rhetoric that Howe had to contend with. With this new knowledge he looked at Tertan's face and wondered how he could have so long deceived himself. Tertan was still talking, and the class had lapsed into a kind of patient unconsciousness, a coma of respect for words which, for all that most of them knew, might be profound. Almost with a suffusion of shame, Howe believed that in some dim way the class had long ago had some intimation of Tertan's madness. He reached out as decisively as he could to seize the thread of Tertan's discourse before it should be entangled further.

"Mr. Tertan says that the blame must be put upon whoever kills the joy of living in another. We have been assuming that Captain Alving was a wholly bad man, but what if we assume that he became bad only because Mrs. Alving, when they were first married, acted toward him in the prudish way she says she did?"

It was a ticklish idea to advance to freshmen and perhaps not profitable. Not all of them were following.

"That would put the blame on Mrs. Alving herself, whom most of you admire. And she herself seems to think so." He glanced at his watch. The hour was nearly over. "What do you think, Mr. De Witt?"

De Witt rose to the idea; he wanted to know if society couldn't be blamed for educating Mrs. Alving's temperament in the wrong way. Casebeer was puzzled, Stettenhover continued to look at his hands until the bell rang.

Tertan, his brows louring in thought, was making as always for a private word. Howe gathered his books and papers to leave quickly. At this moment of his discovery and with the knowledge still raw, he could not engage himself with Tertan. Tertan sucked in his breath to prepare for speech and Howe made ready for the pain and confusion. But at that moment Casebeer detached himself from the group with which he had been conferring and which he seemed to represent. His constituency remained at a tactful distance. The mission involved the time of an assigned essay. Casebeer's presentation of the plea—it was based on the freshmen's heavy duties at the fraternities during Carnival Week—cut across Tertan's preparations for speech. "And so some of us fellow thought," Casebeer concluded with heavy solemnity, "that we could do a better job, give our minds to it more, if we had more time."

Tertan regarded Casebeer with mingled curiosity and revulsion. Howe not only said that he would postpone the assignment but went on to talk about the Carnival, and even drew the waiting constituency into the conversation. He was conscious of Tertan's stern and astonished stare, then of his sudden departure.

Now that the fact was clear, Howe knew that he must act on it. His course was simple enough. He must lay the case before the Dean. Yet he hesitated. His feeling for Tertan must now, certainly, be in some way invalidated. Yet could he, because of a word, hurry to assign to official and reasonable solicitude what had been, until this moment, so various and warm? He could at least delay and, by moving slowly, lend a poor grace to the necessary, ugly act of making his report.

It was with some notion of keeping the matter in his own hands that he went to the Dean's office to look up Tertan's records. In the outer office the Dean's secretary greeted him brightly, and at his request brought him the manila folder with the small identifying photograph pasted in the corner. She laughed. "He was looking for the birdie in the wrong place," she said.

Howe leaned over her shoulder to look at the picture. It was as bad as all the Deans's-office photographs were, but it differed from all that Howe had ever seen. Tertan, instead of looking into the camera, as no doubt he had been bidden, had, at the moment of exposure, turned his eyes upward. His mouth, as though conscious of the trick played on the photographer, had the sly superior look that Howe knew.

The secretary was fascinated by the picture. "What a funny boy," she said. "He looks like Tartuffe!"

And so he did, with the absurd piety of the eyes and the conscious slyness of the mouth and the whole face bloated by the bad lens.

"Is he *like* that?" the secretary said.

"Like Tartuffe? No."

From the photograph there was little enough comfort to be had. The records themselves gave no clue to madness, though they suggested sadness enough. Howe read of a father, Stanislaus Tertan, born in Budapest and trained in engineering in Berlin, once employed by the Hercules Chemical Corporation—this was one of the factories that dominated the sound end of the town—but now without employment. He read of a mother Erminie (Youngfellow) Tertan, born in Manchester, educated at a Normal School at Leeds, now housewife by profession. The family lived on Greenbriar Street which Howe knew as a row of once elegant homes near what was now the factory district. The old mansion had long ago been divided into small and primitive apartments. Of Ferdinand himself there was little to learn. He lived with his parents, had attended a Detroit high school and had transferred to the local school in his last year. His rating for intelligence, as expressed in numbers, was high, his scholastic record was remarkable, he held a college scholarship for his tuition.

Howe laid the folder on the secretary's desk. "Did you find what you wanted to know? " she asked.

The phrases from Tertan's momentous first theme came back to him. "Tertan I am, but what is Tertan? Of this time, of that place, of some parentage, what does it matter?"

"No, I didn't find it," he said.

Now that he had consulted the sad, half-meaningless record he knew all the more firmly that he must not give the matter out of his own hands. He must not release Tertan to authority. Not that he anticipated from the Dean anything but the greatest kindness for Tertan. The Dean would have the experience and skill which he himself could not have. One way or another the Dean could answer the question, "What is Tertan?" Yet this was precisely what he feared. He alone could keep alive—not forever but for a somehow important time—the question, "What is Tertan?" He alone could keep it still a question. Some instinct told him that he must not surrender the question to a clean official desk in a clear official light to be dealt with, settled and closed.

He heard himself saying, "Is the Dean busy at the moment? I'd like to see him."

His request came thus unbidden, even forbidden, and it was one of the surprising and startling incidents of his life. Later when he reviewed the events, so disconnected in themselves, or so merely odd, of the story that unfolded for him that year, it was over this moment, on its face the least notable, that he paused longest. It was frequently to be with fear and never without a certainty of its meaning in his own knowledge of himself that he would recall this simple, routine request, and the feeling of shame and freedom it gave him as he sent everything down the official chute. In the end, of course, no matter what he did to "protect" Tertan, he would have had to make the same request and lay the matter on the Dean's clean desk. But it would always be a landmark of his life that, at the very moment when he was rejecting the official way, he had been, without will or intention, so gladly drawn to it.

After the storm's last delicate flurry, the sun had come out. Reflected by the new snow, it filled the office with a golden light which was almost musical in the way it made all the commonplace objects of efficiency shine with a sudden sad and noble significance. And the light, now that he noticed it, made the utterance of his perverse and unwanted request even more momentous.

The secretary consulted the engagement pad. "He'll be free any minute. Don't you want to wait in the parlor?"

She threw open the door of the large and pleasant room in which the Dean held his Committee meetings, and in which his visitors waited. It was designed with a homely elegance on the masculine side of the eighteenth-century manner. There was a small coal fire in the grate and the handsome mahogany table was strewn with books and magazines. The large windows gave on the snowy lawn, and there was such a fine width of window that the white casements and walls seemed at this moment but a continuation of the snow, the snow but an extension of casement and walls. The outdoors seemed taken in and made safe, the indoors seemed luxuriously freshened and expanded.

Howe sat down by the fire and lighted a cigarette. The room had its intended effect upon him. He felt comfortable and relaxed, yet nicely organized, some young diplomatic agent of the eighteenth century, the newly fledged Swift carrying out Sir William Temple's business. The rawness of Tertan's case quite vanished. He crossed his legs and reached for a magazine.

It was that famous issue of *Life and Letters* that his idle hand had found and his blood raced as he sifted through it, and the shape of his own name, Joseph Howe, sprang out at him, still cabalistic in its power. He tossed the magazine back on the table as the door of the Dean's office opened and the Dean ushered out Theodore Blackburn.

"Ah, Joseph!" the Dean said.

Blackburn said, "Good morning, Doctor." Howe winced at the title and caught the flicker of amusement over the Dean's face. The Dean stood with his hand high on the door-jamb and Blackburn, still in the doorway, remained standing almost under the long arm.

Howe nodded briefly to Blackburn, snubbing his eager deference. "Can you give me a few minutes?" he said to the Dean.

"All the time you want. Come in." Before the two men could enter the office, Blackburn claimed their attention with a long full "er." As they turned to him, Blackburn said, "Can *you* give *me* a few minutes, Doctor Howe?" His eyes sparkled at the little audacity he had committed, the slightly impudent play with hierarchy. Of the three of them Blackburn kept himself the lowest, but he reminded Howe of his subaltern relation to the Dean.

"I mean, of course," Blackburn went on easily, "when you've finished with the Dean."

"I'll be in my office shortly," Howe said, turned his back on the ready "Thank you, sir," and followed the Dean into the inner room.

"Energetic boy," said the Dean. "A bit beyond himself but very energetic. Sit down."

The Dean lighted a cigarette, leaned back in his chair, sat easy and silent for a moment, giving Howe no signal to go ahead with business. He was a young Dean, not much beyond forty, a tall handsome man with sad, ambitious eyes. He had been a Rhodes scholar. His friends looked for great things from him, and it was generally said that he had notions of education which he was not yet ready to try to put into practice.

His relaxed silence was meant as a compliment to Howe. He smiled and said, "What's the business, Joseph?"

"Do you know Tertan—Ferdinand Tertan, a freshman?"

The Dean's cigarette was in his mouth and his hands were clasped behind his head. He did not seem to search his memory for the name. He said, "What about him?"

Clearly the Dean knew something, and he was waiting for Howe to tell him more. Howe moved only tentatively. Now that he was doing what he had resolved not to do, he felt more guilty at having been so long deceived by Tertan and more need to be loyal to his error.

"He's a strange fellow," he ventured. He said stubbornly, "In a strange way he's very brilliant." He concluded, "But very strange."

The springs of the Dean's swivel chair creaked as he came out of his sprawl and leaned forward to Howe. "Do you mean he's so strange that it's something you could give a name to?"

Howe looked at him stupidly. "What do you mean?" he said.

"What's his trouble?" the Dean said more neutrally.

"He's very brilliant, in a way. I looked him up and he has a top intelligence rating. But somehow, and it's hard to explain just how, what he says is always on the edge of sense and doesn't quite make it."

The Dean looked at him and Howe flushed up. The Dean had surely read Wooley on the subject of "the Howes" and the *tour d'ivresse*. Was that quick glance ironical?

The Dean picked up some papers from his desk, and Howe could see that they were in Tertan's impatient scrawl. Perhaps the little gleam in the Dean's glance had come only from putting facts together.

"He sent me this yesterday," the Dean said. "After an interview I had with him. I haven't been able to do more than glance at it. When you said what you did, I realized there was something wrong."

Twisting his mouth, the Dean looked over the letter. "You seem to be involved," he said without looking up. "By the way, what did you give him at mid-term?"

Flushing, setting his shoulders, Howe said firmly, "I gave him A-minus."

The Dean chuckled. "Might be a good idea if some of our nicer boys went crazy—just a little." He said, "Well," to conclude the matter and handed the papers to Howe. "See if this is the same thing you've been finding. Then we can go into the matter again."

Before the fire in the parlor, in the chair that Howe had been occupying, sat Blackburn. He sprang to his feet as Howe entered.

"I said my office, Mr. Blackburn." Howe's voice was sharp. Then he was almost sorry for the rebuke, so clearly and naively did Blackburn seem to relish his stay in the parlor, close to authority.

"I'm in a bit of a hurry, sir," he said, "and I did want to be sure to speak to you, sir."

He was really absurd, yet fifteen years from now he would have grown up to himself, to the assurance and mature beefiness. In banks, in consular offices, in brokerage firms, on the bench, more seriously affable, a little sterner, he would make use of his ability to be administered by his job. It was almost reassuring. Now he was exercising his too great skill on Howe. "I owe you an apology, sir," he said.

Howe knew that he did, but he showed surprise.

"I mean, Doctor, after your having been so kind about letting me attend your class, I stopped coming." He smiled in deprecation. "Extracurricular activities take up so much of my time. I'm afraid I undertook more than I could perform."

Howe had noticed the absence and had been a little irritated by it after Blackburn's elaborate plea. It was an absence that might be interpreted as a comment on the teacher. But there was only one way for him to answer. "You've no need to apologize," he said. "It's wholly your affair."

Blackburn beamed. "I'm so glad you feel that way about it, sir. I was worried you might think I had stayed away because I was influenced by—" he stopped and lowered his eyes.

Astonished, Howe said, "Influenced by what?"

"Well, by—" Blackburn hesitated and for answer pointed to the table on which lay the copy of *Life and Letters*. Without looking at it, he knew where to direct his hand. "By the unfavorable publicity, sir." He hurried on. "And that brings me to another point, sir. I am secretary of Quill and Scroll, sir, the student literary society, and I wonder if you would address us. You could read your own poetry, sir, and defend your own point of view. It would be very interesting."

It was truly amazing. Howe looked long and cruelly into Blackburn's face, trying to catch the secret of the mind that could have conceived this way of manipulating him, this way so daring and inept—but not entirely inept—with its malice so without malignity. The face did not yield its secret. Howe smiled broadly and said, "Of course I don't think you were influenced by the unfavorable publicity."

"I'm still going to take—regularly, for credit—your romantic poets course next term," Blackburn said.

"Don't worry, my dear fellow, don't worry about it."

Howe started to leave and Blackburn stopped him with, "But about Quill, sir?"

"Suppose we wait until next term? I'll be less busy then."

And Blackburn said, "Very good, sir, and thank you."

In his office the little encounter seemed less funny to Howe, was even in some indeterminate way disturbing. He made an effort to put it from his mind by turning to what was sure to disturb him more, the Tertan letter read in the new interpretation. He found what he had always found, the same florid leaps beyond fact and meaning, the same headlong certainty. But as his eye passed over the familiar scrawl it caught his own name, and for the second time that hour he felt the race of his blood.

"The Paraclete," Tertan had written to the Dean, "from a Greek word meaning to stand in place of, but going beyond the primitive idea to mean traditionally the helper, the one who comforts and assists, cannot without fundamental loss be jettisoned. Even if taken no longer in the supernatural sense, the concept remains deeply in the human consciousness inevitably. Humanitarianism is no reply, for not every man stands in the place of every other man for this other comrade's comfort. But certain are chosen out of the human race to be the consoler of some other. Of these, for example, is Joseph Barker Howe, Ph.D. Of intellects not the first yet of true intellect and lambent instructions, given to that which is intuitive and irrational, not to what is logical in the strict word, what is judged by him is of the heart and not the head. Here is one chosen, in that he chooses himself to stand in the place of another for comfort and consolation. To him more than another I give my gratitude, with all respect to our Dean who reads this, a noble man, but merely dedicated, not consecrated. But not in the aspect of the Paraclete only is Dr. Joseph Barker Howe established, for he must be the Paraclete to another aspect of himself, that which is driven and per-secuted by the lack of understanding in the world at large, so that he in himself embodies the full history of man's tribulations and, overflowing upon others, notably the present writer, is the ultimate end."

This was love. There was no escape from it. Try as Howe might to remember that Tertan was mad and all his emotions invalidated, he could not destroy the effect upon him of his student's stern, affectionate regard. He had betrayed not only a power of mind but a power of love. And, however firmly he held before his attention the fact of Tertan's madness, he could do nothing to banish the physical sensation of gratitude he felt. He had never thought of himself as "driven and persecuted" and he did not now. But still he could not make meaningless his sensation of gratitude. The pitiable Tertan sternly pitied him, and comfort came from Tertan's never-to-be-comforted mind.

III

In an academic community, even an efficient one, official matters move slowly. The term drew to a close with no action in the case of Tertan, and Joseph Howe had to confront a curious problem. How should he grade his strange student, Tertan?

Tertan's final examination had been no different from all his other writing, and what did one "give" such a student? De Witt must have his A, that was clear. Johnson would get a B. With Casebeer it was a question of a B-minus or a C-plus, and Stettenhover, who had been crammed by the team tutor to fill half a blue-book with his thin feminine scrawl, would have his C-minus which he would accept with mingled indifference and resentment. But with Tertan it was not so easy.

The boy was still in the college process and his name could not be omitted from the grade sheet. Yet what should a mind under suspicion of madness be graded? Until the medical verdict was given, it was for Howe to continue as Tertan's teacher and to keep his judgment pedagogical. Impossible to give him an F: he had not failed. B was for Johnson's stolid mediocrity. He could not be put on the edge of passing with Stettenhover, for he exactly did not pass. In energy and richness of intellect he was perhaps even De Witt's superior, and Howe toyed grimly with the notion of giving him an A, but that would lower the value of the A De Witt had won with his beautiful and clear, if still arrogant, mind. There was a notation which the Registrar recognized—Inc., for Incomplete, and in the horrible comedy of the situation, Howe considered that. But really only a mark of M for Mad would serve.

In his perplexity, Howe sought the Dean, but the Dean was out of town. In the end, he decided to maintain the A-minus he had given Tertan at mid-term. After all, there had been no falling away from that quality. He entered it on the grade sheet with something like bravado.

Academic time moves quickly. A college year is not really a year, lacking as it does three months. And it is endlessly divided into units which, at their beginning, appear larger than they are—terms, half-terms, months, weeks. And the ultimate unit, the hour, is not really an hour, lacking as it does ten minutes. And so the new term advanced rapidly, and one day the fields about the town were all brown, cleared of even the few thin patches of snow which had lingered so long.

Howe, as he lectured on the romantic poets, became conscious of Blackburn emanating wrath. Blackburn did it well, did it with enormous dignity. He did not stir in his seat, he kept his eyes fixed on Howe in perfect attention, but he abstained from using his notebook, there was no mistaking what he proposed to himself as an attitude. His elbow on the writing-wing of the chair, his chin on the curled fingers of his hand, he was the embodiment of intellectual indignation. He was thinking his own thoughts, would give no public offense, yet would claim his due, was not to be intimidated. Howe knew that he would present himself at the end of the hour.

Blackburn entered the office without invitation. He did not smile; there was no cajolery about him. Without invitation he sat down beside Howe's desk. He did not speak until he had taken the blue-book from his pocket. He said, "What does this mean, sir?"

It was a sound and conservative student tactic. Said in the usual way it meant, "How could you have so misunderstood me?" or "What does this mean for my future in the course?" But there were none of the humbler tones in Blackburn's way of saying it.

Howe made the established reply, "I think that's for you to tell me."

Blackburn continued icy. "I'm sure I can't sir."

There was a silence between them. Both dripped their eyes to the blue-book on the desk. On its cover Howe had penciled: "F. This is very poor work."

Howe picked up the blue-book. There was always the possibility of injustice. The teacher may be bored by the mass of papers and not wholly attentive. A phrase, even the student's handwriting, may irritate him unreasonably. "Well," said Howe, "Let's go through it."

He opened the first page. "Now here: you write, In *The Ancient Mariner,* Coleridge lives in and transports us to a honey-sweet world where all is rich and strange, a world of charm to which we can escape from the humdrum existence of our daily lives, the world of romance. Here, in this warm and honey-sweet land of charming dreams we can relax and enjoy ourselves.' "

Howe lowered the paper and waited with a neutral look for Blackburn to speak. Blackburn returned the look boldly, did not speak, sat stolid and lofty. At last Howe said, speaking gently, "Did you mean that, or were you just at a loss for something to say?"

"You imply that I was just 'bluffing?' " The quotation marks hung palpable in the air about the word.

"I'd like to know. I'd prefer believing that you were bluffing to believing that you really thought this."

Blackburn's eyebrows went up. From the height of a great and firm-based idea he looked at his teacher. He clasped the crags for a moment and then pounced, craftily, suavely. "Do you mean, Doctor Howe, that there aren't two opinions possible?"

It was superbly done in its air of putting all of Howe's intellectual life into the balance. Howe remained patient and simple. "Yes, many opinions are possible, but not this one. Whatever anyone believes of *The Ancient Mariner,* no one can in reason believe that it represents a—a honey-sweet world in which we can relax."

"But that is what I *feel,* sir."

This was well-done, too, Howe said, "Look, Mr. Blackburn. Do you really relax with hunger and thirst, the heat and the sea-serpents, the dead men with staring eyes, Life in Death and the skeletons? Come now, Mr. Blackburn."

Blackburn made no answer, and Howe pressed forward. "Now, you say of Wordsworth, 'Of peasant stock himself, he turned from the effete life of the salons and found in the peasant the hope of a flaming revolution which would sweep away all the old ideas. This is the subject of his best poems.' "

Beaming at his teacher with youthful eagerness, Blackburn said, "Yes, sir, a rebel, a bringer of light to suffering mankind. I see him as a kind of Prothemeus."

"A kind of what?"

"Prothemeus, sir."

"Think, Mr. Blackburn. We were talking about him only today and I mentioned his name a dozen times. You don't mean Prothemeus. You mean—" Howe waited, but there was no response.

"You mean Prometheus."

Blackburn gave no assent, and Howe took the reins. "You've done a bad job here, Mr. Blackburn, about as bad as could be done." He saw Blackburn stiffen and his genial face harden again. "It shows either a lack of preparation or a complete lack of understanding." He saw Blackburn's face begin to go to pieces and he stopped.

"Oh, sir," Blackburn burst out, "I've never had a mark like this before, never anything below a B, never. A thing like this has never happened to me before."

It must be true, it was a statement too easily verified. Could it be that other instructors accepted such flaunting nonsense? Howe wanted to end the interview. "I'll set it down to lack of preparation," he said. "I know you're busy. That's not an excuse, but it's an explanation. Now, suppose you really prepare, and then take another quiz in two weeks. We'll forget this one and count the other."

Blackburn squirmed with pleasure and gratitude. "Thank you, sir. You're really very kind, very kind."

Howe rose to conclude the visit. "All right, then—in two weeks."

It was that day that the Dean imparted to Howe the conclusion of the case of Tertan. It was simple and a little anti-climactic. A physician had been called in, and had said the word, given the name.

"A classic case, he called it," the Dean said. "Not a doubt in the world," he said. His eyes were full of miserable pity, and he clutched at a word. "A classic case, a classic case." To his aid and to Howe's there came the Parthenon and the form of the Greek drama, the Aristotelian logic, Racine and the Well-Tempered Clavichord, the blueness of the Aegean and its clear sky. Classic—that is to say, without a doubt, perfect in its way, a veritable model, and, as the Dean had been told, sure to take a perfectly predictable and inevitable course to a foreknown conclusion.

It was not only pity that stood in the Dean's eyes. For a moment there was fear too. "Terrible," he said, "it is simply terrible."

Then he went on briskly. "Naturally, we've told the boy nothing. And, naturally, we won't. His tuition's paid by his scholarship, and we'll continue him on the rolls until the end of the year. That will be kindest. After that the matter will be out of our control. We'll see, of course, that he gets into the proper hands. I'm told there will be no change, he'll go on like this, be as good as this, for four to six months. And so we'll just go along as usual."

So Tertan continued to sit in Section 5 of English 1A, to his classmates still a figure of curiously dignified fun, symbol to most of them of-the respectable but absurd intellectual life. But to his teacher he was now very different. He had not changed—he was still the greyhound casting for the scent of ideas, and Howe could see that he was still the same Tertan, but he could not feel it. What he felt as he looked at the boy sitting in his accustomed place was the hard blank of a fact. The fact itself was formidable and depressing. But what Howe was chiefly aware of was that he had permitted the metamorphosis of Tertan from person to fact.

As much as possible he avoided seeing Tertan's upraised hand and eager eye. But the fact did not know of its mere factuality, it continued its existence as if it were Tertan, hand up and eye questioning, and one day it appeared in Howe's office with a document.

"Even the spirit who lives egregiously, above the herd, must have its relations with the fellowman," Tertan declared. He laid the document on Howe's desk. It was headed "Quill and Scroll Society of Dwight College. Application for Membership."

"In most ways these are crass minds," Tertan said, touching the paper. "Yet as a whole, bound together in their common love of letters, they transcend their intellectual lacks since it is not a paradox that the whole is greater than the sum of its parts."

"When are the elections?" Howe asked.

"They take place tomorrow."

"I certainly hope you will be successful."

"Thank you. would you wish to implement that hope?" A rather dirty finger pointed to the bottom of the sheet. "A faculty recommender is necessary," Tertan said stiffly, and waited.

"And you wish me to recommend you?"

"It would be an honor."

"You may use my name."

Tertan's finger pointed again. "It must be a written sponsorship, signed by the sponsor." There was a large blank space on the form under the heading, "Opinion of Faculty Sponsor."

This was almost another thing and Howe hesitated. Yet there was nothing else to do and he took out his fountain pen. He wrote, "Mr. Ferdinand Tertan is marked by his intense devotion to letters and by his exceptional love of all things of the mind." To this he signed his name, which looked bold and assertive on the white page. It disturbed him, the strange affirming power of a name. With a businesslike air, Tertan whipped up the paper, folding it with decision, and put it into his pocket. He bowed and took his departure, leaving Howe with the sense of having done something oddly momentous.

And so much now seemed odd and momentous to Howe that should not have seemed so. It was odd and momentous, he felt, when he sat with Blackburn's second quiz before him, and wrote in an excessively firm hand the grade of C-minus. The paper was a clear, an indisputable failure. He was carefully and consciously committing a cowardice. Blackburn had told the truth when he had pleaded his past record. Howe had consulted it in the Dean's office. It showed no grade lower that a B-minus. A canvass of some of Blackburn's previous instructors had brought vague attestations to the adequate powers of a student imperfectly remembered, and sometimes surprise that his abilities could be questioned at all.

As he wrote the grade, Howe told himself that his cowardice sprang from an unwillingness to have more dealings with a student he disliked. He knew it was simpler than that. He knew he feared Blackburn; that was the absurd truth. And cowardice did not solve the matter after all. Blackburn, flushed with a first success, attacked at once. The minimal passing grade had not assuaged his feelings and he sat at Howe's desk and again the blue-book lay between them. Blackburn said nothing. With an enormous impudence, he was waiting for Howe to speak and explain himself.

At last Howe said sharply and rudely, "Well?" His throat was tense and the blood was hammering in his head. His mouth was tight with anger at himself for his disturbance.

Blackburn's glance was almost baleful. "This is impossible, sir."

"But there it is, " Howe answered.

"Sir?" Blackburn had not caught the meaning but his tone was still haughty.

Impatiently Howe said, "There it is, plain as day. Are you going to complain again?"

"Indeed I am, sir." There was surprise in Blackburn's voice that Howe should ask the question.

"I shouldn't complain if I were you. You did a thoroughly bad job on your first quiz. This one is a little, only a very little, better." This was not true. If anything, it was worse.

"That might be a matter of opinion, sir."

"It is a matter of opinion. Of my opinion."

"Another opinion might be different, sir."

"You really believe that?" Howe said.

"Yes." The omission of the "sir" was monumental.

"Whose, for example?"

"The Dean's, for example." Then the fleshy jaw came forward a little. "Or a certain literary critic's, for example."

It was colossal and almost too much for Blackburn himself to handle. The solidity of his face almost crumpled under it. But he withstood his own audacity and went on. "And the Dean's opinion might be guided by the knowledge that the person who gave me this mark is the man whom a famous critic, the most eminent judge of literature in this country, called a drunken man. The Dean might think twice about whether such a man is fit to teach Dwight students."

Howe said in quiet admonition, "Blackburn, you're mad," meaning no more than to check the boy's extravagance.

But Blackburn paid no heed. He had another shot in the locker. "And the Dean might be guided by the information, of which I have evidence, documentary evidence,"—he slapped his breast pocket twice—"that this same person personally recommended to the college literary society, the oldest in the country, that he personally recommended a student who is crazy, who threw the meeting into an uproar—a psychiatric case. The Dean might take that into account."

Howe was never to learn the details of that "uproar." He had always to content himself with the dim but passionate picture which at that moment sprang into his mind, of Tertan standing on some abstract height and madly denouncing the multitude of Quill and Scroll who howled him down.

He sat quiet a moment and looked at Blackburn. The ferocity had entirely gone from the student's face. He sat regarding his teacher almost benevolently. He had played a good card and now, scarcely at all unfriendly, he was waiting to see the effect. Howe took up the blue-book and negligently sifted through it. He read a page, closed the book, struck out the C-minus and wrote an F.

"Now you may take the paper to the Dean," he said. "You may tell him that after reconsidering it, I lowered the grade."

The gasp was audible. "Oh, sir!" Blackburn cried. "Please!" His face was agonized. "It means my graduation, my livelihood, my future. Don't do this to me."

"It's done already."

Blackburn stood up. "I spoke rashly, sir, hastily. I had no intention, no real intention, of seeing the Dean. It rests with you—entirely, entirely. I *hope* you will restore the first mark."

"Take the matter to the Dean or not, just as you choose. The grade is what you deserve and it stands."

Blackburn's head dropped. "And I will be failed at mid-term, sir?"

"Of course."

From deep out of Blackburn's great chest rose a cry of anguish. "Oh, sir, if you want me to go down on my knees to you, I will, I will."

Howe looked at him in amazement.

"I will, I will. On my knees, sir. This mustn't, mustn't happen."

He spoke so literally, meaning so very truly that his knees and exactly his knees were involved and seeming to think that he was offering something of tangible value to his teacher, that Howe, whose head had become icy clear in the nonsensical drama, thought, "The boy is mad," and began to speculate fantastically whether something in himself attracted or developed aberration. He could see himself standing absurdly before the Dean saying, "I've found another. This time it's the vice-president of the Council, the manager of the debating team and secretary of Quill and Scroll."

One more such discovery, he thought, and he himself would be dis-covered! And there, suddenly, Blackburn was on his knees with a thump, his huge thighs straining his trousers, his hand outstretched in a great gesture of supplication.

With a cry, Howe shoved back his swivel chair and it rolled away on its casters half across the little room. Blackburn knelt for a moment to nothing at all, then got to his feet.

Howe rose abruptly. He said, "Blackburn, you will stop acting like an idiot. Dust your knees off, take your paper and get out. You've behaved like a fool and a malicious person. You have half a term to do a decent job. Keep your silly mouth shut and try to do it. Now get out."

Blackburn's head was low. He raised it and there was a pious light in his eyes. "Will you shake hands, sir?" he said. He thrust out his hand.

"I will not," Howe said.

Head and hand sank together. Blackburn picked up his blue-book and walked to the door. He turned and said, "Thank you, sir." His back, as he departed, was heavy with tragedy and stateliness.

IV

After years of bad luck with the weather, the College had a perfect day for Commencement. It was wonderfully bright, the air so transparent, the wind so brisk that no one could resist talking about it.

As Howe set out for the campus he heard Hilda calling from the back yard. She called, "Professor, professor," and came running to him.

Howe said, "What's this professor business?"

"Mother told me," Hilda said. "You've been promoted. And I want to take your picture."

"Next year," said Howe. "I won't be a professor until next year. And you know better than to call anybody 'professor.' "

"It was just in fun," Hilda said. She seemed disappointed.

"But you can take my picture if you want. I won't look much different next year." Still, it was frightening. It might mean that he was to stay in this town all his life.

Hilda brightened. "Can I take it in this?" she said, and touched the gown he carried over his arm.

Howe laughed. "Yes, you can take it in this."

"I'll get my things and meet you in front of Otis," Hilda said. "I have the background all picked out."

On the campus the Commencement crowd was already large. It stood about in eager, nervous little family groups. As he crossed, Howe was greeted by a student, capped and gowned, glad of the chance to make an event for his parents by introducing one of his teachers. It was while Howe stood there chatting that he saw Tertan.

He had never seen anyone quite so alone, as though a circle had been woven about him to separate him from the gay crowd on the campus. Not that Tertan was not gay, he was the gayest of all. Three weeks had passed since Howe had last seen him, the weeks of examination, the lazy week before Commencement, and this was now a different Tertan. On his head he wore a panama hat, broadbrimmed and fine, of the shape associated with South American planters. He wore a suit of raw silk, luxurious, but yellowed with age and much too tight, and he sported a whangee cane. He walked sedately, the hat tilted at a devastating angle, the stick coming up and down in time to his measured tread. He had, Howe guessed, outfitted himself to greet the day in the clothes of that ruined father whose existence was on record in the Dean's office. Gravely and arrogantly he surveyed the scene—in it, his whole bearing seemed to say, but not of it. With his haughty step, with his flashing eye, Tertan was coming nearer. Howe did not wish to be seen. He shifted his position slightly. When he looked again, Tertan was not in sight.

The chapel clock struck the quarter hour. Howe detached himself from his chat and hurried to Otis Hall at the far end of the campus. Hilda had not yet come. He went up into the high portico and, using the glass of the door for a mirror, put on his gown, adjusted the hood on his shoulders and set the mortarboard on his head. When he came down the steps, Hilda had arrived.

Nothing could have told him more forcibly that a year had passed than the development of Hilda's photographic possessions from the box camera of the previous fall. By a strap about her neck was hung a leather case, so thick and strong, so carefully stitched and so molded to its contents that it could only hold a costly camera. The appearance was deceptive, Howe knew, for he had been present at the Aikens' pre-Christmas conference about its purchase. It was only a fairly good domestic camera. Still, it looked very impressive. Hilda carried another leather case from which she drew a collapsible tripod. Decisively she extended each of its gleaming legs and set it up on the path. She removed the camera from its case and fixed it to the tripod. In its compact efficiency the camera almost had a life of its own, but Hilda treated it with easy familiarity, looked into its eye, glanced casually at its gauges. Then from a pocket she took still another leather case and drew from it a small instrument through which she looked first at Howe, who began to feel inanimate and lost, and then at the sky. She made some adjustment on the instrument, then some adjustment on the camera. She swept the scene with her eye, found a spot and pointed the camera in its direction. She walked to the spot, stood on it and beckoned to Howe. With each new leather case, with each new instrument, and with each new adjustment she had grown in ease and now she said, "Joe, will you stand here?"

Obediently Howe stood where he was bidden. She had yet another instrument. She took out a tape-measure on a mechanical spool. Kneeling down before Howe, she put the little metal ring of the tape under the tip of his shoe. At her request, Howe pressed it with his toe. When she had measured her distance, she nodded to Howe who released the tape. At a touch, it sprang back into the spool. "You have to be careful if you're going to get what you want," Hilda said. "I don't believe in all this snap-snap-snapping," she remarked loftily. Howe nodded in agreement, although he was beginning to think Hilda's care excessive.

Now at last the moment had come. Hilda squinted into the camera, moved the tripod slightly. She stood to the side, holding the plunger of the shutter-cable. "Ready," she said. "Will you relax, Joseph, please?" Howe realized that he was standing frozen. Hilda stood poised and precise as a setter, one hand holding the little cable, the other extended with curled dainty fingers like a dancer's, as if expressing to her subject the precarious delicacy of the moment. She pressed the plunger and there was the click. At once she stirred to action, got behind the camera, turned a new exposure. "Thank you," she said. "Would you stand under that tree and let me do a character study with light and shade?"

The childish absurdity of the remark restored Howe's ease. He went to the little tree. The pattern the leaves made on his gown was what Hilda was after. He had just taken a satisfactory position when he heard in the unmistakable voice, "Ah, Doctor! Having your picture taken?"

Howe gave up the pose and turned to Blackburn who stood on the walk, his hands behind his back, a little too large for his bachelor's gown. Annoyed that Blackburn should see him posing for a character study in light and shade, Howe said irritably, "Yes, having my picture taken."

Blackburn beamed at Hilda. "And the little photographer?" he said. Hilda fixed her eyes on the ground and stood closer to her brilliant and aggressive camera. Blackburn, teetering on his heels, his hands behind his back, wholly prelatical and benignly patient, was not abashed at the silence. At last Howe said. "If you'll excuse us, Mr. Blackburn, we'll go on with the picture."

"Go right ahead, sir. I'm running along." But he only came closer. "Docter Howe," he said fervently, "I want to tell you how glad I am that I was able to satisfy your standards at last."

Howe was surprised at the hard, insulting brightness of his own voice, and even Hilda looked up curiously as he said, "Nothing you have ever done has satisfied me, and nothing you could ever do would satisfy me, Blackburn."

With a glance at Hilda, Blackburn made a gesture as if to hush Howe—as though all his former bold malice had taken for granted a kind of understanding between himself and his teacher, a secret which must not be betrayed to a third person. "I only meant, sir," he said, "that I was able to pass your course after all."

Howe said, "You didn't pass my course. I passed you out of my course. I passed you without even reading your paper. I wanted to be sure the college would be rid of you. And when all the grades were in and I did read your paper, I saw I was right not to have read it first."

Blackburn presented a stricken face. "It was very bad, sir?"

But Howe had turned away. The paper had been fantastic. The paper had been, if he wished to see it so, mad. It was at this moment that the Dean came up behind Howe and caught his arm. "Hello, Joseph," he said. "We'd better be getting along, it's almost late."

He was not a familiar man, but when he saw Blackburn, who approached to greet him, he took Blackburn's arm, too. "Hello, Theodore," he said. Leaning forward on Howe's arm and on Blackburn's, he said, "Hello, Hilda dear." Hilda replied quietly, "Hello, Uncle George."

Still clinging to their arms, still linking Howe and Blackburn, the Dean said, "Another year gone, Joe, and we've turned out another crop. After you've been a here a few years, you'll find it reasonably upsetting—you wonder how there can be so many graduating classes while you stay the same. But of course you don't stay the same." Then he said, "Well," sharply, to dismiss the thought. He pulled Blackburn's arm and swung him around to Howe. "Have you heard about Teddy Blackburn?" he asked. "He has a job already, before graduation—the first man of his class to be placed." Expectant of congratulations, Blackburn beamed at Howe. Howe remained silent.

"Isn't that good?" the Dean said. Still Howe did not answer and the Dean, puzzled and put out, turned to Hilda. "That's a very fine-looking camera, Hilda." She touched it with affectionate pride.

"Instruments of precision," said a voice. "Instruments of precision." Of the three with joined arms, Howe was the nearest to Tertan, whose gaze took in all the scene except the smile and the nod which Howe gave him. The boy leaned on his cane. The broad-brimmed hat, canting jauntily over his eye, confused the image of his face that Howe had established, suppressed the rigid lines of the ascetic and brought out the baroque curves. It made an effect of perverse majesty.

"Instruments of precision," said Tertan for the last time, addressing no one, making a casual comment to the universe. And it occurred to Howe that Tertan might not be referring to Hilda's equipment. The sense of the thrice-woven circle of the boy's loneliness smote him fiercely. Tertan stood in majestic jauntiness, superior to all the scene, but his isolation made Howe ache with a pity which Tertan was more the cause than the object, so general and indiscriminate was it.

Whether in his sorrow he made some unintended movement toward Tertan which the Dean checked, or whether the suddenly tightened grip on his arm was the Dean's own sorrow and fear, he did not know. Tertan watched them in the incurious way people watch a photograph being taken, and suddenly the thought that, to the boy, it must seem that the three were posing for a picture together made Howe detach himself almost rudely from the Dean's grasp.

"I promised Hilda another picture," he announced—needlessly, for Tertan was no longer there, he had vanished in the last sudden flux of visitors who, now that the band had struck up, were rushing nervously to find seats.

"You'd better hurry," the Dean said. "I'll go along, it's getting late for me." He departed and Blackburn walked stately by his side.

Howe again took his position under the little tree which cast its shadow over his face and gown. "Just hurry, Hilda, won't you?" he said. Hilda held the cable at arm's length, her other arm crooked and her fingers crisped. She rose on her toes and said "Ready," and pressed the release. "Thank you," she said gravely and began to dismantle her camera as he hurried off to join the procession.

THE DEVIL WAS
THE JOKER

J. F. Powers

Mr. McMaster, a hernia case convalescing in one of the four-bed wards, was fat and fifty or so, with a candy-pink face, sparse orange hair, and popeyes. ("Eyes don't permit me to read much," he had told Myles Flynn, the night orderly, more than once.) On his last evening in the hospital, as he lay in his bed smoking, his hands clasped over a box of havanas that rested on the soft dais of his stomach, he called Myles to his bedside. He wanted to thank him, he said, and, incidentally, he had no use for "that other son of a bitch"—meaning the other orderly, an engineering student, who had prepped him for surgery. "A hell of a fine engineer he'll make. You, though, you're different—more like a doctor than an orderly—and I was surprised to hear from one of the Sisters today that you're not going into the medical field." Mr. McMaster said he supposed there must be other reasons for working in a hospital, but he didn't sound as though he knew any.

Myles said he'd been four years in a seminary, studying for the priesthood—until "something happened." There he stopped.

Mr. McMaster grinned. "To make a long story short," he said.

Myles shook his head. He'd told Mr. McMaster all there was for him to tell—all he knew. He'd simply been asked to leave, he said, and since that day, three months before, he'd just been trying to make himself useful to society, here in the hospital. Mr. McMaster suddenly got serious. He wondered, in a whisper, whether Myles was "a cradle Catholic," as if that had something to do with his expulsion, and Myles said, "Yes. Almost have to be with a name like mine." "Not a-tall," said Mr. McMaster. "That's the hell of it. The other day I met a Jew by the name of Buckingham. Some Buckingham!"

Scenting liquor on the patient's breath, Myles supposed that Mr. McMaster, like so many salesmen or executives on their last evening wanted to get a good night's rest, to be ready for the morrow, when he would ride away in a taxicab to the daily battle of Chicago.

Again Mr. McMaster asked if Myles was a cradle Catholic, and when Myles again told him he was, Mr. McMaster said, "Call me Mac," and had Myles move the screen over to his bed. When they were hidden from the others in the ward, Mac whispered, "We don't know who they may be, whatever they say." Then he asked Myles if he'd ever heard of the Clementine Fathers. Myles had. "I'm with them," Mac said. "In a goodwill capacity." He described the nature of his work, which was meeting the public, lay and clerical (the emphasis was on the latter), and "building good will" for the Clementine order and finding more readers for the *Clementine,* the family-type magazine published by the Fathers.

Myles listened patiently because he considered it part of his job to do so, but the most he could say for the magazine was that it was probably good— of its kind. Yes, he'd heard the Fathers' radio program. The program, "Father Clem Answers Your Question," was aimed at non-Catholics but it had many faithful listeners among the nuns at the hospital. And the pamphlets put out by the Fathers, many of them written by Father Clem— Myles knew them well. In the hospital waiting rooms, they were read, wrung, and gnawed upon by their captive audience. "Is Father Clem a real person?" Myles asked. "Yes, and no," Mac said, which struck Myles as descriptive of the characters created by Father Clem, an author who tackled life's problems through numberless Joans, Jeans, Bobs, and Bills, clear-thinking college kids who, coached from the wings by jolly nuns and priests, invariably got the best of the arguments they had with the poor devils they were always meeting—atheists, euthanasianists, and the like. "Drive a car?" Mac asked. Myles said yes.

Mac then said he wanted it understood he wasn't making Myles any promises, but he thought there might be a job opening up with the Fathers soon, a job such as his own. "Think it over," Mac said, and Myles did—needing only a moment. He thought of his correspondence with the hierarchy, of the nice replies, all offering him nothing. For his purposes, the job with the fathers, unsuited as he was to it, could be ideal. Traveling around from diocese to diocese, meeting pastors and even bishops face to face in the regular course of the work, he might make the vital connection that would lead him, somehow, to the priesthood. Without a bishop he'd never get into another seminary—a bishop was more necessary than a vocation—but Myles had more than meeting the right bishop to worry about. He had lost his clerical status, and was now 1-A in the draft. The call-up might come any day.

Working with Mac would be action of a positive sort, better than continuing his fruitless correspondence, better than following such advice as he'd had from acquaintances—or even from the confessional, where, too hopefully, he'd taken his problems. There he had been told to go into business or science and get ahead, or into government and make a success of *that,* after which, presumably, he could come—tottering—before the bishops of the land as a man of proved ability and, what was more important, a man of stability. When the wise old confessor realized, however, that Myles not only had been cast aside by the Church but was likely to be wanted soon by the State, there had been no problem at all. His counsel had flowed swift and sure: "Enlist! Don't wait to be drafted!"

"Don't think of it as just a job," Mac said now. "Try to think of it as the Fathers do, and as I hope I do. Think of it as the Work."

Myles, thinking of it as a steppingstone to ordination, said he'd like to be considered for the job.

Mac said that of course the Fathers would have the last say, but his word would carry some weight with them, since Myles, if accepted, would be working under him—at first, anyway. He then asked Myles to bring a glass of ice water, and easy on the water. Myles, returning with a glass of ice, noted a bottle in bed with Mac, tucked under the sheet at his side like a nursing infant. He left them together, behind the screen.

Two days later Myles was summoned by telegram to an address in the Loop. He found the place, all right—an old building with grillwork elevators affording passengers a view of the cables. Mac was waiting for Myles at the cigar stand downstairs. As they rode up to the Fathers' floor, he advised Myles to forget all about his past as a seminarian, reasoning that if this was mentioned to the Fathers, it might make a bad impression. Myles had to agree with that, if reluctantly.

At the fifth floor, which the Fathers shared with a number of tailors, publishers, and distributors of barbers' supplies, Mac hustled Myles into the washroom. Myles' black overcoat, suit, and tie were all wrong, Mac said. He told Myles to take off his coat and then he suggested that they switch ties. This they did, morosely. Mac's suit, a double-breasted Glen plaid with a precipitous drape and trousers that billowed about his disproportionately thin legs, would "just carry" the black tie, he said, and presumably his tie, with its spheres, coils and triangles suggesting the spirit of Science and Industry, would carry Myles' black suit. "Don't want 'em to think they're hiring a creep," Mac said.

There was no trouble at all with the Fathers. Mac evidently stood high with them. He told them that Myles had gone to the University of Illinois for a time, which was news to Myles. He let it pass, though, because he remembered a conversation at the hospital during which, assuming Illinois to be Mac's old school, he had said that he'd once attended a football game at Illinois—or almost had. He had been dragooned into joining the Boy Scouts, Myles had explained, and had marched with his troop to the stadium for the season opener, admission free to Scouts, but on reaching the gates, he had remained outside, in a delayed protest against the Scouts and all their pomps. He had spent the afternoon walking under the campus elms. "Then you were there," Mac had said, which Myles had taken to mean that Mac felt as he did about those beautiful old trees.

Mac delivered a little pep talk, chiefly for the benefit of the three Fathers in the office, Myles suspected, although the words were spoken to him. He could think of nothing to say. He was more impressed by the charitable than the catechetical aspects of the Fathers' work. And yet, little as he might value their radio program, their pamphlets, their dim magazine, it would be work with which he could associate himself with some enthusiasm. It would suit his purposes far better than going into business or staying on at the hospital.

"The Work is one hundred per cent apostolic," said one of the Fathers.

Myles remembered that the Fathers ran several institutions for juvenile delinquents. "I know something of your trade schools," he said quickly.

"Would that we had more of them," said the Father sitting behind the desk. He had bloodied his face and neck in shaving. "You have to move with the times." He seemed to be the boss. On the wall behind him hung a metal crucifix, which could have come off a coffin, and a broken airplane propeller, which must have dated from the First World War. "How do you stand in the draft?" he asked Myles.

"All clear," said Mac, answering for him. Myles let that pass, too. He could tell Mac the facts later.

When Myles heard what the salary would be, he was glad he had other reasons for taking the job. The money would be the least important part of it, Mac put in, and Myles could see what he meant. But Myles didn't care about the money; he'd live on bread and water—and pamphlets. The salary made him feel better about not telling Mac and the Fathers that he intended to use his new position, if he could, to meet a bishop. The expense allowance, too, impressed him as decidedly pre-war. Mac, however, seemed to be hinting not at its meanness but at Myles' possible profligacy when, in front of two more Fathers, who had come in to meet Myles, he said, "You'll have to watch your expenses, Flynn. Can't have you asking for reimbursements, you understand." As Myles was leaving, one of the new arrivals whispered to him, "I was on the road myself for a bit and I'd dearly love to go out again. Mr. McMaster, he's a grand companion. You'll make a great team."

Three days later the team was heading north in Mac's car, a lightweight black Cadillac, a '41—a good year for a Cadillac, Mac said, and the right car for the job: impressive but not showy, and old enough not to antagonize people.

Myles was not sorry to be leaving Chicago. The nuns and nurses at the hospital had been happy to see him go—happy, they said, that he'd found a better job. This showed Myles how little they had ever understood him and his reasons for being at the hospital; he'd known all along that they had very little sense of vocation.

Speaking of the nurses, Myles told Mac that the corporal works of mercy had lost all meaning in the modern world, to which Mac replied that he wouldn't touch nursing with a ten-foot pole. Nursing might be a fine career for a girl, he allowed, and added, "A lot of 'em marry above themselves— marry money."

They were like two men in a mine, working at different levels, in different veins, and lost to each other. Mac, who apparently still thought of Myles as a doctor, wanted to know how much the internes and nurses knocked down and what their private lives were like—said he'd heard a few stories. When Myles professed ignorance, Mac seemed to think he was being secretive, as if the question went against the Hippocratic oath. He tried to discuss medicine, with special reference to his diet, but failed to interest Myles. He asked what the hospital did with the stiffs, and received no pertinent information, because the question happened to remind Myles of the medieval burial confraternities and he sailed into a long discussion of their blessed work, advocating its revival in the modern world.

"All free, huh?" Mac commented. "The undertakers would love that!"

Myles strove in vain for understanding, always against the wind. Mac had got the idea that Myles, in praising the burial fraternities, was advocating a form of socialized medicine, and he held on to it. "Use logic," he said. "What's right for the undertakers is right for the doctors."

They rode in silence for a while. Then Mac said, "What you say about the nurses may be true, but you gotta remember they don't have it easy." He knew how Myles felt about hospital work, he said, but instead of letting it prey on his mind, Myles should think of other things—of the better days ahead. Mac implied that Myles' talk about the corporal works was just a cover-up for his failure to get into anything better.

Myles restated his position. Mac, with noticeable patience, said that Myles was too hard on people—too critical of the modern world. "Give it time," he said. When Myles persisted, Mac said, "Let's give it a rest, huh? You wanna take it awhile?" He stopped the car and turned the wheel over to Myles. After watching him pass a Greyhound bus, he appeared to be satisfied that the car was in good hands, and went to sleep.

The first night on the road they stopped in a small town, at the only hotel, which had no bar, and Mac suggested that they go out for a drink. In a tavern, the bartender, when he found out they were from Chicago, showed them his collection of matchbooks with nudes on the cover.

"I have a friend that'll get you all that you want," Mac said to him. "You better avert your eyes, son," he said to Myles. "This is some of that modern world you don't like. He doesn't like our modern world," Mac said to the bartender.

"Maybe he don't know what he's missing."

The bartender seemed anxious to make a deal until Mac asked him to put down a little deposit "as evidence of good faith."

"Do I have to?"

"To me it's immaterial," Mac said. "But I notice it sometimes speeds delivery."

"I can wait."

"All right, if you're sure you can. You write your name and address on a slip of paper and how many you want." While the bartender was doing this, Mac called over to him, "Don't forget your zone number."

"We don't have 'em in this town."

"Oh," Mac said. He gave Myles a look, the wise, doped look of a camel.

The bartender brought the slip of paper over to Mac. "They gotta be as good as them I got—or better," he said, and walked away.

Mac, watching him, matched him word for step: "When-you-gonna-get-those-corners-sawed-off-your-head?"

Leaving the tavern with Mac, Myles saw the wind take the slip of paper up the street.

"My friend can do without that kind of business," Mac said.

Mac began operations on a freezing cold day in central Wisconsin, and right away Myles was denied his first opportunity. While Mac went into a chancery office to negotiate with the bishop, who would (or would not) grant permission to canvass the diocese, Myles had to wait outside in the car, with the engine running; Mac said he was worried about the battery. This bishop was one with whom Myles had already corresponded unsuccessfully, but that was small consolation to him, in view of his plan to plead his case before as many bishops as possible, without reference to past failures. How he'd manage it with Mac in attendance, he didn't know. Perhaps he could use the initial interview for analysis only and, attempting to see the bishop as an opponent in a game, try to uncover his weakness, and then call back alone later and play upon it. Myles disapproved of cunning, and rather doubted whether he could carry out such a scheme. But he also recalled that puzzling but practical advice, "Be ye therefore wise as serpents and simple as doves," the first part of which the bishops themselves, he believed, were at such pains to follow in their dealings with him.

The next day Mac invited Myles to accompany him indoors when he paid his calls upon the pastors. The day was no warmer but Mac said nothing about the battery. He said, "You've got a lot to learn, son," and proceeded to give Myles some pointers. In some dioceses, according to Mac, the bishop's permission was all you needed; get that, and the pastors—always excepting a few incorrigibles—would drop like ripe fruit. Unfortunately, in such dioceses the bishop's permission wasn't always easy to obtain. Of course you got in to see bishops personally (this in reply to a question from Myles), but most of the time you were working with pastors. There were two kinds of pastors, Mac said—those who honestly believed they knew everything and those who didn't. With the first, it was best to appear helpless (as, in fact, you were) and try to get them interested in doing your job for you. With the other kind, you had to appear confident, promise them the moon—something they were always looking for anyway—tell them a change might come over their people if they were exposed to the pamphlets and the *Clementine*. Of course, no pastor had a right to expect such a miracle, but many did expect it even so, if the pamphlets and the *Clementine* hadn't been tried in the parish before. You'd meet some, though, Mac said, who would be cold, even opposed, to the Work, and offensive to you, and with them you took a beating—but cheerfully, hoping for a change of heart later. More than one of that kind had come around in the end, he said, and one of them had even written a glowing letter to the Fathers, complimenting them on the high type of layman they had working for them, and had placed an order for a rack of pamphlets on condition that Mac received credit for it. Then there were the others—those who would do everything they could to help you, wanted to feed you and put you up overnight, but they, for some reason, were found more often in the country, or in poor city parishes, where little could be accomplished and where you seldom went.

On the third day out, they came across one of the incorrigibles. He greeted them with a snarl. "You guys're a breed apart," he said. Myles was offended, but Mac, undaunted, went into his routine for cracking hard nuts. "Don't know much about this job, I'm ashamed to say," he said, "but it's sure a lot of fun learning." The pastor, instead of going out of his way to help a cheerful soul like Mac (and a nervous one like Myles), ordered them out of the rectory, produced a golf club when they didn't go and, when they did, stood at the front window, behind a lace curtain, until they drove off.

Before the end of the first week, Myles discovered that Mac wasn't really interested in getting permission to canvass a parish house-to-house. He said he just didn't care that much about people. What he liked was co-operation; he liked to have a pastor in the pulpit doing the donkey work and the ushers in the aisles dispensing pencil stubs and subscription blanks, with him just sitting at a card table in the vestibule after Mass, smiling at the new sub-scribers as they passed out, making change, and croaking, "God love you." That was what Mac called "a production." He operated on a sliding scale— a slippery one, Myles thought. In a big, well-to-do parish, where the take would be high, Mac cut prices. He was also prepared to make an offering toward the upkeep of the church, or to the pastor's favorite charity (the latter was often the former), and to signify his intention beforehand. He had to hustle, he said, in order to meet the stiff competition of the missionaries; a layman, even if he represented a recognized religious order, was always at a disadvantage. Fortunately, he said, there were quite a few secular pastors who, though they didn't care for the orders, didn't consider the struggling Clementines a menace. But there weren't many pastors with flourishing parishes who would co-operate with Mac or with anybody. They were sitting pretty, Mac said, and they knew it. If he now and then succeeded with one of them, it was only because he was liked personally—or, as it seemed to Myles, because of what Mac called "the package deal." The package deal didn't actually involve the Work, Mac was careful to explain, but it sometimes helped it. And, Myles felt, compromised it.

The package deal always began with Mac's opening his bag of tricks. It was a Gladstone bag, which he had got from a retired cooky salesman. When open, it looked like a little stadium, and where the cookies had once been on display, in their individual plastic sections, ranged in tiers, there were now rosaries, medals, scapulars—religious goods of the usual quality, which didn't catch the eye in many rectories. But there were also playing cards with saints as face cards—in one deck the Devil was the joker—and these were new to some priests, as they were to Myles, and had strong educational appeal. Children could familiarize themselves with the lives of the saints from them, and there were other decks, which taught Christian doctrine. Mac had a new kind of rosary, too. It was made of plastic, to fit the hand, and in function and appearance it was similar to an umpire's ball-and-strike indicator. Each time a little key was punched, the single dial, which showed the Mysteries—Sorrowful, Joyful, and Glorious—revolved a notch, and for the Ave Marias there was a modest tick, for the Pater Nosters an authoritative click. Mac had difficulty explaining the new rosary's purpose to some priests—*not* to replace the old model, the traditional beads on a string, but to facilitate prayer while driving, for the new rosary was easily attached to the steering wheel. "Of course, you still have to say the prayers," Mac would say.

Mac gave freely from his bag. Other things, however, he sold—just as an accommodation, he said, to priests, whose work naturally left them little time for shopping. He seemed to have a friend in every business that a parish priest might have to deal with. Myles saw him take large orders for automatic bingo cards (with built-in simulated corn counters), and the trunk of the car was full of catalogues and of refills for the grab bag. "There's one for you, Father," he'd say, presenting a pastor with one of the new rosaries. Later, speaking earnestly of power lawnmowers, of which he happened to have a prospectus showing pictures and prices, he'd say, "That's practically cost minus, Father. He"—referring to a friend—"can't do better than that, I know."

One day, when they were driving along, Myles, at the wheel, asked about Mac's friends.

"Friends? Who said I had any?" Mac snapped.

"I keep hearing you talking about your friends."

"Is that *so?*" Some miles later, after complete silence, Mac said, "I'm a man of many friends—and I don't make a dime on any of 'em." Still later, "The Fathers know all about it."

This Myles doubted. The Fathers were forbidden to engage in business for profit, he knew, and he believed that Mac, as their representative, was probably subject to the same prohibition. It was a question, though, whether Mac was primarily the Fathers' representative or his friends' or his own. It was hard to believe that *everyone* was only breaking even. And Myles felt sure that if the Fathers knew about the package deal, they'd think they had to act. But a replacement for Mac would be hard to find. The *Clementine*, as Myles was discovering, was not an easy magazine to sell. The pamphlets weren't moving well, either.

Without knowing it at the time, Myles saw a variation of the package deal worked on a pastor who met them in his front yard, baying, "I know all about you! Go!" Myles was more than ready to go, but Mac said, "You know, Monsignor, I believe you do know about me." "Don't call me Monsignor!" "My mistake, Father." Mac's voice was as oil being poured out. "Father, something you said just now makes me want to say something to you, only it's not anything I care to say in front of others." "Whatever you have to say can be said now," the pastor mumbled. "Believe me, Father, I can't say it—not in front of this boy," Mac said, nodding at Myles. Then, in a stage whisper to Myles, "You better go, son." Myles hesitated, expecting to hear the pastor overrule Mac, but nothing of the sort happened, and Myles went out and sat in the car. Mac and the pastor, a fierce-looking, beak-nosed Irish type, began to walk slowly around the yard, and presently disappeared behind the rectory. Then, after a bit, there was Mac, coming out the front door and calling to Myles from the porch, "Come on in!" Myles went in and shook hands with the pastor, actually a gentle silver-haired man. He asked them to stay for lunch, but Mac graciously refused, insisting it would be too much trouble for the housekeeper. On the following Sunday morning, this same pastor, a marvelous speaker, preached in behalf of the Work, calling the *Clementine* "that dandy little magazine" at all five Masses. Myles attended them all, while Mac hobnobbed with the ushers in the vestibule. Between Masses, the two of them, sitting at the card table, worked like bookmakers between races. Afterward, when they were driving away, Mac announced that the team had had its most successful day. That evening, in a new town, relaxing in the cocktail lounge of their hotel, Mac gave up his secret. He said he had diagnosed the pastor perfectly and had taken the pledge from him—that was all. Seeing that Myles disapproved, he said, "It so happened I needed it." Myles, who was getting to know Mac, couldn't quarrel with that.

Mac and Myles moved constantly from town to town and diocese to diocese, and almost every night Myles had the problem of locating suitable accommodations. He soon saw that he would not be able to afford the hotels and meals to which Mac was accustomed, and finally he complained. Mac looked hurt. He said, "We don't do the Work for profit, you know." He only got by himself, he said, by attributing part of his living expenses to the car. He wasn't misusing the swindle sheet, though; he was adapting it to circumstances beyond his control. There really *were* expenses. "I don't have to tell you that," he said "The Fathers, God love 'em, just don't understand how prices have gone up." Myles' predecessor, a fellow named Jack, had put up in "the more reasonable hotels and rooming houses," and Mac suggested that Myles do the same, for a while. "Later, when you're doing better, you could stay in regular hotels."

"Is that what Jack did—later?" Myles asked.

"No. Jack seemed to like the kind of places he stayed in." Jack, in fact, had quit the Work in order to stay on in one of them, and was now engaged to the landlady. "In some ways, Jack wasn't meant for the Work," Mac added. "But we had some fine times together and I hated to see him go. He was a damn fine driver. Not that that's everything."

It had become an important part of Myles' job to do all the driving and put the car away at night and bring it around to the hotel in the morning for Mac and his luggage. More and more, Mac rode in the back seat. (he said he preferred the ashtray there.) But there was no glass between the front and back seats, and the arrangement did not interfere with conversation or alter Mac's friendliness. Occasionally, they'd arrive in a town late at night—too late for Myles to look for one of the more reasonable places— and Mac would say, mercifully, "Come on. Stay with me." And on those nights Mac would pick up the tab. This could also happen even when they arrived in plenty of time for Myles to look around, provided the drive had been a long one and Myles had played the good listener.

The association between the two was generally close, and becoming closer. Mac talked frankly about his ex-friends, of whom there were many—mostly former associates or rivals in the general-merchandise field, double-crossers to a man. The first few times this happened, Myles controlled his desire to tell Mac that by damning others, as he did, he damned the whole human race—damned himself, in fact. One day, after Mac had finished with his old friends and with his wife (who was no good), and was beginning to go to work on the Jews (who also had given him nothing but trouble), Myles did tell him. He presented an idea he held to be even greater than the idea of brotherhood. It was the doctrine of the Mystical Body of Christ. Humanity was one great body, Myles explained, all united with Christ, the Saviour. Mac acted as though the doctrine were a new one on him. "One great body, huh? Sounds like the Mystical Knights of the Sea," he said, and talked for a while of Amos and Andy and of the old days when they'd been Sam and Henry. That was the afternoon that Mac got onto the subject of his dream.

Mac's dream—as he spoke, the snow was going from gray to ghostly blue and the lights were coming on in the houses along the way—was to own a turkey ranch and a church-goods store. What he really wanted was the ranch, he said, but he supposed he'd have to play it safe and have the store, too. Turkeys could be risky. With the general revival of interest in religion, however, a well-run church-goods store would be sure to succeed. He'd sell by mail, retail and wholesale, and there'd be discounts for everybody—not just for the clergy, though, of course, he'd have to give them the usual break. The store would be a regular clearinghouse: everything from holy cards to statues—products of all the leading manufacturers.

"Sort of a supermarket?" Myles asked, thinking of chalices and turkeys roosting all in a row.

"That's the idea."

"It'd be nice if there were one place in this country where you could get an honest-piece of ecclesiastical art," Myles said.

"I'd have that, too, later," Mac said. "A custom department."

They were getting along very well, different as they were. Mac *was* a good traveling companion, ready wherever they went with a little quick information about the towns ("Good for business," "All Swedes," "Wide open"), the small change of real knowledge.

One day, when they were passing through Superior, Wisconsin, Mac said that originally the iron-ore interests had planned to develop the town. Property values had been jacked up, however, by operators too smart for their own good, and everything had gone to Duluth, with its relatively inferior harbor. That was how Superior, favored by nature, had become what it was, a small town with the layout of a metropolis.

"It's easier to move mountains than greedy hearts," Myles commented.

"I wouldn't know," Mac said.

Myles found the story of Superior instructive—positively Biblical, he said. Another case of man's greed. The country thereabouts also proved interesting to Myles, but difficult for Mac when Myles began to expound on the fished-out lakes (man's greed), the cut-over timberland (man's greed), the poor Indians (the *white* man's greed). The high-grade ore pits, Mac foolishly told him, were almost exhausted.

"Exhausted for what?" Myles asked.

"Steel," said Mac, who didn't realize the question had been rhetorical.

"This car!" said Myles, with great contempt. "War!" Looking into the rearview mirror, he saw Mac indulging in what was becoming a habit with him—pulling on his ear lobes.

"What *are* you?" Mac finally demanded. "Some kind of a new damn fool?"

But Myles never gave up on him. He went right on making his points, laying the ground for an awakening; it might never come to Mac, but Myles carried on as if it might at any moment. Mac, allied with the modern world for better or worse, defended the indefensible and fought back. And when logic failed him, he spluttered, "You talk like you got holes in your head," or, "Quit moanin'!" or, "Who you think you are, buster—the Pope?"

"This is when you're *really* hard to take!" Mac said one day, when the news from Korea was bad and Myles was most telling, Myles continued obliviously, perceiving moral links between Hiroshima and Korea and worse things to come, and predicting universal retribution, weeping, and gnashing of teeth. "And why?" he said. "Greed!"

"Greed! Greed! Is that all you can think about? No wonder they had to get rid of you!"

A few miles of silence followed, and then a few well-chosen words from Mac, who had most certainly been thinking, which was just what Myles was always trying to get him to do. "Are you sure the place you escaped from was a seminary?" he asked.

But Myles let him see he could take even this, turning the other cheek so gracefully that Mac could never know his words were touching a sore spot.

Later that day, in the middle of a sermon from Myles, they passed a paddy wagon and Mac said, "They're looking for you." Ever after, if Myles discoursed too long or too well on the state of the modern world, there came a tired but amiable croaking from the back seat, "They're looking for you."

At night, however, after the bars closed, it was *Mac* who was looking for Myles. If they were staying at the same hotel, he'd knock at Myles' door and say, "Care to come over to the room for a drink?" At first, Myles, seeing no way out of it, would go along, though not for a drink. He drank beer when he drank, or wine, and there was never any of either in Mac's room. It was no fun spending the last hour of the day with Mac. He had a lot of stories, but Myles often missed the point of them, and he knew none himself—none that Mac would appreciate, anyway. What Cardinal Merry del Val had said to Cardinal Somebody Else—the usual seminary stuff. But Mac found a subject to interest *him*. He began denying that Myles was a cradle Catholic. Myles, who had never seen in this accident of birth the personal achievement that Mac seemed to see, would counter, "All right. What if I weren't one?"

"You see? You see?" Mac would say, looking very wise and drunk. Then, as if craving and expecting a confession, he'd say, "You can tell *me*."

Myles had nothing to tell, and Mac would start over again, on another tack. Developing his thought about what he called Myles' "ideas," he would arrive at the only possible conclusion: Myles wasn't a Catholic at all. He was probably only a smart-aleck convert who had come into the Church when the coming was good, and only *thought* he was in.

"Do you deny the possibility of conversion?" Myles would ask, though there was small pleasure in theologizing with someone like Mac.

Mac never answered the question. He'd just keep saying, "You call yourself a *Catholic*—a *cradle* Catholic?"

The first time Myles said no to Mac's invitation to come over and have one, it worked. The next time, Mac went back to his room only to return with his bottle, saying "Thought you might like to have one in your pajamas." That was the night Myles told Mac, hopefully, that whiskey was a Protestant invention; in Ireland, for example, it had been used, more effectively than the penal laws, to enslave the faithful. "Who're you kiddin'!" Mac wailed.

Mere admonishment failed with Mac. One day, as they were driving through primitive country, Myles delivered a regular sermon on the subject of drink. He said a man possessed by drink was a man possessed by the Devil. He said that Mac, at night, was very like a devil, going about hotel corridors "as a roaring lion goeth about seeking whom he may devour." This must have hit Mac pretty hard, for he said nothing in his own defense; in fact, he took it very well, gazing out at the pine trees, which Myles, in the course of his sermon, had asked him to consider in all their natural beauty. That afternoon, they met another hard nut—and Mac took the pledge again, which closed the deal for a production on the following Sunday, and also, he seemed to think, put him into Myles' good graces. "I wish I could find one that could give it to me and make it stick," he said.

"Don't come to me when I'm a priest," said Myles, who had still to see his first bishop.

That night Mac and the bottle were at the door again. Myles, in bed, did not respond. This was a mistake. Mac phoned the office and had them bring up a key and open Myles' door, all because he thought Myles might be sick. "I love that boy!" he proclaimed, on his way back to his room at last. Later that night Myles heard him in the corridor, at a little distance, with another drunk. Mac was roaring, "I'm seein' who I may devour!"

More and more, Myles and Mac were staying together in the same hotels, and Myles, though saving money by this arrangement (money, however, that he never saw), wondered if he wasn't paying too much for economy. He felt slightly kept. Mac only wanted him handy late at night, it seemed, so as to have someone with whom to take his pleasure, which was haranguing. Myles now understood better why Jack had liked the places he stayed in. Or was this thing that Mac was doing to him nightly something new for Mac? Something that Myles had brought upon himself? He was someone whom people looking for trouble always seemed to find. It had happened to him in the hospital, in the seminary, in the Boy Scouts. If a million people met in one place, and he was there, he was certain that the worst of them would rise as a man and make for him.

But Mac wasn't always looking for trouble. One afternoon, for no reason at all, he bought Myles a Hawaiian sports shirt. "For next summer," Mac said, as if they would always be together. The shirt was a terrible thing to look at—soiled merchandise picked up at a sale—but it might mean something. Was it possible that Mac, in his fashion, liked him?

"A fellow like you might handle that end of it,"Mac said one day in the car. He had been talking about the store part of his dream and how he would put out a big catalogue in which it would be wise for manufacturers—and maybe religious orders, too—to buy advertising if they expected to do business with him. "Interested?" he asked.

Myles was definitely not interested, but he was touched by the offer, since it showed that Mac trusted him. It was time to put matters straight between them. Myles spoke then of *his* dream—of the great desire he had to become a priest. Not a punch-drunk seminary professor or a fat cat in a million-dollar parish, he said, but a simple shepherd ministering gently to the poorest of God's poor. He wouldn't mind being a priest-worker, like those already functioning so successfully in France, according to reports reaching him. "That can't happen here," Mac said. Myles, however, saw difficult times ahead for the nation—Here Mac started to open his mouth but grabbed instead for his ears. Myles felt pretty sure that there would soon be priest-workers slaving away in fields and factories by day and tending to the spiritual needs of their poor fellow-workers by night.

"Poor?" Mac asked. "What about the unions? When I think what those boys take home!"

Myles then explored the more immediate problem of finding a bishop to sponsor him.

Mac said he knew several quite well and he might speak to them.

"I wish you would," Myles said. "The two I've seen looked impossible." Then, having said that much—too much—he confessed to Mac his real reason for taking the job: the urgency of his position with regard to Selective Service.

Immediately, Mac, who had not been paying much attention, released an ear for listening. He appeared ill-disposed toward Myles' reluctance to serve in the armed forces, or, possibly, toward such frankness.

"I can't serve two masters," Myles said, Mac was silent; he'd gone absolutely dead. "Are you a veteran?" Myles asked.

"Since you ask," Mac said, "I'll tell you. I served and was wounded—honorably—in both World Wars. If there's another one, I hope to do my part. Does that answer your question?" Myles said that it did, and he could think of nothing to say just then that wouldn't hurt Mac's feelings.

That night, Mac, in his cups, surpassed himself. He got through with the usual accusations early and began threatening Myles with "exposure." "Dodgin' the draft!" Mac howled. "I oughta turn you in."

Myles said he hadn't broken the law *yet*.

"But you *intend* to," Mac said. "I oughta turn you in."

"I'll turn myself in when the time comes," Myles said.

"Like hell you will. You'll go along until they catch up with you. Then they'll clap you in jail—where you belong."

"Maybe you're right," Myles said, thinking of St. Paul and other convicts.

"Then you'll wish you were in the Army—where you belong. I'm not sure it's not my duty to report you. Let's see your draft card."

Myles let him see it.

" 'Flynn, Myles'—that you? How do I know you're not somebody else by the same name?"

Myles made no reply. Had prohibition been so wrong, he wondered.

"Don't wanna incriminate yourself, huh? Hey, you're 1-A! Didja see that?"

Myles explained, as he had before, that he was awaiting his induction notice.

"Bet you are! Bet you can hardly wait! I'd better hold onto this." Mac slipped Myles' draft card into his pocket.

In the morning, Myles got the card back. Mac, sober, returned it, saying he'd found it in his room, where Myles (who had not been there) must have dropped it. "Better hold on to that," Mac said.

The next night Myles managed to stay in a rooming house, out of reach, but the following night they were together again, and Mac asked to see Myles' draft card again. Myles wouldn't give it up. "I deny your authority," he said, himself emboldened by drink—two beers.

"Here's my authority!" Mac cried. He loosened his trousers and pulled up his shirt in front, exposing a stomach remarkably round, smooth, veined, and, in places, blue, like a world globe. There was a scar on it. "How d'ya think I got that?"

"Appendicitis," Myles said.

There was no doubt of it. The scar testified to Mac's fraudulence as nothing else had, and for once Mac seemed to know it. He'd strayed into a field in which he believed Myles to be supreme. Putting his stomach away, he managed a tone in which there was misgiving, outrage, and sarcasm. "That's right. That's right. You know everything. You were a bedpan jockey. I forgot about that."

Myles watched him, amused. Mac might have saved himself by telling the truth or by quickly laughing it off, but he lied on. "Shrapnel—some still inside," he said. He coughed and felt his stomach, as if his lungs were there, but he didn't get it out again. "Not asking *you* to believe it," he said. "Won't show *you* my other wound."

"Please don't," said Myles. He retired that night feeling that he had the upper hand.

One week later, leaving a town in Minnesota where they had encountered a difficult bishop, Mac ordered Myles to stop at a large, gabled rectory of forbidding aspect. As it turned out, however, they enjoyed a good dinner there, and afterward the pastor summoned three of his colleagues for a little game of blackjack—in Mac's honor, Myles heard him say as the players trooped upstairs.

Myles spent the evening downstairs with the curate. While they were eating some fudge the curate had made that afternoon, they discovered that they had many of the same enthusiasms and prejudices. The curate wanted Myles to understand that the church was not his idea, loaded up, as it was, with junk. He was working on the pastor to throw out most of the statues and all the vigil lights. It was a free-talking, free-swinging session, the best evening for Myles since leaving the seminary. In a nice but rather futile tribute to Myles, the curate said that if the two of them were pastors, they might, perhaps, transform the whole diocese. He in no way indicated that he thought there was anything wrong with Myles because he had been asked to leave the seminary. He believed, as Myles did, that there was no *good* reason for the dismissal. He said he'd had trouble getting through himself and he thought that the seminary, as an institution, was probably responsible for the way Stalin, another aspirant to the priesthood, had turned out. The curate also strongly disapproved of Mac, and of Myles' reasons for continuing in the Work. He said the Clementines were a corny outfit, and no bishop in his right mind, seeing Myles with Mac, would ever take a chance on him. The curate thought that Myles might be playing it too cautious. He'd do better, perhaps, just to go around the country, hitchhiking from see to see, washing dishes if he had to, but calling on bishops personally—as many as he could in the time that remained before he got his induction notice.

"How many bishops have you actually seen?" the curate asked.

"Three. But I couldn't say anything with Mac right there. I would've gone back later, though, if there'd been a chance at all with those I saw."

The curate sniffed. "How could you tell?" he asked. "I thought you were desperate. You just *can't* be guided entirely by private revelation. You have a higher injunction: 'Seek, and you shall find.' Perhaps you still haven't thought this thing *through*. I wonder. Perhaps you don't pray enough?"

Myles, noticing in the curate a tendency to lecture and feeling that he'd suffered one "perhaps" too many, defended himself, saying, "The man we met today wouldn't let us set foot on church property in his diocese. What can you do with a bishop like that?"

"The very one you should have persevered with! Moses, you may remember, had to do more than look at the rock. He had to strike it."

"Twice, unfortunately," murmured Myles, not liking the analogy. Moses, wavering in his faith, had struck twice and had not reached the Promised Land; he had only seen it in the distance and died.

"It may not be too late," the curate said. "I'd try that one again if I were you."

Myles laughed. "*That* one was your own bishop," he said.

"The bishop said that?" The curate showed some alarm and seemed suddenly a lot less friendly. "Is that why you're here, then—why Mac's here, I mean?"

"I couldn't tell you why I'm here," Myles said. In Mac's defense, he said, "I don't think he's mentioned the Work here." It was true. Mac and the pastor had hit it off right away, talking of other things.

"I heard him trying to sell the pastor a new roof—a copper one. Also an oil burner. Does he deal in *those* things?" the curate asked.

"He has friends who do." Myles smiled. He wanted to say more on this subject to amuse the curate, if that was still possible; he wanted to confide in him again; he wanted to say whatever would be necessary to save the evening. But the shadow of the bishop had fallen upon them. There were only crumbs on the fudge plate; the evening had ended. It was bedtime, the curate said. He offered Myles a Coke, which Myles refused, then showed him to a couch in the parlor, gave him a blanket, and went off to bed.

Some time later—it was still night—Mac woke Myles and they left the rectory. Mac was sore; he said he'd lost a bundle. He climbed into the back seat and wrapped himself in the car rug. "A den of thieves. I'm pretty sure I was taken. Turn on the heater." And then he slept while Myles drove away toward the dawn.

The next day, as they were having dinner in another diocese, another town, another hotel—Mac looked fresh; he'd slept all day—Myles told him that he was quitting.

"Soon?" said Mac.

"Right away."

"Give me a little time to think about it."

After dinner, Mac drew one of his good cigars out of its aluminum scabbard. "What is it? Money? Because if it is—" Mac said, puffing on the cigar, and then, looking at the cigar and not at Myles, he outlined his plans. He'd try to get more money for Myles from the Fathers, more take-home dough and more for expenses. He'd sensed that Myles had been unhappy in some of those flea bags; Myles might have noticed that they'd been staying together oftener. Ultimately, if the two of them were still together and everything went right, there might be a junior partnership for Myles in the store. "No." Mac said, looking at Myles. "I can see that's not what you want." He turned to the cigar again and asked, "Well, why not?" He invited Myles up to his room, where, he said, he might have something to say that would be of interest to him.

Upstairs, after making himself a drink, Mac said that he just might be able to help Myles in the only way he wanted to be helped. He was on fairly good terms with a number of bishops, as Myles might have gathered, but an even better bet would be the Clementines. Myles could join the order as a lay brother—*anybody* could do that—swiftly win the confidence of his superiors, then switch to the seminary, and thus complete his studies for the priesthood. "I might be able to give you such a strong recommendation that you could go straight into the seminary," Mac said. "It would mean losing you, of course. Don't like that part. Or *would* it? What's to stop us from going on together, like now, after you get your degree?"

"After *ordination?*" Myles asked.

"There you are!" Mac exclaimed. "Just shows it's a natural—us working as a team. What I don't know, you do."

While Mac strengthened his drink just a little—he was cutting down—Myles thanked him for what he'd done to date and also for what he was prepared to do. He said that he doubted, however, that he was meant for the Clementines or for the community life, and even if he were, there would still be the problem of finding a bishop to sponsor him. "Oh, *they'd* do all that," Mac said. Myles shook his head. He was quitting. He had to intensify his efforts. He wasn't getting to see many bishops, was he? Time was of the essence. He had a few ideas he wanted to pursue on his own (meaning he had one—to have another crack at the curate's bishop). The induction notice, his real worry, might come any day.

"How d'ya know you're all right physically?" Mac asked him. "You don't look very strong to me. I took you for a born 4-F. For all you know, you might be turned down and out lookin' for a job. In the circumstances, I couldn't promise to hold this one open forever."

With the usual apprehension, Myles watched Mac pour another drink. Could Mac want so badly for an underpaid chauffeur, he wondered. Myles' driving was his only asset. As a representative of the Fathers, he was a flop, and he knew it, and so did Mac. Mac, in his own words, was the baby that delivered the goods. But no layman could be as influential as Mac claimed to be with the Fathers, hard up though they were for men and money. Mac wouldn't be able to help with any bishop in his right mind. But Mac did want him around, and Myles, who could think of no one else who did, was almost tempted to stay as long as he could. Maybe he *was* 4-F.

Later that evening Mac, still drinking, put it another way, or possibly said what he'd meant to say earlier. "Hell, you'll never pass the mental test. Never let a character like you in the Army." The Fathers, though, would be glad to have Myles, if Mac said the word.

Myles thanked him again. Mac wanted him to drive the car, to do the Work, but what he wanted still more, it was becoming clear, was to have a boon companion, and Myles knew he just couldn't stand to be it.

"You're not my type," Mac said. "You haven't got it—the velocity, I mean—but maybe that's why I like you."

Myles was alone again with his thoughts, walking the plank of his gloom.

"Don't worry," Mac said. "I'll always have a spot in my heart for you. A place in my business."

"In the supermarket?"

Mac frowned. Drinking, after a point, made him appear a little cross-eyed. "I wish you wouldn't use that word," he said distinctly. "If y'wanna know, your trouble's words. Make y'self harda take. Don't *have* to be jerk. Looka you. Young. Looka me. Dead. Not even Catholic. Bloody Orangeman 'S truth."

Myles couldn't believe it. And then he could, almost. He'd never seen Mac at Mass on Sundays, either coming or going, except when they were working, and then Mac kept to the vestibule. The bunk that Mac had talked about Myles' being a cradle Catholic began to make sense.

"Now you're leaving the Work, I tell you," Mac was saying. "Makes no difference now." They were in Minnesota, staying in a hotel done in the once popular Moorish style, and the ceiling light and the shades of the bed lamps, and consequently the walls and Myles' face, were dead orange and Mac's face was bloody orange.

Myles got up to leave.

"Don't go," Mac said. He emptied the bottle.

But Myles went, saying it was bedtime. He realized as he said it that he sounded like the curate the night before.

Ten minutes later Mac was knocking at Myles' door. He was in his stocking feet, but looked better, like a drunk getting a hold on himself.

"Something to read," he said. "Don't feel like sleeping."

Myles had some books in his suitcase, but he left them there. "I didn't get a paper," he said.

"Don't want that," Mac said. He saw the Gideon Bible on the night stand and went over to it. "Mind if I swipe this?"

"There's probably one in your room."

Mac didn't seem to hear. He picked up the Gideon. "The Good Book," he said.

"I've got a little Catholic Bible," Myles said. The words came out of themselves—the words of a diehard proselytizer.

"Have you? Yeah, that's the one I want."

"I can't recommend it," Myles said, on second thought. "You better take the other one, for reading. It's the King James."

"Hell with that!" Mac said. He put the King James from him.

Myles went to the suitcase and got out his portable Bible. He stood with it at the door, making Mac come for it, and then, still withholding it, led him outside into the corridor, where he finally handed it over.

"How you feel now, about that other?" Mac asked.

For a moment, Myles thought he was being asked about his induction, which Mac ordinarily referred to as "that other," and not about Mac's dark secret. When he got Mac's meaning, he said, "Don't worry about me. I won't turn you in."

In the the light of his activities, Mac's not being a Catholic was in his favor, from Myles' point of view; as an honest faker Mac was more acceptable, though many would not see it that way. There was something else, though, in Mac's favor—something unique; he was somebody who liked Myles just for himself. He had been betrayed by affection—and by the bottle, of course.

Myles watched Mac going down the corridor in his stocking feet toward his room, holding the Bible and swaying just a little, as if he were walking on calm water. He wasn't so drunk.

The next morning Mac returned the Bible to Myles in his room and said, "I don't know if you realize it or not, but I'm sorry about last night. I guess I said a lot of things I shouldn't have. I won't stand in your way any longer." He reached into his pocket and took out his roll. "You'll need some of this," he said.

"No thanks," Myles said.

"You sure?"

Myles was sure.

"Forget anything I might have said." Mac eased over to the window and looked out upon the main street. "I don't know what, but I might have said something." He came back to Myles. He was fingering his roll, holding it in both hands, a fat red squirrel with a nut. "You sure now?"

Myles said yes, he was sure, and Mac reluctantly left him.

Myles was wondering if that had been their good-by when, a few minutes later, Mac came in again. His manner was different. "I'll put it to you like this," he said. "You don't say anything about me and I won't say anything about you. Maybe we both got trouble. You know what I'm talking about?"

Myles said that he thought he knew and that Mac needn't worry.

"They may never catch you," Mac said, and went away again. Myles wondered if *that* had been their good-by.

Presently Mac came in again. "I don't remember if I told you this last night or not. I know I was going to, but what with one thing and another last night, and getting all hung up—"

"Well?"

"Kid"—it was the first time Mac had called him that—"I'm not a Catholic."

Myles nodded.

"Then I did say something about it?"

Myles nodded again. He didn't know what Mac was trying now, only that he was trying something.

"I don't know what I am," Mac said. "My folks weren't much good. I lost 'em when I was quite young. And you know about my wife." Myles knew about her. "No damn good."

Myles listened and nodded while all those who had ever failed Mac came in for slaughter. Mac ordinarily did this dirty work in the car, and it had always seemed to Myles that they threw out the offending bodies, one by one, making room for the fresh ones. It was getting close in the room. Mac stood upright amid a wreckage of carcasses—with Myles.

"You're the only one I can turn to," he said. "I'd be afraid to admit to anyone else what I've just admitted to you—I mean to a priest. As you know, I'm pretty high up in the Work, respected, well thought of, and all that, and you can imagine what your average priest is going to think if *I* come to him—to be baptized!"

The scene rather appealed to Myles, but he looked grave.

"I know what you're thinking," Mac said. "Don't think I don't know the awful risk I'm taking now, with my immortal soul and all. Gives me a chill to think of it. But I still can't bring myself to do the right thing. Not if it means going to a priest. Sure to be embarrassing questions. The Fathers could easily get wind of it back in Chicago."

Myles was beginning to see what Mac had in mind.

"As I understand it, you don't have to be a priest to baptize people," Mac continued. "*Anybody* can do it in an emergency. You know that, of course."

Myles, just a step ahead of him, was thinking of the pastors who'd been deceived into giving Mac the pledge. It looked a lot like the old package deal.

"We could go over there," Mac said. glancing at the wash-bowl in the corner. "Or there's my room, if it'd be more appropriate." He had a bathroom.

Myles hardened. "If you're asking *me* to do it," he said, "the answer's no." Myles was now sure that Mac had been baptized before—perhaps many times, whenever he had need of it. "I couldn't give you a proper certificate anyway," Myles added. "You'd want that."

"You mean if I wanted to go on with it and come into the Catholic Church? All the way in? Is that what you mean?"

Myles didn't mean that at all, but he said, "I suppose so."

"Then you do get me?" Mac demanded.

Myles stiffened, knowing that he was in grave danger of being in on

Mac's conversion, and feeling, a moment later, that this—this conversion—like the pledge and baptism, must have happened before. He hastened to say, "No, I don't get you and I don't *want* to."

Mac stood before him, silent, with bowed head, the beaten man, the man who'd asked for bread and recieved a stone, who'd asked for a fish and got a serpent.

But no, Mac wasn't that at all, Myles saw. He was the serpent, the nice old serpent with Glen-plaid markings, who wasn't *very* poisonous. He'd been expecting tenderness, but he had caught the forked stick just behind the head. The serpent was quiet. Was he dead? "I give you my word that I'll never tell anybody what you've told me," Myles said. "So far as I'm concerned, you're a Catholic—a cradle Catholic if you like. I hold no grudge against you for anything you've said, drunk or sober. I hope you'll do the same for me."

"I will that," Mac said, and began to speak of their "relationship," of the inspiration Myles had been to him from the very first. There was only one person responsible for the change in his outlook, he said, and it might interest Myles to know that *he* was that person.

Myles saw that he'd let up on the stick too soon. The serpent still had plenty left. Myles pressed down on him. "I want out, Mac," he said. "I'm not a priest yet. I don't *have* to listen to this. If you want me to spill the beans to the Fathers, just keep it up."

The serpent was very quiet now. Dead?

"You do see what I mean?" Myles said.

"Yeah, now I see, Mac said. He was looking only a little hurt; the flesh above his snow-white collar was changing pinks, but he was looking much better, seemingly convinced that Myles, with an excuse to harm him, and with the power to do so would not. Mac was having his remarkable experience after all—almost a conversion. "Had you wrong," he confessed. "Thought sure you'd squeal. Thought sure you'd be the type that would. Hope you don't mind me saying that. Because you got my respect now."

Myles could see, however, that Mac liked him less for having it. But he had Mac's respect, and it was rare, and it made the day rare.

"Until I met you, why—Well, *you* know." Mac stopped short.

Myles, with just a look, had let him feel the stick.

"We'll leave it at that," Mac said.

"If you will, I will," said Myles. He crossed the room to the washbowl, where he began to collect his razor, his toothbrush, and the shaving lotion that Mac had given him. When he turned around with these things in his hands, he saw that Mac had gone. He'd left a small deposit of gray ash on the rug near the spot where he'd coiled and uncoiled.

Later that morning Myles, as a last service and proof of good will, went to the garage and brought Mac's car around to the hotel door, and waited there with it until Mac, smoking his second cigar of the day, appeared, Myles helped him stow his luggage and refused his offer to drive him to the railroad station, if that was where Myles wanted to go. Myles had not told Mac that he intended to hitchhike back to the last town, to confront the difficult bishop and strike the rock a second time. After shaking hands, Mac began, "If I hear of anything—" but Myles silenced him with a look, and then and there the team split up.

Mac got into the Cadillac and drove off. Watching, Myles saw the car, half a block away, bite at the curb and stop. And he saw why. Mac, getting on with the Work, was offering a lift to two men all in black, who, to judge by their actions, didn't really want one. In the end, though, the black car consumed them, and slithered out of view.

THE DEATH OF THE
BALL TURRET GUNNER

Randall Jarrell

From my mother's sleep I fell into the State,
And I hunched in its belly till my wet fur froze.
Six miles from earth, loosed from its dream of life,
I woke to black flak and the nightmare fighters.
When I died they washed me out of the turret with a hose.   5

GULLS LAND AND
CEASE TO BE

John Ciardi

Spread back across the air, wings wide,
    legs out, the wind delicately
dumped in balance, the gulls ride
    down, down, hang, and exactly
touch, folding not quite at once   5

Permission to reprint granted by Mrs. Randall Jarrell.

From *Person to Person* by John Ciardi. © 1964 by Rutgers, The State University. Reprinted by permission of the author.

into their gangling weight, but
taking one step, two, wings still askance,
reluctantly, at last, shut,
twitch one look around
and are aground.   10

LINES COMPOSED
A FEW MILES ABOVE
TINTERN ABBEY

On Revisiting The Banks Of The Wye During A Tour.
July 13, 1798

William Wordsworth

Five years have past; five summers, with the length
Of five long winters! and again I hear
These waters, rolling from their mountain-springs
With a soft inland murmur.—Once again
Do I behold these steep and lofty cliffs,   5
That on a wild secluded scene impress
Thoughts of more deep seclusion; and connect
The landscape with the quiet of the sky.
The day is come when I again repose
Here, under this dark sycamore, and view   10
These plots of cottage-ground, these orchard-tufts,
Which at this season, with their unripe fruits,
Are clad in one green hue, and lose themselves
'Mid groves and copses. Once again I see
These hedge-rows, hardly hedge-rows, little lines   15
Of sportive wood run wild: these pastoral farms,
Green to the very door; and wreaths of smoke
Sent up in silence from among the trees!
With some uncertain notice, as might seem
Of vagrant dwellers in the houseless woods,   20
Or of some Hermit's cave, where by his fire
The Hermit sits alone.

                    These beauteous forms,
Through a long absence, have not been to me
As is a landscape to a blind man's eye:
But oft, in lonely rooms, and 'mid the din   25
Of towns and cities, I have owed to them,

In hours of weariness, sensations sweet,
Felt in the blood, and felt along the heart;
And passing even into my purer mind,
With tranquil restoration:—feelings too   30
Of unremembered pleasure: such, perhaps,
As have no slight or trivial influence
On that best portion of a good man's life,
His little, nameless, unremembered, acts
Of kindness and of love. Nor less, I trust,   35
To them I may have owed another gift,
Of aspect more sublime; that blessed mood,
In which the burthen of the mystery,
In which the heavy and weary weight
Of all this unintelligible world,   40
Is lightened:—that serene and blessed mood,
In which the affections gently lead us on,—
Until the breath of this corporeal frame
And even the motion of our human blood
Almost suspended, we are laid asleep   45
In body, and become a living soul:
While with an eye made quiet by the power
Of harmony, and the deep power of joy,
We see into the life of things.

                    If this
Be but a vain belief, yet, oh! how oft—   50
In darkness and amid the many shapes
Of joyless daylight; when the fretful stir
Unprofitable, and the fever of the world,
Have hung upon the beatings of my heart—
How oft, in spirit, have I turned to thee,   55
O sylvan Wye! thou wanderer thro' the woods,
How often has my spirit turned to thee!

And now, with gleams of half-extinguished thought,
With many recognitions dim and faint,
And somewhat of a sad perplexity,   60
The picture of the mind revives again:
While here I stand, not only with the sense
Of present pleasure, but with pleasing thoughts
That in this moment there is life and food
For future years. And so I dare to hope,   65
Though changed, no doubt, from what I was when first
I came among these hills; when like a roe
I bounded o'er the mountains, by the sides

Of the deep rivers, and the lonely streams,
Wherever nature led: more like a man   70
Flying from something that he dreads than one
Who sought the thing he loved. For nature then
(The coarser pleasures of my boyish days,
And their glad animal movements all gone by)
To me was all in all.—I cannot paint   75
What then I was. The sounding cataract
Haunted me like a passion: the tall rock,
The mountain, and the deep and gloomy wood,
Their colours and their forms, were then to me
An appetite; a feeling and a love,   80
That had no need of a remoter charm,
By thought supplied, nor any interest
Unborrowed from the eye.—That time is past,
And all its aching joys are now no more,
And all its dizzy raptures. Not for this   85
Faint I, nor mourn nor murmur; other gifts
Have followed; for such loss, I would believe,
Abundant recompense. For I have learned
To look on nature not as in the hour
Of thoughtless youth; but hearing oftentimes   90
The still, sad music of humanity,
Nor harsh nor grating, though of ample power
To chasten and subdue. And I have felt
A presence that disturbs me with the joy
Of elevated thoughts; a sense sublime   95
Of something far more deeply interfused,
Whose dwelling is the light of setting suns,
And the round ocean and the living air,
And the blue sky, and in the mind of man:
A motion and a spirit, that impels   100
All thinking things, all objects of all thought,
And rolls through all things. Therefore am I still
A lover of the meadows and the woods,
And mountains; and of all that we behold
From this green earth; of all the mighty world   105
Of eye, and ear,—both what they half create,
And what perceive; well pleased to recognise
In nature and the language of the sense
The anchor of my purest thoughts, the nurse,
The guide, the guardian of my heart, and soul   110
Of all my moral being.

              Nor perchance,
If I were not thus taught, should I the more
Suffer my genial spirits to decay:
For thou art with me here upon the banks

Of this fair river; thou my dearest Friend,   115
My dear, dear Friend; and in thy voice I catch
The language of my former heart, and read
My former pleasures in the shooting lights
Of thy wild eyes. Oh! yet a little while
May I behold in thee what I was once,   120
My dear, dear Sister! and this prayer I make,
Knowing that Nature never did betray
The heart that loved her; 'tis her privilege,
Through all the years of this our life, to lead
From joy to joy: for she can so inform   125
The mind that is within us, so impress
With quietness and beauty, and so feed
With lofty thoughts, that neither evil tongues,
Rash judgments, nor the sneers of selfish men,
Nor greetings where no kindness is, nor all   130
The dreary intercourse of daily life,
Shall e'er prevail against us, or disturb
Our cheerful faith, that all which we behold
Is full of blessings. Therefore let the moon
Shine on thee in thy solitary walk;   135
And let the misty mountain-winds be free
To blow against thee: and, in after years,
When these wild ecstasies shall be matured
Into a sober pleasure; when thy mind
Shall be a mansion for all lovely forms,   140
Thy memory be as a dwelling-place
For all sweet sounds and harmonies; oh! then,
If solitude, or fear, or pain, or grief,
Should be thy portion with what healing thoughts
Of tender joy wilt thou remember me,   145
And these my exhortations! Nor, perchance—
If I should be where I no more can hear
Thy voice, nor catch from thy wild eyes these gleams
Of past esixtence—wilt thou then forget
That on the banks of this delightful stream   150
We stood together; and that I, so long
A worshipper of Nature, hither came
Unwearied in that service: rather say
With warmer love—oh! with far deeper zeal
Of holier love. Nor wilt thou then forget   155
That after many wanderings, many years
Of absence, these steep woods and lofty cliffs,
And this green pastoral landscape, were to me
More dear, both for themselves and for thy sake!

115   The person addressed is the poet's sister, Dorothy Wordsworth.

MY PAPA'S WALTZ

Theodore Roethke

The whiskey on your breath
Could make a small boy dizzy;
But I hung on like death:
Such waltzing was not easy.

We romped until the pans   5
Slid from the kitchen shelf;
My mother's countenance
Could not unfrown itself.

The hand that held my wrist
Was battered on one knuckle;   .   10
At every step you missed
My right ear scraped a buckle.

You beat time on my head
With a palm caked hard by dirt,
Then waltzed me off to bed   15
Still clinging to your shirt.

IN MEMORY OF
W. B. YEATS

W. H. Auden

1 He disappeared in the dead of winter:
The brooks were frozen, the airports almost deserted,
And snow disfigured the public statues;
The mercury sank in the mouth of the dying day.
O all the instruments agree   5
The day of his death was a dark cold day.

Far from his illness
The wolves ran on through the evergreen forests,
The peasant river was untempted by the fashionable quays;
By mourning tongues   10
The death of the poet was kept from his poems.

But for him it was his last afternoon as himself,
An afternoon of nurses and rumors;
The provinces of his body revolted,
The squares of his mind were empty,   15
Silence invaded the suburbs,
The current of his feeling failed: he became his admirers.

Now he is scattered among a hundred cities
And wholly given over to unfamiliar affections;
To find his happiness in another kind of wood   20
And be punished under a foreign code of conscience.
The words of a dead man
Are modified in the guts of the living.

But in the importance and noise of tomorrow
When the brokers are roaring like beasts on the floor of the Bourse,   25
And the poor have the sufferings to which they are fairly accustomed,
And each in his cell of himself is almost convinced of his freedom;
A few thousand will think of this day
As one thinks of a day when one did something slightly unusual.
O all the instruments agree   30
The day of his death was a dark cold day.

2 You were silly like us: your gift survived it all;

The parish of rich women, physical decay,
Yourself; mad Ireland hurt you into poetry.
Now Ireland has her madness and her weather still,   35
For poetry makes nothing happen: it survives
In the valley of its saying where executives
Would never want to tamper; it flows south
From ranches of isolation and the busy griefs,
Raw towns that we believe and die in; it survives,   40
A way of happening, a mouth.

3 Earth, receive an honored guest;

William Yeats is laid to rest:
Let the Irish vessel lie
Emptied of its poetry.   45

Time that is intolerant
Of the brave and innocent,
And indifferent in a week
To a beautiful physique,

Worships language and forgives   50
Everyone by whom it lives;
Pardons cowardice, conceit,
Lays its honors at their feet.

Time that with this strange excuse
Pardoned Kipling and his views,   55
And will pardon Paul Claudel,
Pardons him for writing well.

In the nightmare of the dark
All the dogs of Europe bark,
And the living nations wait,   60
Each sequestered in its hate;

Intellectual disgrace
Stares from every human face,
And the seas of pity lie
Locked and frozen in each eye.   65

Follow, poet, follow right
To the bottom of the night,
With your unconstraining voice
Still persuade us to rejoice;

With the farming of a verse   70
Make a vineyard of the curse,
Sing of human unsuccess
In a rapture of distress;

In the deserts of the heart
Let the healing fountain start,   75
In the prison of his days
Teach the free man how to praise.

THE SILKEN TENT

Robert Frost

She is as in a field a silken tent
At midday when a sunny summer breeze
Has dried the dew and all its ropes relent,
So that in guys it gently sways at ease,
And its supporting central cedar pole,   5
That is its pinnacle to heavenward
And signifies the sureness of the soul,
Seems to owe naught to any single cord,

But strictly held by none, is loosely bound
By countless silken ties of love and thought   10
To everything on earth the compass round,
And only by one's going slightly taut
In the capriciousness of summer air
Is of the slightest bondage made aware.

THE WINDHOVER:
TO CHRIST OUR LORD

Gerard Manley Hopkins

I caught this morning morning's minion, king-
        dom of daylight's dauphin, dapple-dawn-drawn Falcon, in his
        riding
    Of the rolling level underneath him steady air, and striding
High there, how he rung upon the rein of a wimpling wing
In his ecstasy! then off, off forth on swing,   5
    As a skate's heel sweeps smooth on a bow-bend: the hurl and
        gliding
    Rebuffed the big wind. My heart in hiding
Stirred for a bird,—the achieve of, the mastery of the thing!

Brute beauty and valour and act, oh, air, pride, plume, here
    Buckle! AND the fire that breaks from thee then, a billion   10
Times told lovelier, more dangerous, O my chevalier!

No wonder of it: shéer plód makes plough down sillion
Shine, and blue-bleak embers, ah my dear,
    Fall, gall themselves, and gash gold-vermilion.

SPRING AND FALL: TO A YOUNG CHILD

Gerard Manley Hopkins

Márgarét, are you gríeving
Over Goldengrove unleaving?
Leáves, líke the things of man, you
With your fresh thoughts care for, can you?
Ah! ás the heart grows older   5
It will come to such sights colder
By and by, nor spare a sigh
Though worlds of wanwood leafmeal lie;
And yet you wíll weep and know why.
Now no matter, child, the name: 10
Sórrow's spríngs áre the same.
Nor mouth had, no nor mind, expressed
What heart heard of, ghost guessed:
It ís the blight man was born for,
It is Margaret you mourn for.   15

THAT TIME OF YEAR

William Shakespeare

That time of year thou mayst in me behold
When yellow leaves, or none, or few, do hang
Upon those boughs which shake against the cold,
Bare ruined choirs where late the sweet birds sang.
In me thou see'st the twilight of such day   5
As after sunset fadeth in the west,
Which by and by black night doth take away,
Death's second self, that seals up all in rest.

12 *sillion:* furrow

"The Windhover: To Christ Our Lord" and "Spring and Fall: To a Young Child" by Gerard Manley Hopkins from *Sound and Sense,* edited by L. Perrine. Reprinted by permission of Oxford University Press.

In me thou see'st the glowing of such fire,
That on the ashes of his youth doth lie   10
As the deathbed whereon it must expire,
Consumed with that which it was nourished by.
    This thou perceivest, which makes thy love more strong,
    To love that well which thou must leave ere long.

TERENCE, THIS IS STUPID STUFF

A. E. Housman

    "Terence, this is stupid stuff:
You eat your victuals fast enough;
There can't be much amiss, 'tis clear,
To see the rate you drink your beer.
But oh, good Lord, the verse you make,   5
It gives a chap the belly-ache.
The cow, the old cow, she is dead;
It sleeps well the horned head:
We poor lads, 'tis our turn now
To hear such tunes as killed the cow.   10
Pretty friendship 'tis to rhyme
Your friends to death before their time
Moping melancholy mad:
Come, pipe a tune to dance to, lad."

    Why, if 'tis dancing you would be,   15
There's brisker pipes than poetry.
Say, for what were hop-yards meant,
Or why was Burton built on Trent?
Oh many a peer of England brews
Livelier liquor than the Muse,   20
And malt does more than Milton can
To justify God's way to man.
Ale, man, ale's the stuff to drink
For fellows whom it hurts to think:
Look into the pewter pot   25
To see the world as the world's not.

And faith, 'tis pleasant till 'tis past:
The mischief is that 'twill not last.
Oh I have been to Ludlow fair
And left my necktie God knows where,   30
And carried half-way home, or near,
Pints and quarts of Ludlow beer:
Then the world seemed none so bad,
And I myself a sterling lad;
And down in lovely muck I've lain,   35
Happy till I woke again.
Then I saw the morning sky:
Heigho, the tale was all a lie;
The world, it was the old world yet,
I was I, my things were wet,   40
And nothing now remained to do
But begin the game anew.

   Therefore, since the world has still
Much good, but much less good than ill,
And while the sun and moon endure
Luck's a chance, but trouble's sure,   45
I'd face it as a wise man would,
And train for ill and not for good.
'Tis true, the stuff I bring for sale
Is not so brisk a brew as ale: 50
Out of a stem that scored the hand
I wrung it in a weary land.
But take it: if the smack is sour,
The better for the embittered hour;
It should do good to heart and head   55
When your soul is in my soul's stead;
And I will friend you, if I may,
In the dark and cloudy day.

   There was a king reigned in the East:
There, when kings will sit to feast,   60
They get their fill before they think
With poisoned meat and poisoned drink.
He gathered all that springs to birth
From the many-venomed earth;
First a little, thence to more,   65
He sampled all her killing store;
And easy, smiling, seasoned sound,
State the king when healths went round.
They put arsenic in his meat

And stared aghast to watch him eat;   70
They poured strychnine in his cup
And shook to see him drink it up:
They shook, they stared as white's their shirt:
Them it was their poison hurt.
—I tell the tale that I heard told.   75
Mithridates, he died old.

COLLOQUY
IN BLACK ROCK

Robert Lowell

Here the jack-hammer jabs into the ocean;
My heart, you race and stagger and demand
More blood-gangs for your nigger-brass percussions,
Till I, the stunned machine of your devotion,
Clanging upon this cymbal of a hand,   5
Am rattled screw and footloose. All discussions

End in the mud-flat detritus of death.
My heart, beat faster, faster. In Black Mud
Hungarian workmen give their blood
For the martyre Stephen, who was stoned to death.   10

Black Mud, a name to conjure with: O mud
For watermelons gutted to the crust,
Mud for the mole-tide harbor, mud for mouse,
Mud for the armored Diesel fishing tubs that thud
A year and a day to wind and tide; the dust   15
Is on this skipping heart that shakes my house,

House of our Savior who was hanged till death.
My heart, beat faster, faster. In Black Mud
Stephen the martyre was broken down to blood:
Our ransom is the rubble of his death.   20

Christ walks on the black water. In Black Mud
Darts the kingfisher. On Corpus Christi, heart,
Over the drum-beat of St. Stephen's choir

I hear him, *Stupor Mundi,* and the mud
Flies from his hunching wings and beak—my heart,   25
The blue kingfisher dives on you in fire.

A VALEDICTION FORBIDDING MOURNING

John Donne

As virtuous men pass mildly away,
    And whisper to their souls to go,
Whilst some of their sad friends do say,
    The breath goes now, and some say, No:

So let us melt, and make no noise,   5
    No tear-floods, nor sigh-tempests move;
'Twere profanation of our joys
    To tell the laity our love.

Moving of th' earth brings harms and fears,
    Men reckon what it did, and meant;   10
But trepidation of the spheres,
    Though greater far, is innocent.

Dull sublunary lovers' love
    (Whose soul is sense) cannot admit
Absence, because it doth remove
    Those things which elemented it.   15

But we by a love so much refined
    That ourselves know not what it is,
Inter-assurèd of the mind,
    Care less eyes, lips and hands to miss.   20

Our two souls therefore, which are one,
    Though I must go, endure not yet
A breach, but an expansion,
    Like gold to airy thinness beat.

If they be two, they are two so   25
    As stiff twin compasses are two;

Thy soul, the fix'd foot, makes no show
  To move, but doth, if th' other do.

And though it in the centre sit,
  Yet, when the other far doth roam,   30
It leans, and hearkens after it,
  And grows erect, as that comes home.

Such wilt thou be to me, who must,
  Like th' other foot, obliquely run;
Thy firmness makes my circle just,   35
  And makes me end where I begun.

DOVER BEACH

Matthew Arnold

The sea is calm tonight,
The tide is full, the moon lies fair
Upon the straits;—on the French coast the light
Gleams and is gone; the cliffs of England stand,
Glimmering and vast, out in the tranquil bay.   5
Come to the window, sweet is the night-air!
Only, from the long line of spray
Where the sea meets the moon-blanched land,
Listen! you hear the grating roar
Of pebbles which the waves draw back, and fling,   10
At their return, up the high strand,
Begin, and cease, and then again begin,
With tremulous cadence slow, and bring
The eternal note of sadness in.

Sophocles long ago   15
Heard it on the Aegean, and it brought
Into his mind the turbid ebb and flow
Of human misery; we
Find also in the sound a thought,
Hearing it by this distant northern sea.   20

The Sea of Faith
Was once, too, at the full, and round earth's shore
Lay like the folds of a bright girdle furled
But now I only hear
Its melancholy, long, withdrawing roar,   25

Retreating, to the breath
Of the night-wind, down the vast edges drear
And naked shingles of the world.

Ah, love, let us be true
To one another! for the world, which seems   30
To lie before us like a land of dreams,
So various, so beautiful, so new,
Hath really neither joy, nor love, nor light,
Nor certitude, nor peace, nor help for pain;
And we are here as on a darkling plain   35
Swept with confused alarms of struggle and flight,
Where ignorant armies clash by night.

A SOLDIER

Robert Frost

He is that fallen lance that lies as hurled,
That lies unlifted now, come dew, come rust,
But still lies pointed as it plowed the dust.
If we who sight along it round the world,
See nothing worthy to have been its mark,   5
It is because like men we look too near,
Forgetting that as fitted to the sphere,
Our missiles always make too short an arc.
They fall, they rip the grass, they intersect
The curve of earth, and striking, break their own;   10
They make us cringe for metal-point on stone.
But this we know, the obstacle that checked
And tripped the body, shot the spirit on
Further than target ever showed or shone.

28   *naked shingles:* pebbled beaches

BIRCHES

Robert Frost

When I see birches bend to left and right
Across the lines of straighter darker trees,
I like to think some boy's been swinging them.
But swinging doesn't bend them down to stay
As ice-storms do. Often you must have seen them   5
Loaded with ice a sunny winter morning
After a rain. They click upon themselves
As the breeze rises, and turn many-colored
As the stir cracks and crazes their enamel.
Soon the sun's warmth makes them shed crystal shells   10
Shattering and avalanching on the snow-crust—
Such heaps of broken glass to sweep away
You'd think the inner dome of heaven had fallen.
They are dragged to the withered bracken by the load,
And they seem not to break; though once they are bowed   15
So low for long, they never right themselves:
You may see their trunks arching in the woods
Years afterwards, trailing their leaves on the ground
Like girls on hands and knees that throw their hair
Before them over their heads to dry in the sun.   20
But I was going to say when Truth broke in
With all her matter-of-fact about the ice-storm
I should prefer to have some boy bend them
As he went out and in to fetch the cows—
Some boy too far from town to learn baseball,   25
Whose only play was what he found himself,
Summer or winter, and could play alone.
One by one he subdued his father's trees
By riding them down over and over again
Until he took the stiffness out of them,   30
And not one but hung limp, not one was left
For him to conquer. He learned all there was
To learn about not launching out too soon
And so not carrying the tree away
Clear to the ground. He always kept his poise   35

To the top branches, climbing carefully
With the same pains you use to fill a cup
Up to the brim, and even above the brim.
Then he flung outward, feet first, with a swish,
Kicking his way down through the air to the ground.   40
So was I once myself a swinger of birches.
And so I dream of going back to be.
It's when I'm weary of considerations,
And life is too much like a pathless wood
Where your face burns and tickles with the cobwebs   45
Broken across it, and one eye is weeping
From a twig's having lashed across it open.
I'd like to get away from earth awhile
And then come back to it and begin over.
May no fate willfully misunderstand me   50
And half grant what I wish and snatch me away
Not to return. Earth's the right place for love:
I don't know where it's likely to go better.
I'd like to go by climbing a birch tree,
And climb black branches up a snow-white trunk   55
Toward heaven, till the tree could bear no more,
But dipped its top and set me down again.
That would be good both going and coming back.
One could do worse than be a swinger of birches.

PASSAGE TO INDIA

Walt Whitman

I

Singing my days,
Singing the great achievements of the present,
Singing the strong light works of engineers,
Our modern wonders, (the antique ponderous Seven outvied,)
In the Old World the east the Suez canal,   5
The New by its mighty railroad spann'd,
The seas inlaid with eloquent gentle wires;
Yet first to sound, and ever sound, the cry with thee O soul,
The Past! the Past! the Past!

The Past—the dark unfathom'd retrospect!   10
The teeming gulf—the sleepers and the shadows!
The past—the infinite greatness of the past!
For what is the present after all but a growth out of the past?

(As a projectile form'd, impell'd, passing a certain line, still keeps on,
So the present, utterly form'd, impell'd by the past.)   15

II

Passage O soul to India!
Eclaircise the myths Asiatic, the primitive fables.

Not you alone proud truths of the world,
Nor you alone ye facts of modern science,
But myths and fables of eld, Asia's, Africa's fables,   20
The far-darting beams of the spirit, the unloos'd dreams,
The deep diving bibles and legends,
The daring plots of the poets, the elder religions;
O you temples fairer than lilies pour'd over by the rising sun!
O you fables spurning the known, eluding the hold of the known, mounting to
     heaven!   25
You lofty and dazzling towers, pinnacled, red as roses, burnish'd with gold!
Towers of fables immortal fashion'd from mortal dreams!
You too I welcome and fully the same as the rest!
You too with joy I sing.

Passage to India!   30
Lo, soul, seest thou not God's purpose from the first?
The earth to be spann'd, connected by network,
The races, neighbors, to marry and be given in marriage,
The oceans to be cross'd, the distant brought near,
The lands to be welded together.   35

A worship new I sing,
You captains, voyagers, explorers, yours,
You engineers, you architects, machinists, yours,
You, not for trade or transportation only,
But in God's name, and for thy sake O soul.   40

III

Passage to India!
Lo soul for thee of tableaus twain,
I see in one the Suez canal initiated, open'd,
I see the procession of steamships, the Empress Eugenie's leading the van,
I mark from on deck the strange landscape, the pure sky, the level sand in the
     distance,   45
I pass swiftly the picturesque groups, the workmen gather'd,
The gigantic dredging machines.
In one again, different, (yet thine, all thine, O soul, the same,)
I see over my own continent the Pacific railroad surmounting every barrier,

I see continual trains of cars winding along the Platte carrying freight and
    passengers,   50
I hear the locomotives rushing and roaring, and the shrill steam-whistle,
I hear the echoes reverberate through the grandest scenery in the world,
I cross the Laramie plains, I note the rocks in grotesque shapes, the buttes,
I see the plentiful larkspur and wild onions, the barren, colorless, sage-deserts,
I see in glimpses afar or towering immediately above me the great mountains,
    I see the Wind river and the Wahsatch mountains,   55
I see the Monument mountain and the Eagle's Nest, I pass the Promontory, I
    ascend the Nevadas,
I scan the noble Elk mountain and wind around its base,
I see the Humboldt range, I thread the valley and cross the river,
I see the clear waters of lake Tahoe, I see forests of majestic pines,
Or crossing the great desert, the alkaline plains, I behold enchanting mirages
    of waters and meadows,   60
Marking through these and after all, in duplicate slender lines,
Bridging the three or four thousand miles of land travel,
Tying the Eastern to the Western sea,
The road between Europe and Asia.

(Ah Genoese thy dream! thy dream!   65
Centuries after thou art laid in thy grave,
The shore thou foundest verifies thy dream.)

IV

Passage to India!
Struggles of many a captain, tales of many a sailor dead,
Over my mood stealing and spreading they come,   70
Like clouds and cloudlets in the unreach'd sky.

Along all history, down the slopes,
As a rivulet running, sinking now, and now again to the surface rising,
A ceaseless thought, a varied train—lo, soul, to thee, thy sight, they rise,
The plans, the voyages again, the expeditions;   75
Again Vasco da Gama sails forth,
Again the knowledge gain'd, the mariner's compass,
Lands found and nations born, thou born America,
For purpose vast, man's long probation fill'd,
Thou rondure of the world at last accomplish'd.   30

V

O vast Rondure, swimming in space,
Cover'd all over with visible power and beauty,

Alternate light and day and the teeming spiritual darkness,
Unspeakable high processions of sun and moon and countless stars above,
Below, the manifold grass and waters, animals, mountains, trees,   8₅
With inscrutable purpose, some hidden prophetic intention,
Now first it seems my thought begins to span thee.

Down from the gardens of Asia descending radiating,
Adam and Eve appear, then their myriad progeny after them,
Wandering, yearing, curious, with restless explorations,   90
With questionings, baffled, formless, feverish, with never-happy hearts,
With that sad incessant refrain, *Wherefore unsatisfied soul?* and *Whither O
    mocking life?*

Ah who shall soothe these feverish children?
Who justify these restless explorations?
Who speak the secret of impassive earth?   95
Who bind it to us? what is this separate Nature so unnatural?
What is this earth to our affections? (unloving earth, without a throb to answer
    ours,
Cold earth, the place of graves.)

Yet soul be sure the first intent remains, and shall be carried out,
Perhaps even now the time has arrived.   100

After the seas are all cross'd, (as they seem already cross'd,)
After the great captains and engineers have accomplish'd their work,
After the noble inventors, after the scientists, the chemist, the geologist,
    ethnologist,
Finally shall come the poet worthy that name,
The true son of God shall come singing his songs.   105

Then not your deeds only O voyagers, O scientists and inventors shall be
    justified,
All these hearts as of fretted children shall be sooth'd,
All affection shall be fully responded to, the secret shall be told,
All these separations and gaps shall be taken up and hook'd and link'd
    together,
The whole earth, this cold impassive, voiceless earth, shall be completely
    justified,   110
Trinitas divine shall be gloriously accomplish'd and compacted by the true son
    of God, the poet,
(He shall indeed pass the straits and conquer the mountains,
He shall double the cape of Good Hope to some purpose,)

Nature and Man shall be disjoin'd and diffused no more,
The true son of God shall absolutely fuse them.   115

VI

Year at whose wide-flung door I sing!
Year of the purpose accomplish'd!
Year of the marriage of continents, climates and oceans!
(No mere doge of Venice now wedding the Adriatic,)
I see O year in you the vast terraqueous globe given and giving all,   120
Europe to Asia, Africa join'd, and they to the New World,
The lands, geographies, dancing before you, holding a festival garland,
As brides and bridegrooms hand in hand.

Passage to India!
Cooling airs from Caucasus far, soothing cradle of man,   125
The river Euphrates flowing, the past lit up again.
Lo soul, the retrospect brought forward,
The old, most populous, wealthiest of earth lands,
The streams of the Indus and the Ganges and their many affluents,
(I my shores of America walking to-day behold, resuming all,)   130
The tale of Alexander on his warlike marches suddenly dying,
On one side China and on the other side Persia and Arabia,
To the south the great seas and the bay of Bengal,
The flowing literatures, tremendous epics, religions, castes,
Old occult Brahma interminably far back, the tender and junior Buddha,   135
Central and southern empires and all their belongings, possessors,
The wars of Tamerlane, the reign of Aurungzebe,
The traders, rulers, explorers, Moslems, Venetians, Byzantium, the Arabs,
          Portuguese,
The first travelers famous yet, Marco Polo, Batouta the Moor,
Doubts to be solv'd, the map incognita, blanks to be fill'd,   140
The foot of man unstay'd, the hands never at rest,
Thyself O soul that will not brook a challenge.

The medi 2val navigators rise before me,
The world of 1492, with its awaken'd enterprise,
Something swelling in humanity now like the sap of the earth in spring,   145
The sunset splendor of chivalry declining.

And who art thou sad shade?
Gigantic, visionary, thyself a visionary,
With majestic limbs and pious beaming eyes,
Spreading around with every look of thine a golden world,   150
Enhuing it with gorgeous hues.

As the chief histrion,
Down to the footlights walks in some great scena,
Dominating the rest I see the Admiral himself,
(History's type of courage, action, faith,)   155
Behold him sail from Palos leading his little fleet,
His voyage behold, his return, his great fame,
His misfortunes, calumniators, behold him a prisoner, chain'd,
Behold his dejection, poverty, death.

(Curious in time I stand, noting the efforts of heroes,   160
Is the deferment long? bitter the slander, poverty, death?
Lies the seed unreck'd for centuries in the ground? lo, to God's due occasion,
Uprising in the night, it sprouts, blooms,
And fills the earth with use and beauty.)

VII

Passage indeed O soul to primal thought,   165
Not lands and seas alone, thy own clear freshness,
The young maturity of brood and bloom,
To realms of budding bibles.

O soul, repressless, I with thee and thou with me, E,
Thy circumnavigation of the world begin,   170
Of man, the voyage of his mind's return,
To reason's early paradise,
Back, back to wisdom's birth, to innocent intuitions,
Again with fair creation.

VIII

O we can wait no longer,   175
We too take ship O soul,
Joyous we too launch out on trackless seas,
Fearless for unknown shores on waves of ecstasy to sail,
Amid the wafting winds, (thou pressing me to thee, I thee to me, O soul,)
Caroling free, singing our song of God,   180
Chanting our chant of pleasant exploration.

With laugh and many a kiss,
(Let others deprecate, let others weep for sin, remorse, humiliation,)
O soul thou pleasest me, I thee.
Ah more than any priest O soul we too believe in God,   185
But with the mystery of God we dare not dally.

O soul thou pleasest me, I thee,
Sailing these seas or on the hills, or waking in the night,
Thoughts, silent thoughts, of Time and Space and Death, like waters flowing,
Bear me indeed as through the regions infinite,   190
Whose air I breathe, whose ripples hear, lave me all over,
Bathe me O God in thee, mounting to thee,
I and my soul to range in range of thee.

O Thou transcendent,
Nameless, the fibre and the breath,   195
Light of the light, shedding forth universes, thou centre of them,
Thou mightier centre of the true, the good, the loving,
Thou moral, spiritual fountain—affection's source—thou reservoir,
(O pensive soul of me—O thirst unsatisfied—waitest not there?
Waitest not haply for us somewhere there the Comrade perfect?)   200
Thou pulse—thou motive of the stars, suns, systems,
That, circling, move in order, safe, harmonious,
Athwart the shapeless vastnesses of space,
How should I think, how breathe a single breath, how speak, if, out of myself,
I could not launch, to those, superior universes?   205

Swiftly I shrivel at the thought of God,
At Nature and its wonders, Time and Space and Death,
But that I, turning, call to thee O soul, thou actual Me,
And lo, thou gently masterest the orbs,
Thou matest Time, smilest content at Death,   210
And fillest, swellest full the vastnesses of Space.

Greater than stars or suns,
Bounding O soul thou journeyest forth;
What love than thine and ours could wider amplify?
What aspirations, wishes, outvie thine and ours O soul?   215
What dreams of the ideal? what plans of purity, perfection, strength?
What cheerful willingness for others' sake to give up all?
For others' sake to suffer all?

Reckoning ahead O soul, when thou, the time achiev'd,
The seas all cross'd, weather'd the capes, the voyage done,   220
Surrounded, copest, frontest God, yieldest, the aim attain'd,
As filled with friendship, love complete, the Elder Brother found,
The Younger melts in fondness in his arms.

Passage to more than India!
Are thy wings plumed indeed for such far flights?   225
O soul, voyagest thou indeed on voyages like those?
Disportest thou on waters such as those?

Soundest below the Sanscrit and the Vedas?
Then have thy bent unleash'd.

Passage to you, your shores, ye aged fierce enigmas!   230
Passage to you, to mastership of you, ye strangling problems!
You, strew'd with the wrecks of skeletons, that, living, never reach'd you.

Passage to more than India!
O secret of the earth and sky!
Of you O waters of the sea! O winding creeks and rivers!   235
Of you O woods and fields! of you strong mountains of my land!
Of you O prairies! of you gray rocks!
O morning red! O clouds! O rain and snows!
O day and night, passage to you!

O sun and moon and all you stars! Sirius and Jupiter!   240
Passage to you!
Passage, immediate passage! the blood burns in my veins!
Away O soul! hoist instantly the anchor!
Cut the hawsers—haul out—shake out every sail!
Have we not stood here like trees in the ground long enough?   245
Have we not grovel'd here long enough, eating and drinking like mere brutes?
Have we not darken'd and dazed ourselves with books long enough?

Sail forth—steer for the deep waters only,
Reckless O soul, exploring, I with thee, and thou with me,
For we are bound where mariner has not yet dared to go,   250
And we will risk the ship, ourselves and all.

O my brave soul!
O farther farther sail!
O daring joy, but safe! are they not all the seas of God?
O farther, farther sail!   255

ODE TO THE WEST WIND

Percy Bysshe Shelley

I

O wild West Wind, thou breath of autumn's being,
Thou, from whose unseen presence the leaves dead
Are driven, like ghosts from an enchanter fleeing.

Yellow, and black, and pale, and hectic red,
Pestilence-stricken multitudes: O thou,   5
Who chariotest to their dark wintry bed

The wingèd seeds. where they lie cold and low,
Each like a corpse within its grave, until
Thine azure sister of the spring shall blow

Her clarion o'er the dreaming earth, and fill   10
(Driving sweet buds like flocks to feed in air)
With living hues and odors plain and hill;

Wild Spirit, which art moving everywhere;
Destroyer and preserver; hear, oh hear!

II

Thou on whose stream, mid the steep sky's commotion,   15
Loose clouds like earths decaying leaves are shed,
Shook from the tangled boughs of Heaven and Ocean,

Angels of rain and lightning: there are spread
On the blue surface of thine aery surge,
Like the bright hair uplifted from the head   20

Of some fierce Maenad, even from the dim verge
Of the horizon to the zenith's height,
The locks of the approaching storm. Thou dirge

Of the dying year, to which this closing night
Will be the dome of a vast sepulchre,   25
Vaulted with all thy congregated might

Of vapors, from whose solid atmosphere
Black rain, and fire, and hail will burst: oh hear!

III

Thou who didst waken from his summer dreams
The blue Mediterranean, where he lay,   30
Lulled by the coil of his crystàlline streams,

21. *Maenad:* nymph in the train of Bacchus, god of wine.

31. *coil:* movement.

Beside a pumice isle in Baiae's bay,
And saw in sleep old palaces and towers
Quivering within the wave's intenser day,

All overgrown with azure moss and flowers   35
So sweet, the sense faints picturing them! Thou
For whose path the Atlantic's level powers

Cleave themselves into chasms, while far below
The sea-blooms and the oozy woods which wear
The sapless foliage of the ocean, know   40

Thy voice, and suddenly grow gray with fear,
And tremble and despoil themselves: oh hear!

IV

If I were a dead leaf thou mightest bear;
If I were a swift cloud to fly with thee;
A wave to pant beneath thy power, and share   45

The impulse of thy strength, only less free
Than thou, O uncontrollable! If even
I were as in my boyhood, and could be

The comrade of thy wanderings over Heaven,
As then, when to outstrip thy skiey speed   50
Scarce seemed a vision; I would ne'er have striven

As thus with thee in prayer in my sore need.
Oh, lift me as a wave, a leaf, a cloud!
I fall upon the thorns of life! I bleed!

A heavy weight of hours has chained and bowed   55
One too like thee: tameless, and swift, and proud.

V

Make me thy lyre, even as the forest is:
What if my leaves are falling like its own!
The tumult of thy mighty harmonies

32. *Baiae:* village on west coast of Italy.

Will take from both a deep, autumnal tone,   60
Sweet though in sadness. Be thou, Spirit fierce,
My spirit! Be thou me, impetuous one!

Drive my dead thoughts over the universe
Like withered leaves to quicken a new birth!
And, by the incantation of this verse,   65

Scatter, as from an unextinguished hearth
Ashes and sparks, my words among mankind!
Be through my lips to unawakened earth

The trumpet of a prophecy! O Wind,
If winter comes, can spring be far behind?   70

THE FALL OF ROME

W. H. Auden

The piers are pummelled by the waves;
In a lonely field the rain
Lashes an abandoned train;
Outlaws fill the mountain caves.

Fantastic grow the evening gowns;   5
Agents of the Fisc pursue
Absconding tax-defaulters through
The sewers of provincial towns.

Private rites of magic send
The temple prostitutes to sleep;   10
All the literati keep
An imaginary friend.

Cerebretonic Cato may
Extoll the Ancient Disciplines,
But the muscle-bound Marines   15
Mutiny for food and pay.

Caesar's double-bed is warm
As an unimportant clerk

Writes I DO NOT LIKE MY WORK
On a pink official form.   20

Unendowed with wealth or pity,
Little birds with scarlet legs,
Sitting on their speckled eggs,
Eye each flu-infected city.

Altogether elsewhere, vast   25
Herds of reindeer move across
Miles and miles of golden moss,
Silently and very fast.

STOPPING BY WOODS
ON A SNOWY EVENING

Robert Frost

Whose woods these are I think I know.
His house is in the village though;
He will not see me stopping here
To watch his woods fill up with snow.

My little horse must think it queer   5
To stop without a farmhouse near
Between the woods and frozen lake
The darkest evening of the year.

He gives his harness bells a shake
To ask if there is some mistake.   10
The only other sound's the sweep
Of easy wind and downy flake.

The woods are lovely, dark and deep,
But I have promises to keep,
And miles to go before I sleep,   15
And miles to go before I sleep.

THE DANCE

William Carlos Williams

In Breughel's great picture, The Kermess,
the dancers go round, they go round and
around, the squeal and the blare and the
tweedle of bagpipes, a bugle and fiddles
tipping their bellies (round as the thick-   5
sided glasses whose wash they impound)
their hips and their bellies off balance
to turn them. Kicking and rolling about
the Fair Grounds, swinging their butts, those
shanks must be sound to bear up under such   10
rollicking measures, prance as they dance
in Breughel's great picture, The Kermess.

William Carlos Williams, *Collected Later Poems*. Copyright 1944 by William Carlos Williams. Reprinted by permission of New Directions Publishing Company.